A WOMAN CONDEMNED

TRUE CRIME HISTORY

A WOMAN CONDEMNED

The Tragic Case of Anna Antonio

James M. Greiner

The Kent State University Press

KENT, OHIO

For Phyllis, Maria, and Frankie

Library of Congress Cataloging-in-Publication Data
Names: Greiner, James M., 1954- author.
Title: A woman condemned : the tragic case of Anna Antonio / James M. Greiner.
Description: Kent, Ohio : Kent State University Press, [2019] | Series: True crime
            history | Includes bibliographical references and index.
Identifiers: LCCN 2019014333 | ISBN 9781606353820 (pbk.)
Subjects: LCSH: Antonio, Anna, 1906-1934. | Murder–New York (State)–Case studies. |
            Trials (Murder)–New York (State)–Albany. | Abused wives–New York (State)–
            Case studies. | Women death row inmates–United States–Case studies.
Classification: LCC HV6533.N5 G74 2019 | DDC 364.152/3092 [B] –dc23
LC record available at https://lccn.loc.gov/2019014333

23 22 21 20 19   5 4 3 2 1

CONTENTS

ACKNOWLEDGMENTS

Authors and historians who do their own research will probably tell you the same thing. While digging and searching for one thing, you stumble upon something else. That's what happened here. While researching material about an unfortunate woman who was hanged for murder in my hometown of Herkimer, I came across the story of Anna Antonio. At that time my knowledge of executed women in nineteenth- and twentieth-century New York was somewhat limited. I was already familiar with the Ruth Snyder case, due in part to the sensational grainy photo of her in the *New York Daily News* when she received that fatal jolt of electricity. The only other woman I had ever heard of was Ethel Rosenberg, victim of the Red Scare of the 1950s. I had never heard of Anna Antonio. My initial reaction after doing a little research was curiosity. What did she do and why did two men follow her to the electric chair at Sing Sing prison? Telling the complete story of the life and times of Anna Antonio would have been impossible had it not been for the support, cooperation, and generosity of a great many people.

Once more I am indebted to Jim Folts and his staff at the New York State Archives in Albany. His friendly and knowledgeable staff couldn't do enough to make my visits there—and there were quite a few—enjoyable. The four volumes of trial transcripts, together with rearguments, Auburn prison records, and Sing Sing prison records, had to be photographed. This involved multiple trips to Albany, and if you don't think that was fun, allow me to introduce my assistant who took all those pictures—my wife Teresa. Equally important as the transcripts is the website called Old Fulton Postcards. Don't let the name fool you. This website is not about postcards; it's all about old newspapers. Established and managed by Tom Tryniski, this unique site provides millions of pages of old newspapers to the public for free.

At the Albany Hall of Records, Craig Carlson and his staff retrieved the police blotters of the Albany County Jail while City of Albany Historian Tony Opalka not only provided me with a wealth of information about the south side of Albany but pointed the way to Jim Davies at the Albany Library, which led to Allison Munsell Napierski of the Albany Institute of Art and History. Through their efforts I was able to obtain 1930s photographs of Albany. Lisa Crompton of the Historic Albany Foundation searched through files of homes in the south end and sent not only photographs of Sam and Anna's apartment on 3 Teunis Street but a two-page history of the dwelling. A few miles away, Melissa Thacke and Dianne Gade retrieved Cappello family material for me from the archives of the Schenectady County Historical Society. On the other side of the state, Brooke Morse sent me information on the checkered past of Sam Faraci archived in the Ontario County Records, Archives and Information Services in Canandaigua. City of Hudson Historian Pat Fenoff provided information on the notorious red-light district of Hudson in the 1930s, and Guy Cheli was literally my "go-to guy" when it came to researching photographs of Sing Sing prison. He directed me to Norm MacDonald, curator of the Ossining Historical Society. Norm located the pictures I requested of the Death House and sent them to me post haste. Dana White, village historian for Ossining, simply amazed me at how quickly she sent me the information I needed on Sing Sing prison matron Lucy Many.

The central repository of information on Sing Sing warden Lewis Lawes is the Lloyd Sealy Library at John Jay College of Criminal Justice. Special Collections librarian Ellen Belcher was insistent that I use a clear digitalized photograph of Lewis Lawes for this book and I am so glad she did. It's a great picture of the warden.

Closer to home, Sue Perkins, executive director of the Herkimer County Historical Society and longtime friend of mine, was always there to help me with census records, genealogical research, and computer work.

Tom Kriger, author of several articles on the New York milk wars of the 1930s, offered his insight into the fierce competition between the milk companies of that era. Unfamiliar with the Steamburg arson,

Kriger said destruction by arson did occur. Although he has yet to un-
cover any evidence that organized crime was making inroads in the
dairy market during that era, he candidly said that he would not have
been the least surprised.

Sometimes in the course of your research you just get lucky. That is
the only way I can explain how I came across the material on the lead investigator of the Antonio case, William Flubacher. When, by chance, I
discovered a picture of Flubacher in his uniform on the New York State
Police Centennial Web site, I was put in contact with Trooper Brian
Gregoire. "What do you want to know about Flubacher?" he asked. I explained what I was doing and he told me he had a trunk that was full of
Flubacher's personal papers. The trunk proved to be a treasure chest.
Mug shots of the suspects, original interview notes, and police reports
added so much more to this project. The information Gregoire provided
to me necessitated the rewriting of several sections in the book, but it
was well worth it and I can't thank him enough.

Retired Herkimer County judge Patrick L. Kirk and his wife Cheryl
are old friends of mine. Both of them wanted to help out on this project
and I'm glad they did. In between basketball games and softball innings
at The Villages in Florida, Pat reviewed the manuscript and offered his
insight on the courtroom activities that I presented. In the meantime,
his wife set aside her golf clubs and put her red pen to work making all
sorts of corrections. In New Jersey, Don Burke took his turn. A journalist by trade, Don painstakingly reviewed each page and offered many
suggestions and corrections. I can only hope that Don has now taken it
upon himself to write his own book.

Another lady who wielded a red pen was Valerie Ahwee, my copy
editor. I am so thankful that Managing Editor Mary Young assigned
this project to such a talented editor. And a big thank you goes to Ac-
quiring Editor William Underwood for his advice and assistance.

Whenever possible I reached out to family members associated with
this story. Charles Cassaro of Port Charlotte, Florida, is a direct descen-
dant of the first Mrs. Sam Antonio, Mary Turano. He passed along to me
several stories that had been passed down to him about Mary. Several
of Dan Prior's relatives couldn't help at all. As all eight of his children
have passed, only grandchildren remain. Daniel Prior III said he wasn't
familiar with the Antonio case, but instead offered a few anecdotes of

his late grandfather's traits and mannerisms. After going through old obituaries, I located the family of the assistant district attorney, Joseph Casey. Only then did I discover that Casey's grandson was a parish priest at a church next door to me in Frankfort, New York. Father Yanas put me in contact with his father John and sister Kathy Yanas. Between the two they overwhelmed me with information about Joseph Casey. Kathy Yanas of Albany provided all the background information on her multitalented grandfather. Imagine my surprise when Dr. John Wands Saca of Troy, New York, told me that his great aunt, Sara Mara, kept a diary. Unfortunately, the district attorney's secretary not only didn't mention the Antonio trial, but she recorded her diary in shorthand. Still, Mr. Saca related many stories of his late "Aunt Sate," which I incorporated into this book. John Crary, son of the same John Crary who drove Sam Antonio to Memorial Hospital, grew up hearing about the Antonio murder and shared several stories with me about this case. Lastly, Kim Noyes of the DeMarco Funeral Home in Rotterdam was very helpful in gathering information on the Anna Antonio funeral.

It took a tremendous amount of courage for members of Anna Antonio's family to step forward and assist me with this book. There are some very special people here, people who wanted the whole story to be told. Diane Boswell, daughter of Frankie, told me what it was like to grow up, not knowing the truth. Only after prodding and doing a little research on her own was Diane able to get a glimpse of what had happened all those years ago. Marie Antonio's daughter, Vicki Moyer Reed, provided me with so many pictures and stories I just don't know where to begin to thank her. Her vivid recollections of her late mother are special.

There is only one person alive today who has any memory of those times and to her I am indebted. To me, she will always be Aunt Phyllis. Speaking to me about her life, the memories she had, and the times she spent with Marie is something I shall never forget. To protect the privacy of this very special lady, I have omitted her last name. Aunt Phyllis, this book is for you, your brother, and your sister. Thank you for letting me tell this story.

James M. Greiner
Herkimer, New York

INTRODUCTION
THE GUT

Alex Williams was a gaslight-era policeman from New York City who was as rough and tough as some of the neighborhoods he was assigned to patrol. He never dodged a fight, was known to instigate a few, and used his nightstick in such a menacing way as to earn him the sobriquet "Clubber." In 1872, after walking the beat in several different neighborhoods in the city, Clubber Williams found himself assigned to the West Thirteenth Street Station near Broadway. At that time the streets nearest the Great White Way were rife with gangs, gambling, opium dens, and prostitutes. The graft and kickbacks he received from these various illegal activities enabled him to enjoy a far better lifestyle than that of an ordinary policeman. "I have had chuck for a long time," he boasted, "and now I am going to eat tenderloin." By the time reform-minded police commissioner Theodore Roosevelt was able to force Williams into retirement, the "Czar of the Tenderloin," as he was known, owned a yacht, a home in Cos Cob, Connecticut, and several other pieces of property.[1] After Williams, the term *Tenderloin* came to signify any part of a metropolitan area with a seedy reputation. Every major city in the country had a Tenderloin, and Albany, New York, was no exception.

In Albany, the Tenderloin was the south end of the city. It was an expanse that ran from Pearl Street right on down to the Hudson River, a distance of about seven long city blocks. The Tenderloin got its first thrashing on the bookshelves from Carl H. Stubig. Before he left town in 1912, the twenty-six-year-old reporter for the *Knickerbocker Press* published *Curses on Albany*. According to Stubig, the vice, corruption, and

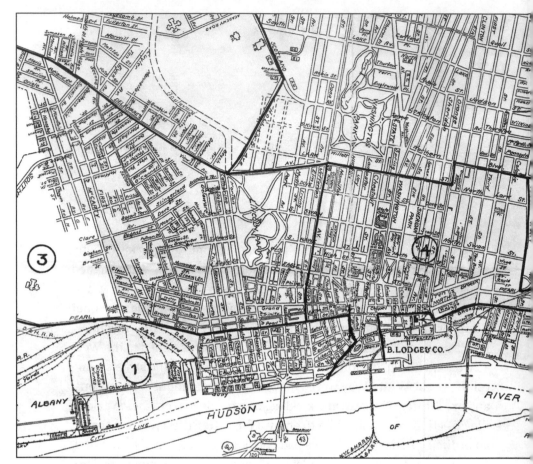

Albany's south end in 1936 (HOLC)

anything else one could imagine that were bad for Albany could be attributed to the Republican Party in general and Billy Barnes in particular.

For close to two decades, William F. Barnes Jr. was the behind-the-scenes power broker in Albany. He never held an elected office, but Boss Barnes ran Albany and held a grip on the Republican Party that would be copied in years to come. Stubig believed that Barnes was a corrupt party leader who did little to alleviate the vice that thrived in the Tenderloin and one who may have in fact profited from its existence. The figures Stubig used in his book to support his claims were impressive, especially when one considers the size of Albany in the year 1912. Of the

1,200 women who lived on the south end, Stubig claimed that one-third were "street walkers." This was a section of town, he claimed, where anything could be bought for a price. One could easily obtain a glass of beer, mixed drinks, or cigarettes, not to mention scores of scantily clad women. In the south end, said Stubig, "a red light burns on nearly every thoroughfare."[2]

Unlike many of the muckraking journalists of the Progressive Era, Stubig failed to stir the masses with his *Curses* exposé. Boss Barnes was furious over its publication, but nothing happened. It was only after the Republicans had lost their edge to the Democrats in 1910 that Barnes was investigated. He survived the investigation, Stubig left town, and the Tenderloin worsened.

On the eve of the First World War a steady stream of immigrants poured into Albany, many of whom found refuge in the poorest quarters of the city. As the Tenderloin swelled, so, too, did the urban issues that had long plagued the south end of the city. Prostitution and gambling houses had always flourished here, but now there was an increased use of narcotics, and Prohibition was just around the corner. The 1920s ushered in a new era, and soon only the old-timers would refer to the south end of Albany as the Tenderloin.

In 1928, *Time* magazine published a small editorial about the south end of Albany in the same unflattering terms Stubig had used sixteen years earlier with one exception. *Time* didn't refer to it as the Tenderloin: "Between capitol Hill and the Hudson River, stretching five or six blocks south of busy important State Street, is that district of Albany known as 'The Gut.' The underworld of many cities knows 'The Gut' and draws gangsters from it, contributes gangsters to it. Women without escorts do not walk through 'The Gut' day or night."

Where Stubig had lashed out against the Republican political machine, *Time* attacked the political power base of the Democrats who had risen to power following the demise of Barnes. "The Gut is segregated," charged the editors of *Time*, "and over it rules a Democratic ward politician, unofficial boss of Albany County, close friend of Lieut. Gov. Edwin Corning by the name of Daniel P. O'Connell."[3]

What prompted this editorial was an ugly incident that made national news when a pair of federal agents led a botched speakeasy raid in the south end. The raid was led by Irving Washburn, a former member of Troop G of the New York State Police. At the age of thirty-four, Washburn resigned from the ranks of the State Police and joined the ranks of the plainclothes "dry" agents of the federal government who had the task of enforcing the Eighteenth Amendment—Prohibition. His partner, two years his junior, was Wilford Grisson.

Early in the morning on July 13, 1928, Washburn and Grisson slowly made their way to Madison Street. It wasn't by chance that the two agents happened upon this street. Through street gossip they were reasonably certain that the ice cream parlor at 73 Madison Street was a front for a speakeasy operated by Barbero Zullo. As the two agents made their way up the street, they noticed a truck parked in front of the ice cream parlor. They had been watching Zullo's establishment for weeks and had never seen this truck in the neighborhood. With Grisson acting as the lookout, Washburn made his way to the rear of the paneled truck. Turning the latch slowly, Washburn opened the door and found his prize. He estimated that there were over two hundred cans of alcohol in the truck. He gently closed the door and signaled to his partner. Grisson was making his way to the back of the truck and by chance noticed that the keys were in the ignition.

The simple plan the two agents envisioned of seizing the truck with its cargo of bootleg booze quickly unraveled when Grisson turned the key. The sputtering of the engine had the same effect as a fire alarm. In an instant five men, all of them armed, rushed out of the ice cream parlor to confront the agents. Washburn held his ground. He announced that he was a federal agent and that he was impounding the truck and its cargo for violating the law. He hadn't finished his short speech when he was rushed by the armed men and tackled to the ground. At the same time, Grisson was pulled from the truck and savagely beaten. Washburn managed to break free of his assailants and was attempting to seek refuge behind the truck when the first shots were fired. Outgunned and outmanned, Washburn was able to get off a single shot before being struck in the abdomen. He reeled backward a few steps and slowly sank to the ground. "Stop him," he cried, "that man shot me."[4]

As men scattered in all directions, Grisson, having been beaten nearly senseless and disarmed by his attackers, got to his feet and gave chase.

He didn't get far as two uniformed Albany policemen suddenly arrived on the scene and apprehended him, believing he was one of the perpetrators. Grisson quickly identified himself as a federal agent and told the officers what had happened. By then the attackers had fled, the truck laden with alcohol had vanished, and only the critically wounded Washburn remained. The three placed Washburn in a police car and then sped to Memorial Hospital on Pearl Street.

When the assistant district attorney, John T. Delaney, learned of the shooting, he immediately went to the hospital to interview the two agents. Despite an excruciatingly painful wound, Washburn never lost consciousness and told Delaney that the man who shot him was Barbero Zullo. Delaney turned to the police officers who had accompanied him to the hospital and told them to bring Zullo to the hospital.

It was 11 P.M., almost sixteen hours after the shooting, when Zullo was brought to the hospital. Standing at the foot of Washburn's hospital bed and flanked by two Albany policemen, Delany shone a flashlight on Zullo's face and asked Washburn if this was his assailant. If the use of the flashlight was meant to distort Washburn's view, it didn't work. He positively identified Zullo. A few hours later, Washburn died.[5]

"Great was the regret of short, round faced Boss O'Connell when the spatter of bullets broke the peace of his demesne on an early morning of last week," was the reaction of *Time* magazine. "Echoes of the shots were heard many miles from Albany. This had been no ordinary Prohibition raid."[6] The editors were correct. News of the shooting spread across the state. Just as quickly, federal agents descended on the Gut to avenge one of their own. Their leader was an angry Lowell R. Smith. "Here after," announced the deputy Prohibition administrator, "my men are going in with drawn guns. I'll throw every available man in my office into the South End and if I had 30 more I would send them down there too."[7]

By the time the Washburn case came to trial, Delaney had four men, including Zullo, under arrest. The eleven-day trial, presided over by judge Earl H. Gallup, was hampered by a lack of evidence and a lack of eyewitnesses. Not a single weapon had been recovered, thus rendering the slug removed from Washburn's body a useless piece of evidence. The same could be said of the eyewitnesses. If anyone was on the street and witnessed the shooting, they did not come forward. Grisson, too, was of little help. Having been beaten to the ground, he admitted on the witness stand that he did not see Zullo shoot his partner. The defense was quick to exploit these weaknesses in the case. Not only had witnesses come forward to defend Zullo's character, the defense suggested that in the street melee, it was Grisson who had mistakenly shot his partner.

Zullo never took the stand, but one of his cohorts, Vincent Boneventuro, did and told an interesting story. Not only did he admit that there was indeed a truck with bootleg alcohol in front of the ice cream parlor on the morning in question, but he said the shooting was the result of an argument that escalated between the dry agents and Zullo. Boneventuro claimed that the agents were attempting to bribe Zullo to get a "take" in exchange for releasing the truck to the bootleggers.[8] The case ultimately collapsed when David Smurl, chief of the Albany Police Department, presented an interesting piece of evidence to Delaney. It was a letter written by Boneventuro while in his custody. In the statement, Boneventuro swore that he witnessed Joseph Zullo, not his brother Barbero, fire the fatal shot.[9]

The trial, which ended in a not-guilty verdict, was variously interpreted. "A very definite understanding had existed between the Federal Agents and Boss O'Connell. If not molested, 'The Gut' had promised to restrain itself from too-overt alcohol smuggling and rowdy boozers," concluded the editors of *Time*. "A slimy trail of vice had crawled to the very steps of the State Capitol."[10] The verdict and the message sent to federal authorities was clear—stay away from the Gut. This was private property and you are certainly not welcome here. The same message was delivered three years later to organized crime. The gangster who received this message was Jack "Legs" Diamond.

No one knows for sure how Jack Diamond came to be called Legs. Some say it was for the prowess he exhibited on the dance floor, while others maintained that it was due to his ability to quickstep his way out of trouble with the law or rival gangs. Either way, by the 1920s Legs Diamond was one of the most famous racketeers in America, if not one of the most dangerous. In his brief career on the opposite side of the law, Diamond managed to get arrested twenty-five times, four of which were for murder. He was, as one headline touted, "Adept in Beating the Rap."[11]

By the summer of 1931, Legs was persona non grata in New York City. The former owner of the Hotsy Totsy Club had been virtually run out of town by rival gangsters. Never one to give up the rackets and the money it generated, Legs decided to relocate to upstate New York. Albany seemed to be the ideal location for Legs to carve out his own niche in underworld activities. Halfway between non-Prohibition Canada and thirsty New York City, the rural roads on the outskirts of Albany offered a perfect setting to hijack trucks with bootleg booze. This would enable him to resell the booze to gangs in New York or funnel it into the Gut. With talk of Prohibition coming to an end, Legs saw this as his last chance to make big money before moving on to something else.

It didn't take him long to get into trouble in his new surroundings. In April 1931, Legs went on trial for the alleged kidnapping and torture of a Cairo, New York, truck driver named Grover Parkes.[12] Diamond knew plenty of lawyers in New York City, but here in upstate New York, he was out of his element. Fortunately for him, an attorney stepped forward and offered his services. His name was Daniel H. Prior.

The Irish gangster and the Irish attorney were a perfect match. Both were highly intelligent individuals who came from different backgrounds but shared the same view of life. Jack Diamond was the son of poor Irish immigrants. He served his apprenticeship on the streets of New York finding comradeship in his gang, the Hudson Dusters. Violence and intimidation were the trademarks of his profession. It earned him the dubious respect of his peers and the absolute loathing of those he double-crossed.

His attorney chose a different path to achieve his brand of success. Not nearly as poor as Diamond, Prior channeled his talents in academics and oratory. Like Diamond, he displayed the same type of ambition and determination to succeed. An honor student at Albany High School, Prior was the recipient of numerous awards for public speaking. Upon graduating, he was accepted at Holy Cross, and after one year he abruptly transferred to Albany Law School. He graduated, passed the bar, entered private practice, and at the age of twenty-five ran for Congress. Prior surprised friends and critics alike as he campaigned in Albany as a seasoned veteran. His speeches focused on all the major issues of the day and for the most part were well received by the Albany press.

Although Prior lost the election to his Democratic opponent by a mere eighty votes, the Republicans were impressed. With their backing, Prior was able to secure a position in the district attorney's office.

Two years later, in 1916, a city judgeship became vacant and Prior received the appointment. He completed the term and campaigned successfully for another. When it appeared to many of his friends that he might make a career out of serving as a city judge, Prior surprised them and announced that he would not seek reelection. He had his reasons, and Boss O'Connell may have been one of them. The Democrats were in power and may have wanted to ease him, a Republican, aside. Another reason might have had to do with money. He may have found it difficult to raise a large family on the fixed income of a city judge. A return to private practice would be more lucrative.[13]

Whatever fee had been agreed upon, Legs Diamond knew right from the beginning that he was going to get his money's worth out of Dan Prior when they walked into the Greene County Courthouse. The first thing Prior did was file a motion to have the trial moved out of the county. The papers he filed with the Supreme Court argued that Diamond could never expect to receive a fair trial in the same county the alleged victim resided. The courts agreed, and the trial was moved to the Rensselaer County Courthouse in Troy, New York. Prior was elated. Not only had he won a minor victory by having a change in venue, but the trial itself would be front-page news in the larger papers of Troy, Schenectady, and Albany.

Diamond was accused of the kidnapping and torture of Grover Parkes in an effort to discover the whereabouts of a still. In the verbal sparring that took place, Prior destroyed one witness after another. When the state maintained that Parkes was "a hard working trucker," and his associate James Duncan "a fine young man, a son of the soil,"[14] Prior shook his head in disbelief. Diamond's past was a matter of public record, but these two men were not the innocent lambs portrayed by the prosecution.

"These two men," scoffed Prior, "are out and out bootleggers."[15]

As was expected, the crowd that gathered outside the courthouse was almost as large as the crowd that managed to get inside it. Everyone wanted to get a glimpse of Legs Diamond. As it turned out, a glimpse is about all they got. The trial lasted two days, and the jury deliberated for three hours and returned a verdict of not guilty. Once more, Legs beat the rap. "I owe it all to Dan," he exclaimed as he exited the courtroom.[16]

The celebration was premature. The powers that controlled the capital city were more determined than ever to rid themselves of Legs Diamond. In December 1931, Legs was brought to trial a second time, this time charged with the assault of Parkes's associate, James Duncan. Prior immediately claimed that this was in violation of his client's Fifth Amendment rights. Surely, contended Prior, this was a case of double jeopardy. The court dismissed the motion almost as quickly as it had been filed. The Grover Parkes affair had been settled—this was about James Duncan.

Prior looked upon this as a minor setback. As many of the witnesses who had testified previously were slated to testify in this trial, he needed little time to prepare. During the trial, Prior was able to produce more witnesses who claimed to have seen Diamond in Albany on the day Duncan claimed to have been assaulted.

It may have been the same witnesses and in some respects the same crime, but it was a different jury. When Prior addressed the jury in his closing remarks, he reiterated the bootleg past of Parkes and Duncan. These two were not pillars of the community. Removing his glasses, Prior rubbed his eyes as if he were tired of the whole affair. The case against his client was weak. Twirling his glasses in a windmill-like fashion, he asked the jury how it was possible to declare his client innocent in June and find him guilty in December for virtually the same offense. His client, seated in the courtroom next to his wife, Alice, was innocent then and innocent now.

All eyes in the courtroom were focused on Diamond. Throughout both trials he had been friendly and courteous with everyone he had come in contact with. Often in the company of Prior, Legs was a recognizable figure in Albany. It was difficult for some people to imagine that this long lanky character with the trademark fedora was, in reality, a heartless killer. While the jury decided his fate, Legs casually leaned back in his chair and offered a few words to those who occupied the seats behind him. "If I beat this rap," he said with a sly grin, "I'm going south—to Florida—and take a long rest. I could get my health back perhaps, if I wasn't always getting into trouble."[17]

He was right. Getting into trouble was the source of many of his health problems. Nobody knows for sure how many times he was involved in shoot-outs, but the "Clay Pigeon" of the underworld or "Mr. Big Shot-at" had miraculously survived four assassination attempts.

It took five and a half hours, but the jury returned with a verdict of not guilty. Cheers, shouts, and applause echoed throughout the court as Diamond walked away, a free man. This was indeed cause for celebration. That night Legs arranged a victory celebration at Freddie Young's speakeasy on Broadway Street. He was there with his wife and Dan Prior and his wife. The celebration was well under way when Legs suddenly excused himself from the table and exited the party. Prior assumed that his client was a little drunk from the party or a little tired given the stress he had been under the last few days.

After leaving the party, Legs hailed a cab and met up with his girl-friend, showgirl and stripper Kiki Roberts. After his tryst with Roberts, Legs took a cab to 67 Dove Street, a rooming house he had rented for the duration of the trial. He made his way upstairs to his room, passed out on the bed, and never woke up. After hearing several gunshots, his landlady went to his room and found him on a blood-soaked bed.

Prior was home, but he made his way as quickly as possible to police headquarters when he received news of Diamond's murder. "It was a great shock," he told a group of waiting reporters, "I don't know any more than you of the entire affair."[18] Once inside headquarters, Prior discovered that the police knew about as much as he did, or so they claimed.

The first person Prior encountered was John T. Delaney. No longer an assistant, he was now the district attorney. He immediately informed Prior that he was leading the investigation and not to expect much. "I have no doubt," said Delaney, "that it was the same gangsters who tried to get Diamond on the other two occasions."[19] The chief of police, David Smurl, was in complete agreement, assuring Prior that he was rounding up suspects, having already locked up Legs's wife, Alice.

Fiery little Alice was as tough as her gangster husband. When she was brought to the station for questioning and taken to a holding cell, she pulled her arm away from her police escort. "Don't you dare lay your hands on me," she snapped.[20] Her insistence at meeting with an attorney was met with Smurl's flat refusal. When Prior learned of this encounter, he was furious. It was a flagrant disregard of individual rights. He made it known to Delaney and Smurl that he was counsel for Alice Diamond and any questions they might have for her would be asked in his presence.[21] Prior knew that Alice Diamond wasn't a suspect. After all, she was at the speakeasy with him for most of the evening. Prior also knew of the on-again, off-again relationship that existed between Alice and Legs. He even suspected that Alice knew all about Kiki Roberts yet remained loyal to her husband.

Prior did have serious doubts about Smurl's assumption that "rival gangs" were responsible for Diamond's murder. When Legs had gone to trial in July, Chief Smurl announced that he was placing a twenty-four-hour armed guard to shadow every move of Albany's resident gangster. "We don't want any baby killings in Albany," declared Smurl in a dramatic statement to the press. "A machine gun fusillade means innocent bystanders—even children might get hurt." What Smurl was alluding to was a tragic incident that occurred, not in Albany, but in New York City. On July 28, 1931, another Irish American gangster, Vincent "Mad Dog" Coll, attempted to kidnap a member of the Dutch Schultz gang in broad daylight on a New York City street. In the ensuing gun battle, five-year-old Michael Vengelli was killed.[22]

Smurl's press release and posturing after the death of Legs Diamond rang hollow with Prior. Throughout the course of both trials there had never been any sign of trouble. Diamond and Prior walked about the streets of Albany unmolested. But a mere six hours after his second trial he was killed. Where was the police presence Smurl had boasted of?

Prior also noticed that no one seemed to be taking credit for the murder. There was no gangland gossip or whispering, not even a hint as to who was responsible. Vincent Coll, interviewed in his jail cell while waiting to go to trial for the murder of Michael Vengelli, claimed no knowledge of the affair. "I feel sorry for anybody who is bumped off," he said, "particularly so soon after he has beaten a trial."[23] The press noted that the funeral of Legs lacked the pomp and flowers associated with a fallen gang member. Days later, the Albany police, citing lack of evidence, ended their investigation.

The Gut was free of Legs Diamond, but his memory lingered. On June 23, 1932, Joseph D'Urgolo, the chief witness for the defense in both Diamond trials, went on trial in Rensselaer County charged with perjury. No one was surprised when Dan Prior stepped forward to defend him. After a two-day trial, in which the jury deliberated a scant forty-nine minutes, D'Urgolo was declared not guilty. Newspaper reporters were anxious to interview Prior, and he was happy to oblige. "This is the last echo of the Diamond case—at least I hope it is. I don't want to be picking up the ends of this case—I want to go out and make some money. But don't for one minute think that I am ashamed of having defended Diamond. What lawyer would not have defended a man who has been twice acquitted by two different juries?"[24] His opposite number, Rensselaer County district attorney Harry Clinton said in begrudging admiration, "Dan Prior is a good trial lawyer. He knows the ins and outs. He's shrewd. He's astute."[25] Prior's successful defense of Legs Diamond had made him the most successful trial lawyer in Albany. He had fame but no money. Legs died before he could pay Dan Prior's fee.

The death of Legs Diamond made good copy for the press. The public was fascinated by the cavalier-like attitude of gangsters like Diamond who flaunted the law to make their fortune in bootleg booze. He was gone, and there were others to take his place. With colorful nicknames that matched their personalities, the public didn't seem to mind this subculture that killed their own. It was only when the Prohibition turf wars claimed the lives of innocent bystanders, like Michael Vengelli, did the public protest. Prohibition was tolerated by the public, but the narcotics trade was loathed. Drinking, whether it be wine, whiskey, or beer, was part of the western European culture that came to America with the immigrants. Narcotics, however, were looked upon with disdain as an eastern pestilence.

A decade before the noble experiment of Prohibition, the trafficking and use of narcotics was fairly widespread in the Gut. On the eve of Prohibition, Albany police chief James Hyatt went as far as to predict that an absence of alcohol in the city might lead to the increased use of narcotics. With no statistics at his disposal to prove or refute this theory, Hyatt realized early on that narcotics was a problem that needed to be addressed.[26] The chief who would have to deal with the narcotics trade in Albany was not Hyatt but his replacement, David L. Smurl.

The biggest mystery surrounding Smurl was the fact that no one ever questioned his meteoric rise in the ranks of the Albany Police Department. Smurl signed on as a patrolman on September 1, 1913, at the relatively old age of thirty-eight. It took him ten years to make sergeant. Then on September 16, 1926, he catapulted over the ranks of lieutenant, captain, and assistant chief and became chief of police. Smurl did not take lightly to criticism, was often difficult to get along with, and, above all, he disliked outside law enforcement officials. With this attitude it came as no surprise that he would clash with federal narcotics agent Richard A. Kelly.

When Richard Kelly transferred to Albany, he brought with him the eternal gratitude of the city of Syracuse. He was the single most important person, according to the *Syracuse Journal*, responsible for ridding the city of narcotics. The newspaper lauded Kelly for his tireless efforts of having "run down every dope peddler in the city and either run him out of town or put him in jail. . . . When Mr. Kelly first came to Syracuse he was given a list of every drug addict and dealer in Syracuse. He has gone religiously down that list and accounted for every one. One or two are dead, several are in jail, more are under indictment and the other balance have left town."[27] Kelly was a no-nonsense, cigar-smoking federal agent who loved his work and had little use for those who could not or would not do their job.

Arriving in Albany, Kelly immediately set his sights on the Gut. Employing the same tactics that had served him well in Syracuse, Kelly watched the little fish and then snagged the bigger ones. "We could have arrested," said Kelly of one drug runner, "several times, but we are after the bigger fellows who used this man."[28] The narcotics trade knew no age, gender, or race. This was made abundantly clear when Kelly conducted a raid on a Chinese laundry on Broadway Street. Five of the Chinese he arrested were in their twenties, and one was seventy-five years old. In no time at all, Kelly was picking up dope peddlers while at the same time picking up headlines.[29]

The Albany press appreciated his efforts in clearing out drug peddlers and began to wonder aloud about the Albany police's apparent lack of effort in performing the same service for the city. When the *Albany Evening News* congratulated Kelly for his capture of a drug peddler in the possession of "dream powder" (opium), on the same page it noted what a difficult time Chief Smurl had with tracking down parking scofflaws.[30] Publicity of this nature only widened the rift between the two.

By September 1930, the Kelly-Smurl feud reached a boiling point. Kelly accused the Albany Police Department of refusing his request to have officers assigned to him for drug raids. Smurl chafed at this meddling into his department and was further outraged to discover that a few of his patrolmen had not only volunteered to assist Kelly but were making raids with him on their off-duty hours. Smurl came under additional pressure when Maj. Joseph Manning, chief narcotics agent for northern New Jersey and New York, publicly denounced Smurl's lack of cooperation. "In most cities," said Manning, "the police department is glad to assign police officers to the federal narcotics officer. That is what we need in Albany."[31]

It appeared that nothing had changed since the early days of Prohibition. The police didn't cooperate with federal dry agents then and they were not about to cooperate with federal narcotics agents now. Smurl downplayed the entire incident, claiming that the dope problem in the south end of Albany wasn't as widespread as Kelly claimed. In response to Manning's statement, Smurl announced that he might be able to lend two officers to Kelly's squad in the near future. "Just as soon as the men I have in mind are through with some special work. They will be put on narcotics suppression. And I believe, they'll turn up something," said Smurl, "if there is any dope in the city."[32]

There was plenty of dope in the Gut, and Kelly was determined to do his job with or without the cooperation of Smurl. He tracked down runners, addicts, and suppliers working by themselves, in pairs, or in groups. With contacts and informants scattered throughout the south end, Kelly began to focus his attention on a pool hall on Madison Avenue and a restaurant on Green Street. He was watching two men. Both of them were employed by the New York Central Railroad and traveled periodically back and forth to New York City. He suspected that they were bringing narcotics up from the city. One of them was Vincent Saetta, and the other was Sam Antonio.

Part I

MARRIAGE AND MURDER

FROM RAILROADS TO THE RACKETS

In small towns scattered up and down the boot of Italy, there always seemed to be at least one townsman who had a brother, uncle, or cousin who had emigrated to America. They arrived in small groups as families, and a few, like twenty-nine-year-old Frank Antonio, made the journey alone. An illiterate laborer with no particular skills, Antonio arrived in New York City in 1884. No one will ever know how many jobs he worked at or the hardships he endured during this time, but it is fair to say Antonio had a dual purpose. He was determined never to go back to the poverty of his homeland and just as determined to bring the family he left behind to America. It took six long years for Frank Antonio to save enough money to bring his wife, two daughters, and a son-in-law to New York City.

While the new arrivals gazed in awe at the New York City skyline, Frank Antonio assured the wearisome Atlantic Ocean travelers that this would not be their home. Antonio was fortunate to have recently obtained a job with the New York Central Railroad in the western part of the state. Their new home, he told them, would be in Savannah, a small rural village in Wayne County.

Situated midway between Rochester and Syracuse, Savannah was, as one resident recalled, "a railroad town." Due to its location, Savannah was denied the commercial benefits that other villages enjoyed from the Erie Canal; however, the New York Central Railroad line that bisected the county served the region well. It was here, a few miles west of Savannah, that Frank Antonio was able to put a small down payment on a fourteen-acre farm on Clyde Road. With a swamp in the far distance, and with railroad tracks south of his home, the farm provided food for his family. At the same time, employment with the railroad was the income he needed to support a growing family, which in 1894 included a son, Sam Antonio.[1]

For the Antonios, life at the Clyde Road farmhouse revolved around family. Frank Antonio never closed the door on family. When his daughter Mary and her husband Peter DeSisto moved out of the farmhouse and took a place in the nearby village of Walcott, Meaka Penta (another sister) and her five children took their place when her marriage dissolved.[2] Young Sam, in the meantime, attended school, worked on the farm, and accompanied his father to the railroad yard.

By 1910, Frank Antonio had become a foreman on the railroad and used his position to get his sixteen-year-old son a job in the telegraph office. From this moment, Sam set education aside and concentrated on a career with the New York Central Railroad. After serving a brief stint in the telegraph office, he worked in the wheel factory and then in 1916 accepted a job as a blacksmith with the railroad in Niagara.[3] Several months after the move to Niagara, Sam crossed the Canadian border into Welland County, Ontario, and married Mary Turano on July 20.

How the two met is a complete mystery. Mary was a recent immigrant from Italy and made her home, with her family, in Brooklyn, New York. Her family maintained that they lost contact with her when she eloped with Sam Antonio. Though difficult to prove, the story cannot be easily dismissed. The wedding was a civil ceremony witnessed by two women from Niagara. The Turano family would have in all probability opposed this union. Aside from the fact that they were Catholic and would have insisted that the marriage take place in a church with their blessing, there was the question of age. On the marriage license, Sam Antonio recorded his age as twenty-two, which was correct, and Mary listed her age as eighteen, which was a lie. She was sixteen years old.[4] After the wedding, Sam brought his new bride to his father and mother's house on Clyde Road.

Dividing his time between railroad work and the family farm, Sam Antonio's lifestyle was almost upset when America entered the First World War. On the same day the Conscription Act was passed on June 5, 1917, Sam reported to the draft office in Savannah. On paper, he appeared to be what every army recruiter dreamed of in a draftee. He was of medium height, with a stocky frame and jet-black hair, blue eyes, and perfect health. However, Sam had no intention of being drafted or enlisting. He made this very clear when he lied to the draft board. Sam claimed that his source of employment was on the family farm, making no mention of his association with the railroad. As an only son needed on the farm, Sam knew that he was exempt from the draft. When his fellow townsmen boarded the trains that would take them to troopships for their journey to France, Sam boarded a train with his wife and moved to Albany.[5]

The couple remained in Albany until Mary's health declined. For over a year his wife suffered from epileptic seizures. By May 1921, these seizures became increasingly frequent and violent. Foregoing the medical facilities in Albany and unable to care for her, Sam moved back to western New York. He brought his ailing wife to the home of his sister, Mary DeSisto, in Wolcott. By the time they had arrived at the DeSisto home, Mary Antonio had experienced several grand mal seizures. A local physician, Dr. T. Sheldon Hicks, was immediately called to the house, but there was little he could do to alleviate her suffering. In the days that followed, convulsions, seizures, together with acute respiratory failure, had sapped every bit of strength from her. Unconscious for almost a week, Mary Antonio died on June 7. Two days later she was buried in Clyde, New York.[6]

Several days later, Sam had a small note of thanks printed in the *Savannah Times*: "I wish to thank the kind friends and neighbors for their assistance to me during the sickness and death of my wife. I also wish to thank those who sent flowers and furnished cars."[7] The only other note he sent was to Mr. and Mrs. Turano, informing them that their daughter had died and was buried at a cemetery in Clyde. It was little comfort to a family that had not seen or heard from their daughter in six years.

The grieving that Sam felt for his first wife did not last long. He returned to Albany and nine months later reappeared in Clyde with his future bride, Anna Cappello. Like his late wife Mary, she, too, was an immigrant and very young.

Anna Cappello was born in 1906 in Alvignon, a tiny village twenty-eight miles north of the port city of Naples. Little is known of her childhood in Italy, but when her mother died, her father entrusted her to the care of cousins, while he made the journey to America to seek work. In wasn't until 1915, with Italy in the midst of the First World War, that her father Ferdinando was able to send for her and two cousins. They arrived at Ellis Island on June 18 and from there her widowed father brought her to a small apartment at 319 Webster Street in Schenectady. It was here that she was reunited with her older brother Pasquale, whom she affectionately called Patsy.[8]

Like many children of Italian immigrants, Anna's schooling was brief. With the equivalent of a fifth-grade education, just enough to grasp the rudimentary workings of a new language, she quit school and went to work. Her father owned a small restaurant and bar in West Albany, and it was here that Anna went to work with an older sister. A frequent customer to the restaurant was a railroad man, Sam Antonio. When Anna and her father relocated to 53 North Jay Street, in the Little Italy section of Schenectady, Sam followed. Of the few suitors she claimed to have had in her teenage years, Anna recalled that her father disapproved of just one—Sam Antonio. The friction between father and daughter led Anna to run away. She went to city hall, obtained a marriage license, and then boarded the train with Sam, bound for Clyde.

On February 22, 1922, Sam and Anna exchanged vows at the Methodist Church in Clyde. Rev. Leslie Farnsworth never questioned why the couple chose his church instead of a Catholic church. The fact that none of her family was present was a clear indication that they disapproved of the union. The ceremony was quick, with only two witnesses—Anna Covell, a parishioner, and Peter DeSisto, Mary's husband. In the same town where his first wife was buried, Sam Antonio recorded on the marriage license that this was his first marriage. Clearly this was not an oversight and his reason for doing this is a mystery. But more disturbing is the fact that he recorded Anna's age as nineteen when, like his first wife, she was in fact sixteen years old.[9]

The newlyweds made their home in Wolcott, with Sam's parents. The family farm on Clyde Road had been sold, and the elderly Antonios had moved to Wolcott to be near Mary and Peter DeSisto. On September 9, 1924, Anna gave birth to her first child. She was christened Phyllis, an Americanization of Felicia, to honor Sam's mother.[10] For a while it appeared that the couple would remain in the western part of the state. However, in 1927, Sam came home and suddenly announced that with his recent promotion to brakeman with the railroad, they would be moving to Albany.

By the 1920s, the Italians were the largest ethnic group in the city of Albany. It didn't take long for families to settle in and occupy apartments that spread from Philip Street by Madison Avenue to Broadway Street and from Second Avenue to Van Zandt Street, give or take a street or two. Here was Albany's Little Italy. It was here that Italian men sought out pick-and-shovel jobs or any work where their minimal skills could be put to use. And it was on Grand Street, for example, where their wives made their way through bakeries, meat markets, and vegetable stands. It was in Little Italy that they escaped the prejudice of the outside world. They spoke their own language, kept alive their old-world traditions, and worked hard to support their families. For Anna, the move to Albany would be almost as if she had relocated back to Jay Street in Schenectady.

With little Phyllis in tow, Anna left the quiet rural surroundings of western New York and returned to city life. They settled into an apartment on 101 Clinton Avenue, remaining there for about two years. From there, it was one move after another. In ten years they had moved in and around the city of Albany eight times.[11]

In almost every instance an Antonio move included other members of the family. When Sam relocated to Albany, his parents joined him and in no time the DeSistos followed in their wake, sharing the same apartment. Living conditions in the apartment swelled when several of Meaka Penta's children joined them.[12] Finally, in 1932, Sam Antonio brought his family to the second floor of a red-brick apartment house at 3 Teunis Street. This move suited their needs in several ways. First, as with their previous moves, it was closer to work. From the apartment doorstep on Teunis Street, it was a little over a mile and a half to Union Station. And, perhaps more importantly, there were fewer mouths to feed. His sister Mary DeSisto and her husband Peter had moved to the Bronx, taking his aged parents with them along with several of the Penta children. It was their last move, but now they were somewhat alone. By the time Sam and Anna moved to 3 Teunis Street, their family had grown. Six-year-old Phyllis was joined by two-and-a-half-year-old Marie and four-month-old Anita. On March 22, 1931, Anna gave birth to a baby boy, Frank. During this time, they had a boarder, Tony Penta. No one knew how long Tony Penta would be living with them. He was one of Meaka's children and had been living with Sam's parents up until then. Tony was about two years older than Anna, and through Sam's influence he had secured a position on the railroad as a tracklayer. Anna and Tony had known each other since she lived in Wolcott and since that time had become close friends. With a house full of little ones and her husband absent for days on end, Anna appreciated the company and assistance of Tony.

After the birth of Frankie, Anna grew more and more concerned about Anita. She appeared lethargic and unresponsive. It was only after she took the infant to Dr. Louis Russo on Delaware Avenue for an examination that she was given devastating news. Dr. Russo told Anna that her little Anita was suffering from the beginning stages of hydrocephalus—water on the brain. Months went by and all Anna could do was watch her helpless child. Each visit to the doctor became less and less encouraging. On August 5, 1931, with Albany in the midst of a brutal heat wave with temperatures soaring into the nineties, Anna gazed helplessly as Anita, whose head had swelled, gasped for each breath. Inside the sweltering apartment, Anna did her best to make her comfortable with damp cloths and cold compresses. When Anita's breathing became more labored, she called for Dr. Russo.

When he arrived, he observed that Anita was quickly failing. As the child struggled for each breath, he could tell that she was in the beginning stages of pneumonia. Dr. Russo stayed by the crib staring at a child he could not save while her mother sobbed nearby. Anita drew her last breath at fifteen minutes after midnight on August 8, 1931. Two days later, the grieving parents buried Anita at Our Lady of Hope Cemetery. Doctor bills and the funeral bill were such that they were unable to put a marker on the grave.[13]

With the death of Anita, Anna sank into a deep depression. She had no close friends or family to lean on at this time. Her father and brother lived in Schenectady, and Tony Penta had moved out of the apartment shortly before Anita had died. As she was a relative newcomer to Teunis Street, the only close friends she had were her upstairs neighbor, Mrs. Margaret Zimmerman, and Julia Altopeda, her daughter Marie's godmother, who lived blocks away on Clinton Street. For now, she had to mask her feelings as she had three small children to raise in a small apartment on a small allowance.

At the end of the summer in 1931, Anna wasn't quite sure if her husband's hours had been reduced with the railroad or he wasn't taking advantage of extra work on the railroad. She began to notice that he was home more frequently but at the same time rarely stayed at home. As a traditional Italian housewife of that era, Anna never asked her husband his affairs. Her place was in the home, particularly the kitchen. She was duty-bound to prepare meals and raise the children. Husbands rarely helped with housework and, above all, their word was law. She soon became accustomed to his parting words to her as he left the apartment "to go out on business." Anna never asked what this business was, but she had her suspicions, especially when she noticed him leaving the apartment with a pistol tucked in his belt.

With her children as her main concern, Anna grew increasingly nervous about the people Sam was inviting to their apartment. She didn't mind preparing meals for his railroad coworkers, but she grew to dislike these other friends who showed up at the apartment at any hour of the day or night. They spoke in low whispers and laughed loudly, and she noted that most of them had guns. The only one she ever recognized was Vincent Saetta. He worked with Sam on the railroad as a brakeman and, not by coincidence, always seemed to be at the apartment when her husband was not working.

Vincent Saetta was a Sicilian who arrived at Ellis Island with his mother and four sisters on June 12, 1912. His father, who arrived in the city a few years earlier, worked in a cigar factory. While his sisters secured employment in the garment district, Vincent drifted in and out of the public schools in Manhattan. Since working beside his father in the cigar factory didn't suit him, and after drifting from one job to the next, Vincent Saetta made the decision to join the army. As it turned out, it was a short, uneventful career. He enlisted and eight months later the war ended before he ever left New York. Following his discharge, Saetta took a job with the New York Central Railroad, eventually becoming a brakeman on the Albany to Hudson line. It was here that he met Sam Antonio.

Saetta's career with the railroad was a little bit longer than his career in the army. In 1931, police arrested Saetta following their investigation into a shooting that took place in West Albany. He called in sick to work the next day, and the railroad promptly dismissed him when they discovered that he was in jail. Although the charges against him were eventually dismissed, Saetta was out of work and out of money.[14]

When the doorbell sounded late in the evening on December 15, 1931, Anna was not surprised to open the apartment door and see Vincent Saetta with another man she had never seen before. As she had done countless times, Anna motioned them into the apartment and pointed toward the living room. She returned to her usual place in the kitchen, and in a backward glance noticed that her husband was seated on the sofa, cleaning a pistol. Saetta, too, seated himself on the sofa next to Sam and proceeded to clean his pistol.

"Well, we will have a good Christmas this year," said Sam. "We will have plenty of money."

"Yes," added Saetta, "we can have some good times."

As the men prepared to leave the apartment, Sam had some last-minute instructions for his wife. He told her to expect a long-distance call in his absence.

"Anna, I am going to call you up from Buffalo. I am just going to say 'all right.'" He then told her to expect another long-distance call, but this one would be from New York City. "When that call comes," he instructed her, "just tell them 'all right' and if they call before I do, why tell them that you have not received the call."[15] He repeated these cryptic instructions to her twice and then hurried out the door. Before he left the apartment, Anna noticed that her husband hadn't packed any luggage for this Buffalo trip. She went to the kitchen window and could just make out all three men getting into a waiting car that sped away into the night.

Several days later, Sam reappeared at 3 Teunis Street. He never asked how Anna or the children fared in his absence, but instead he was anxious to know if she had received a call from New York City. Anna told him that after she had received his call from Buffalo, she received another call at about midnight from New York. Anna told him that she answered with "all right" just as he had instructed. Sam let out a big sigh. He went to the bathroom, washed up, and at 10 A.M. went to bed.

In the afternoon of that same day, Anna heard a knock on the apartment door. Not wishing to disturb her husband, Anna quietly opened the door. It was Vincent Saetta in the company of the same man who went to Buffalo with Sam. Anna told both men that her husband was asleep and she dared not disturb him. She was just about to send them away when the bedroom door swung open. Sam motioned the two men into the living room and Anna to the kitchen.

"You will get your money in a few days," said Sam. This promise was enough for the man whom Anna did not know. He left the apartment, but Saetta remained. Sam told Saetta that he was expecting a call from New York City. Saetta should go home and when he received the call, he would contact him. This wasn't good enough for Vincent Saetta. Against Sam's wishes, he sat on the sofa and waited for the call. Over an hour passed before the phone rang. Instinctively, Anna went to pick up the receiver, only to be eased aside by Saetta, who in turn was outflanked by Sam.

"Will it be alright to come up tonight?" asked Sam.

"No," replied the caller, "tomorrow night. Tomorrow night at Dominick's Restaurant at seven o'clock."

This arrangement suited Sam but not the impatient Saetta.

"Let's go to New York tonight. We done the work. Why can't we get our money now?"

"No," cautioned Sam, "no use going against these people. We will go tomorrow night."[16]

Waiting until the next evening must have seemed like an eternity to the cash-strapped Saetta. Desperate for fast money, and not because Christmas was only a few days away, Saetta owed money to several people, including Sam Antonio. A month earlier Saetta had found himself in financial straits and had asked Sam for a loan. These were lean times for Sam as well, but wishing to help Saetta, he pawned two small diamond rings that belonged to Anna.

Four days before Christmas, Saetta made his way to the Teunis Street apartment to collect his money. When he arrived, he could see the cash spread out over the coffee table in the living room. It was a fifty-fifty split, of sorts. First there was the matter of the rings. Now was time, said Sam, to get the rings out of "hock." The pawnshop was holding the rings for $100, plus interest. He also suggested a slight gratuity.

"You give me $50 of your $500," said Sam, "and I will give $50 of mine and that goes to the kid."[17]

The "kid" was Anna. The money was needed for Christmas, food, and bills. Sam may have hoped that the money would in some way make up for the meals she had prepared for him and his friends over the last few weeks.

Saetta never complained about these stipulations. He took the money and told Sam that he was going to a newsstand on Broadway Street to get a few of the local newspapers. He was curious to see if the press had made note of their latest exploit. He returned momentarily with the *Troy Times,* the *Schenectady Gazette,* and the Albany *Times-Union.* He spread the papers across the kitchen table and with the excitement of a schoolboy reading his name in the paper for the first time, read each paper aloud. It was only then that Anna learned the details of this mysterious job that had nothing to do with Buffalo. As Saetta read each paper, Anna discovered that they had traveled sixty-five miles south of Buffalo to the village of Salamanca and then to nearby Quaker Bridge.

"The main plant of the Steamburg Dairy Products Company at Quaker Bridge, 15 miles southwest of this place was destroyed by fire yesterday with a loss of $100,000," said Saetta, reading from the *Schenectady Gazette.* "Police said firemen found oil-soaked rags in different parts of the building."[18] The other newspapers reported essentially the same thing. The arson, the sixth one in New York, was the result of an ongoing "milk war" that pitted independent milk producers against three of the largest companies in the state.

The plight of the small dairy farmer held little interest for either of the men sitting at the kitchen table. This was a job that had promised big money, and if the job went well, more jobs and more money might come their way. All the reports of the Steamburg arson that they read in the papers indicated that the police had no leads in the case. Both men laughed and congratulated themselves on committing the perfect crime.

"We almost got stuck on the bridge with the fire truck," said Sam, "that bridge is so narrow, we just got by in time."

Their mood changed when Sam took a long look at the papers a second time. Each paper recorded the loss of the dairy plant as $100,000.

Turning to Saetta, he said glumly, "We should have got more money for the job."[19]

This planted a seed of doubt in Saetta's mind. The money they received—$1,000—did seem like a paltry sum for the amount of damage reported by the papers. This bothered him, and he decided to do a little investigating on his own. Bidding the Antonios good-bye, Saetta told them that he had to catch the 8:45 A.M. train to the city as he was spending Christmas with his family. While in New York, Saetta contacted the people Sam had warned him to stay away from. It was an extremely angry and suspicious Vincent Saetta who knocked on the Teunis Street apartment door a week after Christmas.

As she had done so many times before, Anna retired to the kitchen when Saetta arrived. As she prepared lunch, she noticed that this wasn't going to be a friendly meeting. Saetta immediately dispensed with the small talk and got right to the point. He told Sam that he had visited a few people in New York. Saetta now believed that he knew the reason why Sam wanted him to stay away from them.

"You got more money for that, than you split with me, I hear you got $2,500."

"I got a thousand," said Sam, "I split even with you."

"You got $2,500," said Saetta as he stormed out of the apartment.[20]

Startled by the sudden outburst, Sam Antonio let it pass. Vincent Saetta would come back to him because he always did when he ran out of money.

In February 1932, Sam Antonio made another one of his mysterious trips out of town. On this occasion, he went south to New York City at the behest of Vincent Saetta. When Sam returned home, he was immediately confronted by Saetta.

"Did you sell the stuff?"

The "stuff" was narcotics. Saetta was slowly coming to the realization that moving dope in the Gut was becoming more difficult due to the increased efforts of federal agents, led by Richard Kelly. He reasoned that it would be much easier to move drugs in a larger metropolitan area like New York City. Saetta was in for a shock.

"No," replied Sam.

Saetta stared in disbelief as Sam Antonio tried to explain that despite the vastness of the city, there were police and federal agents on every drug corner and in every alleyway. He informed Saetta that he had to dispose of the drugs to avoid being arrested. Saetta seethed with anger, believing that Sam had sold the drugs and kept the money all for himself.

"You are trying to double-cross me, you made a sucker out of me once, you are trying to do the same thing now."[21]

Sam tried to calm his excitable friend, but it was no use. Bitter and angry, Vincent Saetta left the apartment and never returned. The loss of the drugs convinced him that he had been cheated by Sam Antonio all the way around. His business partner, Sam Antonio, would now become his business. If he couldn't get the money out of Sam, he would put pressure on his wife. Surely, timid little Anna would be an easy mark.

2

SAM FARACI

On February 15, 1932, Sam Faraci walked into Louis's Pool Room at 67 Madison Avenue and bought a pack of cigarettes.

"When did you get in?"

Faraci spun around, recognizing the voice immediately from his last visit to the pool hall. Motioning with one hand to the car parked across the street, Faraci, in a thick Italian accent, said, "Just now, pull in with the car."

"I think I know you," said Sam Antonio.

"You know me?" replied Faraci.

"I heard from Vincent Saetta."

"What he told you about me?" said Faraci with a sly grin.[1]

Antonio told him that Saetta had mentioned he would be arriving from Geneva. Faraci may have breathed a sigh of relief if this was all that his friend Saetta had told him. Sam Faraci had been in and out of trouble for the past twenty years.

Like his friend Saetta, Faraci hailed from Sicily. Since he could neither read nor write, his last name would undergo a half-dozen variations in spelling, depending on which reporter happened to be submitting a story or which policeman was writing an arrest report. When he arrived at Ellis Island in 1912, the same year as Saetta, immigration officials recorded his name phonetically.[2] Salvatore Ferruggia became Sam Ferugia and, after a brush with the law, changed it to Sam Faraci. His brother met him at Ellis Island and brought him to Geneva, New York. Here the two brothers labored on a farm, earning enough money in nine months to send for Sam's wife and daughter. When they arrived from Sicily, Sam quit the farm and tried his hand at factory work, mashing cabbage into sauerkraut. This, too, didn't last long. He eventually turned to odd jobs and house painting. All of this was honest work, but it was his other line of work that concerned the local authorities in Geneva.[3]

By 1917, a triangle of crime had been established within the boundaries of Canandaigua, Geneva, and Lyons. The police were asking the public's help in solving a series of petty crimes, burglaries, and strong-armed robberies. The authorities never mentioned the Black Hand but suspected recent Italian immigrants were responsible. In Geneva, the police were aware of one roving gang but thus far had no eyewitnesses or evidence to make an arrest.

The ring leader of one such gang was Sam Faraci. With the assistance of hoodlums who had drifted down from Rochester, Faraci and his gang met at Anthony Saratore's Restaurant located on the outskirts of Geneva at a place called Border City. It was here in December 1917 that they planned their most audacious act. Their target was John Michaelson, a Geneva barber who was also a city alderman. He was well known, well liked, and was known to carry large sums of money. The weapon of choice for Sam Faraci was a fifty-cent baseball bat. Sawing two and a half feet off the bat and wrapping the lower end in newspaper, it could be easily concealed in a coat sleeve or in the folds of a jacket.

The gang struck on Saturday night, December 21. Taking up positions along Exchange Street, one of the gang members signaled that Michaelson was nearby. With their intended target in sight, the gang was just about to call off their attack. Michaelson wasn't alone. The gang lay in wait and soon noticed that Michaelson and the man who was walking with him shook hands and parted company. When Michaelson's friend walked away, the gang made their move. Two men emerged from the shadows and slowly approached him.

The unsuspecting, affable Michaelson commented to the strangers who approached him on what brisk December weather they were experiencing. He was about to bid them good night when he was suddenly struck from behind on the shoulder. Screaming out in pain, Michaelson tried desperately to fend off his attackers. Savagely clubbed on the side of the head, he was then struck across the face with such force that his front teeth were knocked out. At this point, the lookouts on the other side of the street joined in the melee. Amazingly the bloodied and severely wounded alderman never lost consciousness and never stopped screaming for help.

Neighbors, hearing these cries, emerged from their homes to offer aid as the thieves vanished into the night. The police arrived momentarily and gave chase, correctly assuming that the gang would try to rendezvous at Border City. Commandeering city taxis as squad cars, the police raced up and down the streets looking for members of the gang. Standing on the running board of one of the taxis, a police officer noticed one man walking at a quick pace and ordered him to halt. When the stranger broke into a run, the officer leapt from the taxi and gave chase on foot. He tackled the suspect to the ground and in the tussle, the stranger produced a long blade knife and lunged at the officer. Another officer arrived just in time to disarm him.

When the suspect arrived at the police station, he was searched. The only thing he had in his pocket was a wad of bills, $408 to be exact. It was an odd amount of money, but it just so happened to be the exact amount of money Michaelson claimed was stolen. It came as no surprise that the suspect, now in police custody, claimed that he didn't know how he came into the money. The clean-shaven man in his twenties with a large crop of curly red hair told the police that he was new in town and frightened when the police, for he did not know they were police, ordered him to stop. He was from nearby Lyons but had briefly lived in Rochester. The police didn't believe any of this and eventually the man recanted. He said his name was Sam Faraci.[4]

It wasn't until the next day that the police notified Mary Ferugia that her husband was under arrest. When officers brought the pregnant woman to her husband's cell, he stared in disbelief. Some witnesses claimed that Faraci fainted when she was brought to him and could not be revived for almost a half hour. Sam remained in jail awaiting his court date, and Mary went home to spend Christmas with her three children.

It didn't take long for the police to round up the other suspects, and soon all of them stood trial charged with first-degree robbery. On the witness stand, Sam Faraci thought there was a small chance that the charge against him might be dismissed. Although he was apprehended by the police with the money, Michaelson had not positively identified him as one of the assailants. On the witness stand, Faraci tried to distance himself from the assault. He wasn't the one who took the money off the victim, he told the court, it was another one of the gang who gave it to him for safekeeping so it could be divided the next day. The ruse didn't work. All five men were sentenced to a minimum sentence of seven and a half years at Auburn State Prison.[5]

Sam Faraci entered Auburn State Prison with a simple agenda. He was determined to gain an early release. This, of course, could be possible only with good behavior and cooperation. He stayed out of trouble, did as he was told, and in all respects became a model prisoner. As to the cooperation aspect of his plan, it had nothing to do with prison officials. His plan was to cooperate with the man who sentenced him to prison, the Geneva district attorney. Faraci had been in Auburn State Prison for just a few months when he reached out to the district attorney with an offer. Faraci would rat out every known criminal in Geneva in exchange for an early release. The district attorney's office was intrigued by the offer, especially when they learned that the key witness in Faraci's trial had been recently discovered at a railyard in Batavia, a steel pipe near his crushed skull.[6]

The district attorney's office used the information Faraci offered and made a string of arrests. By the latter part of 1920, they were prepared to uphold their part of the bargain and contacted Gov. Nathan Miller.[7] On January 11, 1921, Sam Faraci was paroled from Auburn State Prison having served two years and one month. Whatever joy he felt upon his release was dampened somewhat when the *Auburn Citizen* informed its readers why the parole had been offered. The district attorney "secured the conviction of two Italians interceded with Governor Miller for clemency on the ground that the pair had rendered invaluable assistance in cleaning up a gang of criminals whose acts had terrorized the city of Geneva."[8] When the paper hit the newsstands, everyone in Geneva knew that Sam had turned on some and informed on others in an effort to get out of prison.

Widely unpopular in certain sections of Geneva and Border City, Sam Faraci returned home, fathered more children, and did his best to avoid full-time work by becoming a house painter. This fair-weather work gave him plenty of time to pursue other activities. The trafficking of bootleg booze during Prohibition was his new plan to make easy money.

For Sam Faraci, failure and bad luck were his shadows. One would think that after serving twenty-five months in prison, you would do everything in your power not to return. Ten months later, on November 9, he found himself behind bars in the Ontario County Jail charged with selling alcohol.[9] Faraci didn't need legal counsel to tell him the seriousness of his present situation. He had been paroled from Auburn, not pardoned. One of the conditions of his parole was that if he was later arrested, he would have to complete his original sentence. His usefulness as an informant to the Geneva district attorney's office had long since diminished, so he could expect little in a plea bargain from them. The judge, too, was unsympathetic to his plight after learning the details of his stay in jail before his sentencing.

Knowing full well that he was returning to Auburn, Faraci, the same man who could not orchestrate a successful strong-armed robbery, made plans to escape from the Ontario County Jail. On January 26, 1922, his wife Mary arrived at the jail with a loaf of fresh-baked bread. Deputies casually glanced at the bread in the wicker basket and escorted her into her husband's cell. After she left, the deputies discovered Sam hard at work trying to cut through a steel bar with a hacksaw blade. He told the deputies that his wife was not to blame as it was he who told her to insert the blades into the loaf of bread.[10] The judge told the district attorney to contact Auburn and expect a repeat offender.

Released from prison a second time, on January 9, 1929, Sam told his wife he had several houses lined up to paint, which would keep him busy for most of the summer and fall. He painted a few houses but also managed to get a job running a roadhouse, Fairview Inn, south of Geneva. He remained there for a while, keeping company with a prostitute, Gertrude King, from Oswego, New York.[11]

With her husband away from home more than ever and the lack of money an increasing concern, Mary had to act. With her older children working to support the family, she went to the Ontario Family Court and obtained a court order of support. It was her hope that her errant and irresponsible husband might want to contribute some money to help raise the children he hardly knew. When sheriff's deputies finally tracked him down and served him with the court papers, her husband responded in true Sam Faraci fashion. It was time to get out of town. The day after Valentine's Day, he packed his car and drove away from Geneva, leaving his wife and nine children to fend for themselves. In all respects, Sam Faraci had declared moral bankruptcy. With only a few dollars in his pocket and his prostitute girlfriend by his side, Faraci set out for Albany. Here he could lose himself in the city and at the same time possibly make some money. Remaining in Geneva was simply out of the question. Too many people knew his past and the court order of support carried a penalty. Failure to comply with the court order would once again land him in jail.

After a six-hour drive, Faraci and King arrived in Albany. He was familiar with the Gut, and with the help of an old acquaintance he found a small apartment on Hamilton Street. Still wary of the authorities in Geneva, Faraci and his girlfriend checked in as Mr. and Mrs. King. After they unpacked the car, Faraci told King to stay at the apartment. He told her he was going to Louis's Pool Hall for a pack of cigarettes. It was about 7 P.M. when Faraci parked his car across the street and walked into the pool hall. He gazed about the smoke-filled room in hopes of finding Saetta when he was approached by Sam Antonio. They visited, had a cigarette, and Sam Antonio asked a favor.

"You got your car across the road?"

"Yes."

"What kind a car you got?"

"Oldsmobile coupe."

"Want to do me a favor?"

"Sure, why not, I got no place to go."

"Drive me to Schenectady."[12]

Antonio told Faraci that he didn't have much money but would be able to give a little gas money for this favor. Faraci didn't mind. This was a small trip compared to the six-hour drive he just completed from Geneva. The trip to Schenectady and the return to Albany took a little bit longer than Faraci had anticipated. When they arrived at their destination, Antonio got out of the car and assured him that he would not be all that long. Twenty minutes later Antonio reappeared. He never explained what took so long, but Faraci suspected it had to do with a narcotics delivery.

Back in Albany, a grateful Sam Antonio invited Faraci to dinner. When they arrived at the 3 Teunis Street apartment, Faraci seated himself at the kitchen table while Sam went to the bedroom to get Anna out of bed to cook their meal. She put a pot of coffee on the stove and prepared ham and eggs with toast. She never spoke, but she put the plates on the table and, after serving them, retired to bed.[13]

Sam Faraci could be useful, thought Antonio, more useful than Vincent Saetta. Faraci had an automobile.

3

"ARE WE READY FOR A GOOD TIME?"

Vincent Saetta always believed that he had been cheated out of his fair share of the Steamburg arson money and the money he didn't receive when Sam Antonio allegedly disposed of his narcotics in New York City. Determined to get his money back, or as much as he could, he began making a series of harassing and threatening phone calls to the Teunis Street apartment. Well aware of Sam Antonio's work schedule, Saetta knew when it was best to call the apartment to exert pressure on his wife. When Anna answered the phone, she was at first startled to hear Saetta's voice. Their first conversation was brief.

"Your husband owes me money."

"Why don't you ask him for it?" said Anna.

"I did and he won't give it to me. You got $100 for Christmas."

"That's my money," she replied, ending the conversation.[1]

Anna made it clear that the $50 she received from Saetta and the matching amount she received from her husband was her money. Saetta was taken aback. This was not the mousy little Anna whom he was accustomed to seeing at the apartment. Saetta knew he would have to apply more pressure if he were to get any money out of her. A few days later he placed another call.

"You got a $100, why don't you give it to me? You know your husband owes it to me."

Anna stood her ground. "You gave him the money," snapped Anna, "why should I pay his debt?"[2]

In time, the calls to the apartment in her husband's absence became more frequent. Anna later estimated that in the span of two months, Saetta phoned her almost thirty times demanding money. Each new phone call became more threatening.

"You got $100 that you got for Christmas."

"Yeah, but I'm going to keep that."

"If he don't give me that money he owes me I'm going to kill him."[3]

Staggered by this chilling remark, Anna became worried. Despite the numerous meetings between Vincent Saetta and her husband, with pistols on the coffee table, there had never been talk of killing anyone. She made up her mind to tell her husband the instant he came home.

To her utter surprise, Sam wasn't angry nor did he show the least bit of concern when told of the numerous calls Saetta had placed to their apartment. Sam laughed and told her not to be concerned. He wasn't afraid of Vincent Saetta. Unbeknownst to his wife, Sam had already had an altercation with Vincent Saetta. A week or two earlier, on the sidewalk near a Green Street restaurant, Saetta approached Sam Antonio from behind and sucker punched him in the head. Antonio reeled around and sent Saetta sprawling to the sidewalk with a powerful punch to the eye. Saetta quickly recovered and drew a knife, only to have Antonio kick it out of his hand.

Sam Antonio wasn't worried about Saetta, but he did become concerned when Anna told him of mysterious goings-on downstairs. One evening in January, about a month after the Steamburg arson, Anna heard a commotion outside the apartment in the first-floor foyer. Peeking out her door and looking down the dimly lit staircase, she saw two men. Wearing long overcoats, one of the men confronted upstairs neighbor John Gonyea. Anna distinctly heard one of them say, "He's not the one."[4]

When Anna told her husband about these two mysterious strangers, she later recalled that his whole demeanor changed. She had never

seen him act this way before. Sam became agitated and extremely nervous. In a frightened, serious tone he instructed her never to go into
the basement and fix the furnace. He said he would attend to it when he
got home. He also told her that under no circumstances was she to let
the children out of the apartment unattended. If she could not watch
them, then she should pay someone to do that. "It is better to give them
a half dollar and let someone watch them than to leave them out alone."

Sam was visibly shaken and Anna became increasingly worried. She
began to wonder if these mysterious strangers were in fact hired men
from New York.[5] Saetta told her, in one of his many phone calls, that a
few men were on their way up from the city to help him get his money.

By the first week of March 1932, Saetta became more brazen. Now,
instead of calling Anna, he showed up unannounced at the apartment.
On the pretense that Sam had "paperwork" of his, Saetta pushed the
door and Anna aside. Over her protests, Saetta rifled through the draw-
ers of the desk in the living room. Furious at this intrusion, Anna was
relieved when he left the apartment empty-handed. If the "paperwork"
he had been searching for was money, Anna could have told him he was
wasting his time. Sam never left money in the house or put it in a bank.
He always carried it in his wallet. Afterwards, when Saetta threatened
to show up at the apartment again, Anna reluctantly agreed to meet
him. She told him she had a little Easter shopping to do and agreed to
meet him at the Leland Theater on South Pearl Street.

On the appointed day, Anna went to the Leland Theater and immediately recognized Saetta. As people lined up to get tickets for the afternoon matinee, the two walked to the ice cream parlor that was adjacent
to the theater lobby. Anna ordered a soda and waited only a few seconds for Saetta to recite his oft-repeated phrases.

"You got $100 that you got for Christmas."

"Yes," she said, "and I'm going to keep it."

"If he don't give me the money he owes me I am going to kill him."

Anna couldn't believe that Saetta was still obsessed with the money
given to her at Christmas when Easter was just around the corner. She
couldn't make him understand that there was no money. That money
went to groceries and bills. She was beginning to wonder if this obses-
sion would ever end.

"Your husband double-crossed me on a deal. He owes me about $800 on one deal and he double-crossed me on a dope deal. I am going to get even with him for that."

"If I wanted to get even," said Anna, taking a sip of her soda, "there are a lot of things I could get even with."

"Well," said Saetta in a stern tone, "I'm going to get even."

"So, Vince," said Anna in calm voice in an attempt to change the subject, "you got a black eye."

The comment struck a nerve. "Son of a bitch guinea won't live long. Your husband owes me money, why won't you pay me?"

Anna ignored the last comment and, pushing her soda across the counter, stood up to leave. Before she could take a step, Saetta played his last card. "I know he's got insurance. I'm going to kill him. Will you give me $800?"

Anna shook her head in disbelief. Each conversation with Saetta by phone or even now in person seemed to escalate. First, he asked for money, then demanded money, and was now prepared to kill for money. As his threats increased, so did the amount. In an instant he raised the amount to $800, which could be taken from Sam's insurance. It didn't surprise Anna that Saetta knew Sam had insurance. It was the same $2,800 policy with the Brotherhood of Railway Trainmen that all railroad men were offered.

"I'm tired of all these terrible things between you and Sam," said Anna with a sigh, "don't bother me with it."[6] Anna left Saetta sitting at the counter, walked across the lobby, and bought a movie ticket. She didn't argue with him or encourage him, but, more importantly, she didn't try to stop him. For Saetta, the black eye he sported was proof that he could not take on Sam Antonio alone. If he was going to get rid of Sam Antonio, he would need help. He didn't have to look too far to find a man and a car.

After the first of the year, the lack of money became a real problem for Sam Faraci. Chauffeuring Sam Antonio to Schenectady and other places in the Gut district for narcotic deliveries only netted him a few dollars for gas. Faraci had a few dope customers of his own, but he still needed up-front money to buy the drugs he hoped to sell. Even the money made pimping for Gertrude King in Albany, Binghamton, and

Hudson wasn't enough to satisfy his legitimate creditors. With rent at five dollars a week, they needed food, and unfortunately he hadn't made his twenty-four-dollar car payment in two months. The loss of the car to the finance company would radically alter his lifestyle. The car enabled Faraci to make money. He needed the car, and right now he needed money.

It didn't take much convincing on Saetta's part to enlist Faraci, especially when the conversation turned to money. Saetta promised Faraci $300 if he helped him take care of Sam Antonio. Faraci didn't hesitate or argue about the money. Ever since his days in Geneva he had been lured to the fast dollar. This was more money than he had seen since his days in Geneva. Faraci was aware that a serious rift had developed between the two. After Saetta and Antonio fought on Green Street, Faraci told his friend to be on his guard. While running Sam Antonio back and forth from Schenectady, Faraci reminded Saetta that on a few occasions, their conversations included him. Antonio had second thoughts about how useful Saetta was to his dope-running enterprise. According to Faraci, Sam Antonio alluded to Saetta's questionable usefulness to him and hinted at ending their relationship in a permanent way. When a few more of Saetta's associates corroborated this, he became concerned. After all, with Faraci and a car, his services to Antonio in running dope through the Gut were less important, and he could be deemed expendable. Saetta believed that he had to act. "I don't think the man is worth anything," he said, "it is only time, whether he kills me or I kill him."[7] Saetta believed that the time was now.

"Sam, I have got to kill that man Antonio," Saetta said to Faraci. "He done me dirt and I got to kill him. It is very important, he die or I die. Do you think I should die or do you think he should die?"

"You have always been a good fellow to me, on the level," said Faraci, "he should die."

"Will you help me?"

To the self-centered Faraci, this was opportunity. With Antonio out of the way, he could take on his dope customers. He knew where they lived since he had been driving Antonio all over the Gut and Schenectady. Besides, Saetta would never go after Sam Antonio unless it involved big money similar to the payoff with the Steamburg arson. His financial woes would be put to rest if he could make that kind of money. Besides, to the arrest-prone Faraci, the job held promise. Sam Antonio and Vincent Saetta were never implicated or arrested for the arson.

"Yes, I will be with you."[8]

When Faraci said that he didn't have a weapon, Saetta suggested they go to Uncle Jack's Pawn Shop and Jeweler at 82 Green Street. Proprietor Julius Kommit recognized Saetta immediately when he entered the store. Never one to pass up a dollar, Saetta confronted Kommit and asked if he wasn't entitled to a small commission for assisting in the sale of an item a week or two earlier. The two haggled back and forth until Saetta said that his friend was interested in purchasing a knife. Directed to a few displays beneath a set of glass-topped counters, Kommit removed a tray of knives and placed it in front of Faraci. Among them was a bone-handled hunting knife with a long thin blade. Faraci cradled it in his hand and then tested the strength of the blade by trying to bend it with both hands.

"What do you think of that one?" said Saetta.

"Oh," said Faraci, "that is all right."

"How much?" asked Saetta.[9]

Kommit told them the price was fifty cents. Saetta turned to Faraci and with a simple nod, the sale was complete. Kommit returned the tray and then rolled the knife, as it had no sheath, in a small piece of brown wrapping paper, tying it with string. Saetta instructed Faraci to leave the knife in the sleeve, a pocket inside the car door.

For the next week Saetta and Faraci made plans to lure Sam Antonio out of town. "We will meet all three together," said Saetta. "We will make believe that we are going to Hudson." The plan was to convince Sam Antonio that they were going to the red-light district of Hudson. Either on the way down or on the return trip, whatever worked best, they would do the job. When Faraci asked how it would be done, Saetta said that it would be best if he drove the car and Faraci sat in the middle. "You make believe you have got to take a leak and all three get off. You get out on the other side of the car and I will come around and plug him."[10] Now all they had to do was to wait for the right moment. The Saturday before Easter looked promising.

Early on the morning of March 26, Sam Antonio bundled his brakeman's overalls in a duffle bag and walked down the stairs of his Teunis Street apartment to the street below. He waited a few moments for the cab to arrive that would take him to Union Station on Broadway Street. For the past three months Sam Antonio had been assigned to the Hudson office, so it was necessary for him to make the forty-minute commute from Albany to Hudson. The train pulled away from the Hudson Station at 9:30 A.M. and made stops in Stockport, Newton Hook, and Stuyvesant. After several trips down and back, the train would return to the same yard in Hudson at 9:30 P.M. The hours were long but not steady. "We would take days off," said fellow railroad man Richard Faas, "we had to take time off."[11] Brakemen, as well as conductors, were required by the railroad to stand down after the completion of a twelve-hour shift. The hours were long, yet no one dared to complain. It was the Great Depression, and every railroad man felt thankful to have a job.

Faas had been a railroad man for almost as long as Sam Antonio but had been acquainted with him for only the few months he had been assigned to the Hudson office. In that short time, Faas sensed something about Antonio. Sam Antonio seem distracted, as if his mind were elsewhere and not focused on his job. Lately he noticed that Antonio began shrugging his shoulders and was habitually tugging at his ears. "He was very nervous," observed Faas, "a very nervous person, in fact."[12] The man who knew him best was conductor Henry Mitchell. An employee of the New York Central Railroad since 1906, Mitchell held Sam Antonio in high esteem: "He done his work alright." He had known the first Mrs. Antonio as well as the second, whom he regarded as "a decent respectable woman."

Sam Antonio had been on the job for only an hour when he began to complain that he didn't feel good. Mitchell and Faas were concerned due to the recent outbreaks of influenza. Mitchell suggested that at the next stop, Sam might want get off the train and get to a doctor or a drugstore. Mitchell could then pick him up on the return trip. Sam shook his head. "I will try to work it off," he said.[13]

Mitchell didn't give the incident another thought until they neared Hudson. Antonio told him that he was feeling worse than ever and now that they were in Hudson, he announced that he was going to see a doctor. Mitchell wished him luck and made a notation on the time card that Sam Antonio left the train at 4:50 P.M.

It was almost 6:00 P.M. when Sam Antonio arrived at 3 Teunis Street. His mysterious get-out-of-work-early virus had apparently vanished by the time he climbed the stairs and walked into the apartment. Anna was taken aback that her husband was home from work so early, even more so when he set his best suit of clothes to the side and went into the bathroom to take a bath and shave. It was apparent that he intended to go out that evening. "That is not very nice going out the day before Easter, I asked my brother and sister-in-law, down," protested Anna. Sam reassured her that he would be home by 6 A.M. and wouldn't miss dinner with her family.

After preparing dinner for her husband, Anna asked if she could have a little money so she could purchase an Easter plant for one of her friends. Sam shook his head, reached into his pocket, and displayed a roll of bills. Carefully peeling off ten dollars, he said, "Hurry back, because I'm going out."

Anna went next door and together with her neighbor, Helen Miller, walked to Berberick's florist on Second Avenue. On the way to and from the florist, Anna told her neighbor that they must hurry as her husband had plans. Mrs. Miller wasn't surprised to hear this as it seemed that Sam was always going out. After purchasing a rosebush, the two women returned to Teunis Street just in time to witness Sam Antonio getting into a waiting taxi.

"He has got his new Easter suit on," remarked Anna.

"He must have a heavy date," quipped Mrs. Miller.

"Yes, maybe he has, Helen."[14]

Anna went upstairs to the apartment, fixed supper for the children, and gave all three a bath before sending them off to bed. Having done that, she returned to the kitchen and cleaned the two chickens that were to be their Easter dinner. She went to bed between 10 and 11 P.M. Her day was over; her husband's was just beginning.

That afternoon, while Sam Antonio was feigning illness to leave his job, Saetta and Faraci were also working on a job. For the past several days they were going to pool halls and speakeasies in search of clients who owed them money for alcohol and drugs. Saetta spent most of his time working Hudson and Madison Avenues, while Faraci, in the company of Gertrude King, searched for clients on Sheridan Avenue. Saetta had his sights set on a character he called "Joe the Pollack," eventually cornering him at Willie's Pool Hall. He owed money for alcohol but could produce only two dollars when confronted by Saetta.

Disappointed at not getting more money from Joe, Sam Faraci suggested they go to Paul's Restaurant on Green Street for dinner. Saetta decided to forgo the spaghetti dinner and, leaving Faraci and King, went instead to a speakeasy at 21 Hamilton Street. Here Saetta had a few drinks, played cards, and danced with some of the local girls. It was almost midnight when he left there to meet with Faraci at their prearranged rendezvous.

Saetta walked into the pool hall on Green Street and gazed across the smoke-filled room. Despite the haze he could easily make out Sam Antonio. With a charcoal-gray overcoat draped over one shoulder, Antonio brushed the side of his cream-colored fedora with two fingers when he made eye contact with Saetta. He was the best-dressed man in the place. Standing beside him was Sam Faraci.

When the three got together, Gertrude King having left Faraci after dinner, Saetta asked Antonio for guidance on how to take care of Joe the Pollack. Saetta told Antonio that he wanted to see Joe again, not so much for the money but to make sure he wouldn't be double-crossed.[15] Sam Antonio didn't see this as much of a problem and suggested that they return to Sheridan Avenue and confront Joe. When they arrived at the pool hall, they saw the proprietor, Willie, locking the front door. Leaving the others in the car, Saetta exited the car immediately when he recognized Willie. The two conversed for only a few minutes. Saetta got back in the car and Faraci said, "Are you ready?" Earlier, the two had agreed that this simple phrase indicated that this was the night and that Saetta had his gun. "No I ain't," replied Saetta, "but I will be."[16]

Throughout that evening Saetta was unarmed. He didn't have a holster for his pistol and tucking it into his belt didn't seem like a good idea, especially when he was dancing at 21 Hamilton Street. Faraci understood his response and drove him to his apartment on Columbia Street to collect his weapon. To the unsuspecting Sam Antonio, Saetta was going to his room to freshen up a bit for the remainder of the evening.

Saetta told Faraci not to wait for him and that he would meet him at the pool hall on Green Street. As the two drove out of sight, Saetta, aware of his light-sleeping landlady, slowly tiptoed up the stairs to his room. After gently turning the lock on the door, he entered and with the snap of a light switch dimly lit the room. He made his way to the dresser, opened the top drawer, and removed a bottle of whiskey. Saetta took a long draft and then another. He paused for a moment, took another swig, and set the bottle down. Pushing some articles of clothing aside in the drawer, he took out his revolver. Gently rolling the cylinder of the gun aside revealed five shells. He closed the gun and tucked it into his belt. Saetta glanced one more time around the room, took another swig of whiskey, and placed the half-empty bottle in the dresser drawer.[17]

It was well past midnight when Saetta made his way back to Green Street. Much to his surprise, he discovered that Faraci and Antonio were fast asleep in the car. "Are we ready for a good time?" said Saetta in a voice loud enough to wake the two.

"Don't mind me," said Antonio, "I don't work, tomorrow is Easter Sunday. I don't have to work, so if I stay out all night, it don't make any difference to me."[18]

Saetta said that if they hurried, they might make it down to Hudson in time to get to Black Rose. With the dozen or so brothels in Hudson, Saetta, Faraci, as well as Antonio were familiar with Black Rose or "Nigger Rose." Saetta pushed Faraci aside, got behind the wheel, and drove south out of Albany on Castleton Road. Part of their plan was in place. Faraci was seated in the middle and all they had to do was wait for the right moment. Impatient and somewhat nervous, Faraci blurted out on several occasions, "Stop, I want to piss," only to be ignored by his partner.

By the time the three arrived in Hudson, most of the brothels were either closed or turning away customers. With nothing else to do, they stopped at a small restaurant for coffee, pie, and crullers. When the waiter set the bill on the counter, Sam Antonio picked it up. "No," he said to Faraci, "I know you ain't got much money, I pay for it. I am working, you don't work. It don't make any difference, I will pay."[19]

As they walked back to the car, Faraci whispered to Saetta, "What is the matter you don't stop on the way down?" When Antonio walked around the car to get in the passenger's side, Saetta whispered back, "Well, we didn't have a good chance, I'll stop on the way back."[20]

Less than a mile outside of Hudson, Faraci saw his moment and announced, "Stop, I want to piss." Saetta slowly let up on the accelerator and scanned the horizon. He couldn't make out the glow of any headlights in the distance and a quick look in the rearview mirror revealed only darkness. Now was the time. Gently applying the brake, Saetta brought the coupe to a halt on the shoulder of Castleton Road. Having been nudged in the ribs several times by Faraci, Sam Antonio exited the passenger side door as soon as the car coasted to a stop. While Faraci scurried to the rear of the car to relieve himself, Sam Antonio walked toward the center of the road. It was a cold, crisp morning with a slight chill in the air. Sam Antonio reached into his coat pocket and took out a pack of Camel cigarettes. Looking out at the starless night, he lit a cigarette and tossed the match aside. The only sound, that of the idling car, was suddenly interrupted by Vincent Saetta. "Hey, Sam."

Turning about, Sam Antonio could make out the silhouette of Saetta standing near the headlight of the car. "It's too bad the last time we had a fight, we didn't come out here." A horrified Sam Antonio dropped his cigarette. He knew what this meant. The last time they fought, Saetta had a knife. "Cause then I could have killed you." Saetta pulled the nickel-plated revolver from his belt and leveled it in the direction of Sam Antonio. Five shots rang out into the night.[21]

Mortally wounded, Antonio sank to his knees in the center of the road. Ignoring his moans, Saetta walked to his victim and kicked him over. Sam Antonio wasn't dead and Saetta didn't have any more bullets to administer a coup de grâce. "Get the knife," he shouted to Faraci, "finish him, do your job."

Saetta returned to the driver's seat and watched as Faraci, lit by the headlights, slashed away at Antonio. "Sam," cried the mortally wounded Antonio, "you got to help me out. I never done nothing to you."

The desperate pleas of a man whom he had once befriended didn't affect Faraci as he continued to rapidly thrust the hunting knife into Sam Antonio. "I can't help you," said Faraci, "I have to go through with it, you gotta go, Sam."[22] When he was finished, he rolled the body into a culvert and stabbed him a few more times.

Faraci ran back to the car, jumped in the passenger seat, and breathlessly announced, "He oughta be dead right now."

As they sped away, Saetta handed his gun to Faraci and told him to break apart the weapon. Rolling the cylinder off with its five spent shells, Faraci tossed it out the passenger window, while Saetta tossed the frame of the pistol out his side. It was then that Saetta asked where the knife was.

"I left it in his head," said Faraci.[23]

It didn't take either of them long to comprehend the possible conse-quences of not taking the weapon with them. "Jeeeze," said Faraci, "my fingerprints, on the knife!" The only thing he could hope for would be if the brown paper wrapped on the knife handle was too soggy with morning dew to retain a fingerprint. If it didn't, it would only be a ques-tion of time before his fingerprints were retrieved from Auburn State Prison or the Ontario County Jail.

Speeding their way toward Albany in the daylight hours, Saetta came to realize how brutal Faraci's attack had been on Sam Antonio. "I was not in the mud," recalled Saetta, "but Sam [Faraci], he had mud all over him."[24] Saetta suggested that they go to his apartment to clean up. Faraci had mud caked on his trousers, shirt, and shoes. His hands were bloody and he had blood smears on his face. When they got upstairs to Saetta's room, Faraci went to the bathroom. Taking a towel and wiping the mud from his shoes, he turned to Saetta and said, "Now, get the money for me."

Saetta reached into his pants pocket and showed Faraci a few nickels. "Wait here, I will try to get the party out of bed and get some money." He then stepped lightly down the stairs and drove the Oldsmobile to a tele-phone booth near a restaurant at the corner of Columbia and Broadway Streets. His message was abrupt. "Get yourself a cab and hurry over."[25]

He returned to his apartment, picked up Faraci, and the two raced back to Broadway Street. Faraci, who had picked up Gertrude King at his place on Hamilton Street, remained in the car, and Saetta took up a position by the restaurant door and waited. After a few minutes, a taxi arrived and parked nearby. Anna Antonio got out of the cab and imme-diately recognized Saetta.

"Here is the money," said Anna. Tired of Saetta's constant badgering for money, she hoped that the forty dollars she handed him would put an end to these incessant calls to the apartment. "If Sam hears that you have called me out of the house at this time of the morning he will get even with you for it."

"You don't have to worry about him," he said, "it is all over now."

"What is?"

"I shot him."

"Go on, what are you trying to do, kid me? I don't believe it."[26]

Saetta took the money and watched as Anna returned to the cab and drove away. His next move was to get out of Albany as quickly as possible. As he approached the Oldsmobile coupe, he motioned his accomplice aside. With Gertrude King still in the car, both men conversed in Italian.

"Did you get the money?" asked Faraci.

"Yes."

"How much did you get?"

"Forty dollars."

Faraci was stunned by such a small amount. "Well, cheeses," he cried, "what is that? That ain't nothing."

"Well," said Saetta, "that's all the poor woman could afford to give me." Seeing that Faraci was upset, Saetta became suddenly generous and handed him the forty dollars. What Faraci didn't realize was that Saetta had a good amount of money. After having shot Sam Antonio, he took his wallet and wasn't about to share the contents.

"Why," said an exasperated Faraci, "what could I do with that?"

Saetta said the forty dollars could help with expenses if he wanted to return home to Geneva or bring Gertrude King to her home in Oswego. Faraci shook his head. Oswego perhaps, but definitely not Geneva. The minute he returned to his hometown, he would be immediately arrested for nonpayment of child support.

"I tell you," said Saetta in English, "I tell you what we do. We will go to New York to my people, I haven't been there and it is Easter, and we spend Easter down there."

Faraci nodded in agreement and turned to Gertrude King. "What do you say, do you want to go and see New York? You haven't seen New York?"

"Sure," said King.[27]

4

"MY NAME . . . SAM ANTONIO"

In the early morning hours of March 27, 1932, a four-door LaSalle driven by John C. Crary Jr. slowly made its way north on Castleton Road. The ten or twelve-mile stretch of road bordered the east bank of the Hudson River and linked Albany with the small village of Castle-on-Hudson. Crary, a twenty-two-year-old law student, was coming home from a dance with his girlfriend, Cornelia Halpen. Sitting in the backseat of the sedan was another future attorney and classmate, William L. McDermott. Crary had just brought McDermott's girlfriend to her home in Castleton and was now taking his time on the drive to Albany. Scenic by day, unlit Castleton Road had few guardrails to protect cars if they slid from the cement road into the deep culverts. Crary, driving less than forty miles an hour, had forewarned his father not to expect him home with the family car until the early hours of the morning.

The trio had been on Castleton Road for less than a half hour when the headlights of the LaSalle revealed a shadowy figure in the center of the road raising an outstretched arm. Crary jerked the wheel of the La-Salle to the right to avoid hitting what appeared to be a body in the road and exclaimed, "There was a man!"[1] As soon as he applied the brakes and brought the car to a halt, McDermott leapt from the backseat of the car and rushed to the aid of the man lying in the road. As it was dark, he couldn't immediately make out the extent of the man's injuries. It was only after Crary put the car in reverse, shining the headlights in his direction, that McDermott could see how bad it was. The stranger was lying in a pool of blood.

Leaving Cornelia in the front seat, Crary joined McDermott at the side of the injured man. "I'm shot . . . I'm shot," he said in a low mournful tone, "I'm shot." Gasping for breath and wincing in pain, he kept repeating what at first sounded like "San Antonio." Drawing a long breath, the wounded man cried, "My name . . . Sam Antonio." After repeating his name several more times, Sam Antonio murmured, "three-two, three-two," in an effort to tell them his address: 3 Teunis Street.[2]

The two law students attempted to pick up Antonio but couldn't. At close to two hundred pounds, Antonio was, as McDermott later recalled, simply "dead weight."[3] They dragged Antonio to the side of the car and struggled to pull him into the backseat. Crary got behind the wheel of the car and put the engine in gear to make the ten-mile dash up the river road to Albany. Meanwhile, McDermott had placed himself in the front passenger seat. While Crary and his girlfriend kept their eyes on the road, McDermott turned to the side and never took his eyes off Sam Antonio.

In the backseat, Antonio, writhing in pain, repeated his name over and over, begging to be taken home. "I am gone," he said, "God forgive me, God forgive me." Then he would drift as if unconscious, only to experience a spasm, stiffening all his muscles, drawing him bolt upright in agony. "I can't breathe, I can't breathe. . . . can't you get me to a country doctor?"[4] The thought of a country doctor never entered Crary's mind. He had to get Antonio to Memorial Hospital as quickly as possible. By now it was close to 5 A.M. and streaks of sunlight began to appear on the horizon. With every groan and gasp, Crary pushed the car harder toward Albany. "God forgive me . . . I don't want to die . . . God forgive me. . . . I'm going, I cannot breathe, I don't want to die . . . I am going to die."[5]

In the distance Crary could see the outline of Rensselaer Bridge, which spanned the Hudson. Driving with one hand on the wheel and the other pressed against the horn, he sped across the bridge over to Broadway Street. At that early hour there were few cars to block the way of the horn-blaring LaSalle. From Broadway Street to State Street, Crary drove as fast as he could to get to Memorial Hospital on Pearl Street.[6] He skidded the car to a halt at the emergency room entrance and McDermott exited the car and ran for help. Bursting through the door to the emergency room, McDermott looked about frantically. The switchboard operator noticed him right away, as did Emil Peletier, a hospital orderly. McDermott shouted out that he needed a doctor right away as a man had been shot. Upon hearing this, Peletier immediately set down his cup of coffee on the switchboard desk. Charles Wagner, an ambulance driver who had just walked into the lobby with his cup of coffee, did the same. While Peletier and Wagner retrieved a stretcher, McDermott ran back to the car to assist Crary. At the same time the switchboard operator called for a doctor to report to the emergency room.

It was only after Sam Antonio was placed on a gurney under the lights of the emergency room that Crary and McDermott got a good look at the man they had found on the road. Both were aghast at his appearance. Not only was his face smeared with dried blood, but his thick black hair was matted with blood and mud. His shirt was so saturated with blood that it would have been almost impossible to call it a white dress shirt. The coat and trousers were spattered in mud and his shoes, according to McDermott, had "globs of mud."[7]

The two Good Samaritans were asked to leave the room when Dr. Irving Gage arrived. Dressed in plain white trousers and a sweatshirt, only the stethoscope around his neck gave any indication that he was a doctor. McDermott was somewhat taken aback by his appearance and casually remarked to Crary that it looked as if the doctor had just rolled out of bed. In fact, Dr. Gage had been asleep in one of the empty rooms down the hall when alerted by the switchboard operator. He dressed quickly, pulling up a pair of trousers over his pajamas. No one seemed to notice that he was wearing bedroom slippers and not shoes.[8]

Dr. Gage had almost the same reaction as Crary and McDermott when they saw Antonio in a lit room. The victim was covered from head to toe in mud and blood. Feeling no wrist pulse and detecting only a faint heartbeat, Dr. Gage immediately administered a shot of adrenalin. He then tore open Antonio's shirt to see the extent of his injuries, but it was too late. Sam Antonio had drawn his last breath.[9]

In his official report, Dr. Gage recorded that the victim was already exhibiting signs of "extreme shock and hemorrhage" when he was brought to the emergency room and that he "was practically in a moribund condition."[10] It wasn't until after the clothes had been stripped from the corpse that Dr. Gage had a fair idea of how the victim had suffered. "The wounds were cuts," he said, "some were superficial and some were deep. They were not lacerations, but clean deep wounds."[11] These wounds, about a dozen, were to the scalp, neck, right and left wrists, left shoulder, chest, abdomen, as well as what appeared to be several gunshot wounds. Given the extent of his injuries, he sincerely doubted that anything could have saved this man.

In the emergency room lobby, the three benefactors whispered among themselves speculating as to what had become of the wounded man they had brought to the hospital. Their thoughts darkened sharply when a Catholic priest dashed past them and made his way into the emergency room. Moments later, the priest reappeared. He pushed the door aside while Dr. Gage and Peletier guided the shroud-covered gurney out of the room. Momentarily stunned, Crary, McDermott, and Cornelia Halpen agreed that the events leading up to this had happened in what seemed to be an instant. They were still discussing the details of their adventure when a man in a charcoal-gray uniform approached them. He introduced himself as Corp. William H. Flubacher of the New York State Police.[12]

A nine-and-a-half-year veteran of the state police, Flubacher had been home in bed when he received a call from Troop G headquarters that a shooting victim had been brought to the Pearl Street hospital. When he arrived at the emergency room, Flubacher made his way first to the reception desk. Assured by the receptionist that no calls had been received at her desk with regard to the victim, Flubacher instructed her to keep the phone lines open as he would eventually have to place calls to his superior and the Albany police. When he was informed that the victim had been transported to the morgue, Flubacher turned his attention to the only other people in the lobby.

The two law students were eager to cooperate, but Flubacher quickly discovered that they really didn't have a lot of information to assist him with his investigation. The man they had brought to the hospital was in excruciating pain, so much so that they could barely make out his name—Sam Antonio. As Flubacher jotted down bits and pieces of information in his notepad, Crary asked a favor. Could he possibly take his girlfriend home and then go to his own home to explain to his parents why he was late with the family car? He had told his father that he would be a little late that evening, but now it was early morning. Flubacher hesitated for a moment, glanced at Cornelia Halpen, and nodded. He told the two young men to go home and then get back to the hospital as quickly as possible. He had a few more questions to ask them, and he was certain that the Albany district attorney would want to speak with them.

As the trio exited the lobby, Flubacher saw the anxious expression on the face of the receptionist. With one hand over the telephone receiver, she was waving to him with the other. The caller, said the receptionist, was Mrs. Antonio.

"Funny" is how Flubacher described the moment. How did she know to call the hospital? When he asked her that question, Anna Antonio replied that earlier that morning, she had received an anonymous call instructing her to go to the corner of Columbia and Broadway. This mysterious caller informed her that her husband had been seriously injured. She explained to Flubacher that she did as the caller instructed, but when she didn't find her husband, she returned home. She then received another anonymous call telling her to contact the hospital.

Flubacher didn't know what to make of this story. Her claim to have received two phone calls seemed bizarre. Without revealing any details as to the fate of her husband, Flubacher asked her to come to the hospital. After that he placed two calls. One was to John T. Delaney and the other was to police chief David Smurl. His next stop was the morgue.[13]

Walking down the hall to the morgue, Flubacher noticed ambulance driver Charles Wagner walking toward him with what appeared to be a bundle of soiled clothing. The state policeman stopped him and asked if these were the clothes of the deceased. Wagner said they were and then proceeded to tell Flubacher how he and Emil Peletier had assisted the coroner in disrobing the corpse. When asked what he intended to do with the clothing, Wagner said that he had just asked the undertaker, who was present in the morgue, the exact same question. As the coroner and undertaker had no use for the soiled garments, Wagner was instructed to take the bundle of clothes to the hospital incinerator.

Flubacher took the clothes from Wagner and gave them a cursory examination. The shirt, having been torn open by Dr. Gage, was nothing more than a bloody rag. Flubacher set it aside and studied the suit. He made note of the mud and bloodstains on the trousers and jacket, but he was also interested in the fabric. This was a fine suit of clothes to wear out on the town on a Saturday night. The only thing missing was a wallet, leading Flubacher to believe that the victim had been robbed. There was really nothing of any importance in the pockets to aid in his investigation except a nine-day overdue postal notification. It was for a registered letter from a Louis Pacelli. Whether this was an important lead or a useless piece of paper would have to be determined later. The sleeves and shoulders of the jacket exhibited puncture marks, most likely stab wounds, but it was the bullet holes that interested him. Flubacher ran his finger through the bullet holes and held out hope that a few slugs could be recovered. Inside the jacket pocket was a clean white handkerchief. Odd, thought Flubacher, that here was the only article of clothing that was not soiled or bloodied. He gave all the clothes back to Wagner except the handkerchief. Removing a fountain pen from his front pocket, Flubacher inscribed his initials, "W. F."[14]

When Flubacher returned to the emergency room lobby, he was pleased to see Crary and McDermott waiting for him. The young men gave a detailed account of their early morning adventure on Castleton Road. In excruciating pain, Sam Antonio managed to say his name several times, give his address, prayed out loud, and sometimes mumbled incoherently. The only thing Flubacher wished Antonio had done in his dying breath was to name—or at least give a hint—as to his assailant or assailants. Flubacher scribbled down as many details as he could and then told the young men to go home and get some rest. In a few hours the district attorney and the Albany police would want to speak to them and revisit Castleton Road.

Crary and McDermott left the hospital and drove two blocks to the Waldorf Lunch and Bakery on Broadway Street to get a cup of coffee. It had been an exciting start to their day, and both agreed that this was an interesting start to their law careers. They were seniors at Albany Law School and now were involved in a capital murder case. If whoever did this to Sam Antonio were apprehended, they would no doubt be called as witnesses in the trial. They finished their coffee and drove across town to St. Vincent's Church. It was Easter Sunday.[15]

Meanwhile, Flubacher had completed his interviews of several of the hospital personnel and was about to leave the emergency room when he noticed two women entering the lobby. He noted that one of them appeared more frantic and confused than the other.

"Who are you?" he asked.

"What happened to my husband? My name is Anna Antonio."

Flubacher politely introduced himself and then turned to the other woman and asked who she might be. "Mrs. Miller," she replied. The same Helen Miller who had accompanied Anna to Berberick's to buy an Easter plant had brought her to the hospital. Anna was her neighbor and friend, explained Mrs. Miller, quickly adding that her husband was an Albany policeman.

In what John T. Delaney later characterized as "real police intelligence," Flubacher reacted quickly. Gently drawing Mrs. Miller to one side, he whispered to her that Anna's husband had been brutally murdered. Perhaps receiving such terrible news from a close friend like herself, explained Flubacher, would be easier on her than receiving the news from a total stranger. Mrs. Miller agreed and did as he suggested. When she told Anna what had happened to her husband, Flubacher stood by. Her apparent lack of emotion upon hearing the news disturbed Flubacher. There were no tears or hysterics. In his notebook he wrote, "No emotion." If this wasn't odd, the textbook questions he had for her yielded little. Did he have any enemies? When did you last see him? Where did he go last night? Who were his friends?

"Mrs. Antonio did not know much," concluded Flubacher. However, she did mention that her husband had received a notice for a registered letter. She didn't know who it was from, but she did say that her husband appeared to be genuinely distressed when he received it. Having received his first lead in the case, Anna abruptly asked to return home to her children. Her three children were left in the care of another neighbor. Soon they would be getting out of bed and would need their breakfast. Flubacher shook his head, scribbled "3 Teunis Street" in his notepad, and told her that he would stop by later in the day.[16]

After the two women left the emergency room lobby, Sgt. Thomas Straney appeared. A fellow officer on the police force once described Straney as "more of an inside man, than an outside man."[17] This was a fair assessment. Aside from accompanying other officers to photograph crime scenes, Straney spent most of his time compiling fingerprint registers and filing mug shots. When the camera-toting Straney arrived at the hospital on Pearl Street, Flubacher thanked him for showing up on Easter Sunday and in the same breath apologized. Not only had the victim's clothes been incinerated, but the body was on the way to the undertaker. Still, Flubacher assured Straney that he would need him and his camera before the day was over. At this moment his main concern was contacting the Albany postmaster to retrieve this mysterious letter that Mrs. Antonio claimed had given her husband such great concern.

Straney contacted the postmaster, apprised him of the situation, and in the company of the coroner, Ernst Hein, and Flubacher, agreed to meet at the post office. The postmaster told them that there *had* been a registered letter for Sam Antonio. When Antonio refused to sign for it, the letter was returned. They didn't have the letter, but they did have the name and address of the man who sent it—Louis Pacelli, 37 Rutland Street, Albany.

Before returning to the Albany Police Station and right after he dropped off Hein at Memorial Hospital, Flubacher and Straney drove to the Crary residence at 337 Myrtle Avenue to inspect and take pictures of the LaSalle automobile that had transported Sam Antonio to Memorial Hospital. Flubacher took a long look at the car and couldn't quite come to terms with yet another streak of bad luck. First, Sam Antonio didn't give a hint as to who his assailants were, then there was no wallet, no Pacelli letter, and now this—a showroom-clean car. As soon as her son had arrived home from the hospital, Mrs. Crary washed all the mud off the car and cleaned every spot of blood and mud from the backseat.[18] Flubacher shook his head in disbelief. Any evidence of this savage attack on Antonio was literally washed away. He could only hope that his luck would change when he got to Castleton Road, but he had to hurry. Another snow squall or spring rain could wash away evidence as quickly as Mrs. Crary had done with the car.

Just before 10 A.M., a police cruiser with Flubacher, Straney, Chief Smurl, and district attorney John T. Delaney traveled south on Castleton Road in search of the exact location where Sam Antonio had been found. Their guide was William McDermott. About a mile outside of Castleton, McDermott said he was fairly certain that they were fairly close to the scene of the crime. Straney later said that it was almost impossible to tell who in the squad car shouted first upon seeing the crumpled white fedora on the left-hand side of road. This was the place where Sam Antonio was lured to his death.

The police car lurched to a halt and everyone got out to look for evidence. Straney got to the hat first, examined it closely, and was attempting to place his initials on the headband when someone shouted "blood." On the side of the road were several pools of blood, the largest about ten to twelve inches in diameter.[19] Near the edge of the concrete road a much smaller pool of blood was discovered and lying near it was a knife. Chief Smurl picked it up and handed it to Flubacher.[20] At first it was difficult to determine what kind of knife it was as the top portion of the handle and the blade were wrapped in brown paper and secured with a string. The assailant, reasoned Flubancher, never had time to remove the paper from the blade. This would account for some of the puncture-like stab wounds he observed on Antonio's body in the morgue. Only about two or two and a half inches of the blade were exposed, noted Flubacher, just enough to inflict the stab wounds on Sam Antonio.[21] At last he had a weapon for evidence. Flubacher, as he had done with the handkerchief, removed his fountain pen and placed his initials on the butt of the knife handle.[22]

He placed the knife in the police car and joined Delaney in examining the side of the road. Off the road and into the culvert, Delaney, Smurl, and Flubacher saw that mud had been swept aside and bloodstains were visible, indicating that the mortally wounded Antonio had crawled out of the culvert and onto the road. Flubacher took a small jar and scooped up a portion of mud for analysis. After taking measurements of bloodstains, the width of the road, the depth of the culvert, and the location of the knife relative to the other pools of blood, the team of law enforcement officials was ready to return to Albany. The last person in the police cruiser was Thomas Straney. Taking careful aim with his camera, he snapped one panoramic picture of the scene.

When Delaney returned from Castleton Road, he was told that a patrolman had brought in Louis Pacelli. The registered letter that Mrs. Antonio claimed to have upset her husband was nothing compared to how frightened Louis Pacelli was when he was brought before John Delaney. The grocery store owner said that he had sent a letter to Sam

Antonio, but since he couldn't read or write English, a friend had written it for him. The only reason he sent a registered letter was because Sam Antonio refused to return his phone calls. Pacelli said that on one occasion, Sam's wife answered the phone and hung up with a curt, "He ain't home."[23]

Pacelli tried to impress upon Delaney that the letter he sent to Sam Antonio was in no way threatening. Several months ago, he had loaned Sam Antonio $130. "He had a little child in the hospital, a baby in the hospital," said Pacelli. Reaching into his pocket, Pacelli produced a handwritten note in which Sam Antonio promised to repay the money in thirty days. Months passed, and it was obvious to Pacelli that Sam Antonio had no intention of making good on his promise. Although he had tossed the registered letter in the garbage, Pacelli told Delaney that in essence, if he didn't get his money back, he was prepared to send a complaint to "the company." When Delaney asked him what sort of "company" he had in mind, Pacelli said, "New York Central, for company he work, that is all."[24] Delaney motioned to a nearby patrolman to take Pacelli home. He wasn't a suspect. Delaney didn't believe for one moment that the frightened grocer sitting before him was capable of killing a man over a months-old $130 debt.

Delaney was concerned. Thus far they had evidence of a vicious attack on Sam Antonio and nothing more. No one on the Albany police force had ever heard of Sam Antonio. He had no arrest record and had never run afoul of the law in any way. Delaney needed more information if his investigation were to move forward. He was about to send a detective to 3 Teunis Street to bring in Anna Antonio for questioning when federal narcotics agent Richard Kelly suddenly appeared at the Sixth Precinct.

As his relationship with Chief Smurl had been strained in the past, the cigar-smoking Kelly grinned when he was told that the state police were leading the investigation into the death of someone his department had been shadowing. "Sam Antonio," Kelly told Flubacher, "was mixed up with some dope racket with a dago named Vincent Saetta and some other red head dago." For several weeks, Kelly said, both men had been under surveillance. Sam Antonio and Vincent Saetta had been suspected of using their positions in the New York Central Railroad to ferry narcotics into Schenectady and the Gut. Kelly told Flubacher that he would be in his office the next day and would contact him immediately if he had any new information that might be helpful. As for Vincent Saetta, Kelly had one piece of information that might prove useful. He said Saetta was a frequent visitor "at a dump in Hudson, Black Rose."[25]

In the 1930s, the city of Hudson teemed with bars and brothels. As Castleton Road led to Hudson, Kelly and Flubacher agreed that this may have been on the Saturday night agenda for Antonio and Saetta. Straney, who had been by Flubacher's side all morning, immediately secured a patrol car to make the trip to the most notorious section of Hudson, Diamond Street.

When they arrived in Hudson, Straney turned onto Diamond Street and only had to question a few of the locals to discover the whereabouts of Black Rose. Directed to a large three-story building in the 300 block, Straney parked the car and with Flubacher, Kelly, and Det. Frank Herzog entered the building. Inside there was a large bar, and although it was Easter Sunday, they noticed plenty of women standing by, willing to entertain potential customers. Kelly and Flubacher talked with a few of the girls and were surprised to learn that Black Rose wasn't a place but a person. Just then, a black madam approached them and introduced herself as Black Rose. She told both men that it was common for some of the locals to refer to her as "Nigger Rose."

In his notebook, Flubacher recorded the candor of Black Rose. Unimpressed and not intimidated by the uniformed officer standing before her, Black Rose was friendly and cooperative. Vincent Saetta had been in her place on several occasions, she said, but never alone. He was always in the company of "red Sam." When Flubacher heard the name Sam, he asked her if Sam had a last name. Was it Antonio? Black Rose shook her head. She didn't know red Sam's last name. All the girls in her establishment called him "red" because of his bushy, unkempt mop of red hair. Flubacher wryly recorded in his notebook, "Red Sam cannot be Antonio." Black Rose recalled that red Sam had a car, but she couldn't remember the make, model, color, or license plate number. But as a true madam, she knew the name of the girl red Sam brought to her place. Her name was King.[26]

On the return trip to Albany, Kelly assured Flubacher that when he returned to his office on Monday, he would contact a few of his informants and try to discover the identity of red Sam. That same Monday,

Flubacher and several detectives scoured the Gut unsuccessfully in their search for any clues that might tie Sam Antonio to Vincent Saetta. They believed they had a plausible motive, and the press echoed that sentiment. "Dope Smugglers Sought for Albanian's Murder" was the headline of the *Albany Times Union*. The press surmised that Sam Antonio was most likely "rubbed out because he double crossed associates in a narcotics ring."[27] Chief Smurl, not wishing to be upstaged by Kelly, said that Antonio "apparently had gangster connections" and expressed concern that this recent act of violence would not bring a resurgence of gangster activities in the Albany area "so soon after the death of Legs Diamond."[28]

The next day, Tuesday, Kelly contacted Flubacher and told him that the mystery surrounding red Sam had been solved. In the course of shadowing Sam Antonio, Kelly learned that he was often chauffeured around Schenectady and the Gut in an Oldsmobile coupe. According to Kelly's informants, the driver had bushy red hair and was named Sam Faraci. Kelly didn't know the license plate number of the car, but a quick check with the Motor Vehicle Department revealed that Sam Faraci was from Geneva, New York, and the plate number of the car was 6J67-44.[29]

When Flubacher presented this piece of information to the Albany police, Chief Smurl sent a teletype message across the state for authorities to be on the lookout for Sam Faraci, "wanted in questioning in connection with the murder of Salvatore Antonio, Albany drug peddler, who was taken for a ride."[30]

Now all they could do was wait and hope to get lucky.

5

"MRS. ANTONIO, YOU ARE NOT HELPING US"

Forty-five-year-old Det. Sgt. George Griggs reported to the Third Precinct Station House at 220 North Pearl Street at 3:00 P.M. Entering the station, he realized that he wasn't the only police officer to forego Easter dinner with his family. The place was abuzz with activity as the clicking sounds of manual Underwood typewriters competed with ringing phones and voices in the precinct. A ten-year veteran of the Albany Police Department, Griggs was a plainclothes detective and was familiar with the south end of the city. When Delancy telephoned him at home and told him of the murder of Sam Antonio, Griggs raced to the Third Precinct. To the affable Griggs, foregoing Easter dinner with his family was worth it.[1]

Entering the hallway, Griggs carefully eyed the group of individuals seated on a long bench. There were a few men and one woman. Griggs noticed that even though it was Easter Sunday, this woman could hardly be said to be wearing a new Easter dress as it was worn and faded. Sitting close beside the petite woman was a man who spoke to her in low whispers. He wasn't wearing a suit, but his attire was of a slightly better quality than hers. Griggs didn't know who they were but could venture a guess. Walking down the hall, he paused. Nearby, Flubacher and Kelly were conversing, and a door down he could hear Delaney finishing up his conversation with the Rensselaer district attorney. Griggs overheard Delaney assure the district attorney that his office would conduct the investigation and prosecute those responsible for the vicious attack on Sam Antonio, which had occurred in his county.

After bidding the Rensselaer district attorney good-bye, Delaney turned his attention to Griggs. Presenting him with what little facts were available about the murder, Delaney told Griggs that the first real break in the investigation had come from Richard Kelly. The victim, Sam Antonio, was suspected of peddling dope in the Gut with a character named Vincent Saetta. Delaney told him that his familiarity with the Gut would be essential in this ongoing investigation. The district attorney told him that the only person who could possibly make this connection between Antonio and Saetta was the victim's wife, seated in the hall. When Griggs asked about the gentleman seated beside her, Delaney said that he was of no consequence for the moment. He was Pasquale Cappello, the woman's brother. Right now, said Delaney, it was more important to question her.

In the time it took for Griggs to introduce himself to Anna Antonio, Delaney wasted no time in assembling an array of law enforcement officials in Chief Smurl's office. Seated behind his desk, Smurl kept his own counsel, knowing full well that he really didn't have much to offer in this investigation except the use of the Third Precinct. Delaney sat near a few detectives, and off to one side, away from Smurl, was Richard Kelly. Lastly, there was Flubacher. Delaney reasoned that if Anna Antonio was going to open up and speak to anyone, it would be the first person she had spoken to about her husband's death. For the moment, Delaney would ask the questions.

Never one to stand on any polite formalities, the brusque Delaney began immediately by asking Anna to retrace her husband's movements on the day he was murdered, and in rapid-fire succession he asked who his friends were and if he had enemies. Intimidated at first in this room full of men, Anna spoke softly and slowly, telling them that her husband arrived home from work at about 6 P.M. He took a bath and dressed himself in his finest suit. Before he left the apartment, Anna asked for a little money to buy an Easter plant for a friend. "He never gave me any money," she said, "I had to beg for it." Anna told everyone present that her husband produced, as she recalled, "a roll of bills from his pocket, counted out $450, then took $10," which he gave me. This revelation piqued Flubacher's curiosity. When Sam Antonio's blood-soaked and mud-caked clothes were stripped from him in the morgue, there was no wallet or cash. No brakeman on the New York Central came close to earning this much money. Flubacher was now in complete agreement with Richard Kelly. The murder of Sam Antonio was looking a lot like the result of a bad drug deal or robbery or both.[2]

Anna went on to explain that although she was upset with her husband going out on Saturday night, it was something she had grown to accept. Since Christmas, she estimated that he had not spent one night with her in their apartment. She was returning from the florist with her neighbor, Mrs. Miller, when she saw her husband leave the apartment. After that, she never saw her husband alive again.[3]

When Delaney asked her about the phone calls she received early Sunday morning, Anna repeated the same story she had told Flubacher at Memorial Hospital. The first call, at 5 A.M., instructed her to go to the railroad depot to collect her husband. She didn't recognize the caller's voice, but she called a cab and did as she was instructed. When she arrived at the depot, she waited, and when her husband was nowhere to be found, she had the cab driver take her home. An hour later she received a second call. As with the first call, Anna told Delaney that she didn't recognize the caller's voice. The anonymous caller told her that her husband had been seriously injured and was at the hospital. She then contacted her neighbor, Helen Miller, and together they took a cab to the hospital, where they met Flubacher.

When asked about her husband's friends and, more importantly, his enemies, Anna was less than forthcoming. He had his railroad friends, but she suspected that her husband had crossed others. "I don't know," she replied with a sigh, "he must have had some enemies because he was getting telephone calls from New York; he would get scared and tell me to keep the children off the sidewalks and not to go in the cellar and keep the doors locked. When I would tell me about the calls he received he would say not to pay any attention to them." Throughout the month of February, Anna told her little audience, her husband's fear kept her a virtual prisoner in her own home. On the night he was killed, she overheard her husband say to one of the children as he was preparing to go out for the evening, "Good-bye honey, given I won't live long enough to appreciate you."[4]

When pressed to elaborate on these strange goings-on at 3 Teunis Street, Anna said that all these events seemed to escalate in mid-December when Sam came home with $1,000. The money, she said, was more than she had ever seen in her whole life, and as it was right before Christmas, it was a godsend to the financially pressed household. In addition to rent and other bills, Anna told them that Sam was four months in arrears with his Brotherhood of Railway Trainmen insurance policy. When this policy was paid in full, Anna told Delaney that her husband took out another life insurance policy for $2,500. According to Anna Antonio, her husband was obsessed when it came to the subject of his life insurance. "Keep up my insurance," she recalled him saying on one occasion, "even if you have to go without bread in the house." Odd, thought Flubacher as he jotted the quote down in his notes. How was she to keep up the payments when just a few minutes ago she claimed to have had to beg her husband for money? When Flubacher asked her to explain this discrepancy, Anna replied that she had to pawn her rings to make the payments.[5]

While Griggs and Delaney took notes of what transpired during this interview, the man asking the questions was growing frustrated. Anna had vaguely answered some questions and sidestepped others. He could not believe for one moment that she could not name *anyone*—friend or enemy of her husband—and had no idea how he came into this large amount of cash. When direct questions yielded little information, Delaney changed directions.

"Now, Mrs. Antonio," asked Delaney, "are you sick?"

It was a question Griggs had wanted to ask of the little woman sitting across the table. She was young, but to Griggs, Anna looked tired. Her big eyes didn't appear to be red from tears, but her ashen-gray pallor concerned him. She was either sick, in a weakened state, or could be in a mild state of shock from the events of the day.

"Do you use dope?" inquired the district attorney.

The question startled Anna. Puzzled at first, she replied that not only did she not use dope, she assured all the men present that "I wouldn't know it if I seen it." If they didn't believe her, then they should call for a doctor.[6] Seeing that Anna was irritated by this question, Delaney pushed ahead and asked if her if she thought her husband was peddling narcotics.

"Not that I know of," she said with a deep sigh. "And I don't know any of my husband's business. Italian people are different than other people. The husband never tells his wife anything. The husband's word is law."

"Mrs. Antonio," said a clearly frustrated Delaney, "you are not telling us all you know about this case. We are trying to find out who killed your husband and you are not helping us at all."

"If you find out you will have to find out on your own accord," replied Anna, "and not by me telling you."[7]

To Delaney, this response sparked of noncooperation. Turning to Griggs, Delaney said in a firm tone as he walked from the room, "Lock her up."

A stunned Anna Antonio glared at Griggs. "What are they going to do, hold me?"

With the gruff Delaney out of the room, Griggs tried a gentler approach. As he escorted her from the room, he tried to reassure her that everything would be all right if she cooperated. "Why don't you tell what you know about this thing?" he asked. "They don't want to hold you with the trouble you have in your family. Why don't you tell them what they want to know?"

Anna hesitated for a moment and then looked at Griggs. "I cannot tell them anymore."[8] The wary detective interpreted her comment not as "cannot" but "would not." If she was reluctant to divulge information about her husband's activities, he would look elsewhere. The next day Griggs visited the south end of Albany. With informants scattered throughout the Gut in pool halls, speakeasies, and restaurants, Griggs was confident that he could link Vincent Saetta to Sam Antonio. He visited every place Saetta was known to have frequented and discovered that he had been seen in the company of Sam Antonio on Saturday night. Although the information he gathered from his sources in the Gut was useful, it paled in comparison to the information he received the following day from Richard Kelly. Griggs was taken aback when he learned that the mysterious red Sam everyone was asking about was indeed Sam Faraci. For the past month, Griggs, unbeknownst to Kelly and everyone else in the precinct, had been shadowing Faraci throughout the south end on suspicion of drug trafficking.

Griggs realized that the car, the Oldsmobile coupe belonging to Faraci, was the key. Find the car and you will find Faraci. The teletype sent to all police departments of the description of Faraci, his car, and its license plate might take days to yield results. As it turned out, he didn't have to wait very long. Early Wednesday morning, Griggs was roused from bed by a telephone call from the precinct. They had just received word that Sam Faraci, Vincent Saetta, and a woman, Gertrude King, were being held by the Poughkeepsie police. As Griggs was the only one in the department who could positively identify Sam Faraci, he was instructed to report to the precinct and then proceed to Poughkeepsie. At day's end, Griggs learned that the apprehension of all three was a comedy of errors, complete with bad luck and an equal amount of poor planning.

Saetta planned a murder, but he didn't plan a good escape. The plan to go to New York on the premise of "seeing my people" was in reality a vacation. They visited the Saetta family, did a little shopping, and with Vincent at the wheel of Faraci's car, toured Broadway. All the time they were hampered by the presence of Gertrude King. It was almost impossible for Saetta and Faraci to discuss in detail anything that had transpired before, during, and, most important, after the murder. As long as Gertrude King was at Faraci's side, the two men were unable to rehearse a plausible alibi.

Between family visits and sightseeing, Saetta made only one telephone call. He asked his landlady not to let his room go as he was out of town. He told her he would be returning and as soon as he got back to Albany, he would settle up with her on the overdue rent. One phone call? Saetta should have made several calls. He should have called the pool halls and speakeasies he frequented to pick up any local gossip or street rumors regarding the death of Sam Antonio. The Monday after the murder, the murder on Castleton Road was in all the local newspapers. It was here that Saetta made a costly error. The same man who relied on the newspaper coverage of the Steamburg dairy arson to learn that authorities had no leads in the arson failed to ask anyone how the press reported the death of Sam Antonio. If he had asked any of his friends in Albany, Saetta would have learned that the police were looking for him and Faraci.

Throughout their brief stay in the city, a confident Vincent Saetta at the wheel of the Oldsmobile assured his friend that he knew the streets of New York. Saetta may have known the city, but he didn't know Poughkeepsie. They arrived at Poughkeepsie at about 1:30 A.M. and became disoriented. Saetta was driving slowly along the 200 block of Main Street, hoping that a streetlight might illuminate a sign that could lead them to Albany Post Road. He made a turn two blocks too early into a narrow alley. Realizing his mistake, Saetta brought the car to a slow stop. He looked on either side of the car and discovered that the alley was not wide enough to turn the car around.

Across the street, patrolman John Campion had just checked the door handle and lock on the front door of 235 Main Street when he spied a car in the alley slowly coming to a halt. The car didn't look familiar, but something about the license plate did. Before he left the station house to walk his main street beat, he had copied the license plate number from the most recent teletype from Albany. Removing a small black notebook from his pocket, Campion opened it and looked at the numbers: 6J67-44. He couldn't believe his luck—the car was right in front of him.[9]

Returning the notebook to his pocket, Campion casually walked across the street. Approaching the driver's side of the car, Campion asked if he could be of any assistance. Saetta said that they must have taken a wrong turn as they were trying to get to Albany. Campion shook his head and with a laugh said, "You'll never get to Albany going in that alley." Stepping onto the running board of the Oldsmobile, Campion guided Saetta out of the alley. "I'll show you the way."[10]

Two blocks down and to the right would lead them to Albany Post Road. Campion directed Saetta to drive two blocks down and make a left turn. This led directly to the front door of the Poughkeepsie Police Department. In his twenty-nine years on the police force, John Campion never encountered anything quite like this. He never raised his voice and never drew his service revolver. Campion told Saetta to turn off the ignition and told all of them that they were needed inside to answer a few questions.

Once inside the station house, Campion asked the standard questions: "What is your name?" "Where are you from?" "Where are you going?" The three were cooperative and polite, but this changed when Saetta and Faraci asked why they were being held. Campion looked at both men and said, "We are detaining you for the Albany police."[11]

The demeanor of both men instantly changed when they heard "Albany police." The color quickly faded from Saetta's face. His stomach churned, and he belched several times. "Ulcers," he explained and asked for water.[12] Faraci said nothing, but it was clear that he, too, was highly agitated. Fidgeting in his chair, he moved restlessly from side to side as his eyes darted about the room. As more uniformed officers entered the room, Faraci and Saetta realized that they were trapped.

Led upstairs to separate rooms to spend the remaining morning hours, Gertrude King was confused. She knew that she hadn't done anything in Albany to give the police reason to pick her up for questioning, but she couldn't say the same for her two traveling companions. After observing their behavior downstairs, she suspected that they were in trouble. She just didn't know how serious it was.

Meanwhile, preparations were under way to extradite Saetta, Faraci, and King to Albany. By the time Griggs arrived at the Third Precinct, his boss, Chief Smurl, had assembled a motorcade of cars to transport two patrolmen, a sergeant, a lieutenant, and three detectives to retrieve the fugitives. They arrived at Poughkeepsie at about 7 A.M. and left within the hour. Since the three were being held and were not formally charged with a crime, the paperwork for their release was minimal. While one officer made arrangements to drive Faraci's car with the luggage to Albany police headquarters, Griggs made the decision to separate the suspects. Since he was familiar with Faraci, Griggs thought it best to be in the same car as Saetta. When he noticed how close King and Faraci were, he thought it best to separate them as well. She would ride in the same car with Saetta. As they departed from Poughkeepsie and drove north, Gertrude King remained nervously silent. Saetta, however, acted as if he were on a leisurely drive through the country. Amiable and polite, he asked the officers if he was allowed to smoke. "Why certainly," said one officer, "go ahead and smoke." After excusing himself for belching several times because of his ulcers, Saetta lit a cigarette. He gazed out the window, admiring the countryside and shook his head. "Nice day," he said, "it is a good day for a ride, it is a nice trip down and back." Then, glancing about the interior of the car that would eventually take him to jail, Saetta exclaimed, "This is a nice car you got here. You could get about a good ways if you had a car like this."[13]

In the other car the conversation wasn't as lighthearted. Faraci stared out the window as if deep in thought with an expressionless look on his face. One officer made note of the fact that Faraci didn't utter a single word from Poughkeepsie to Albany.[14]

6

LIES, ALIBIS, AND GERTRUDE KING

The funeral service for Sam Antonio was held on the second floor of 3 Teunis Street, followed by the internment at Our Lady of Christian Help Cemetery in Glenmont. Before the burial, Anna presented funeral director John M. Zwack with an envelope containing her husband's insurance policy from the Brotherhood of Railway Trainmen to help defray the funeral expenses. She wasn't sure if the Metropolitan policy was valid, but she included that as well. A month earlier her husband had met with a Metropolitan agent and after some convincing decided to take out a Metropolitan insurance policy, with the idea of eventually dropping the Brotherhood policy. As only one premium had been paid to Metropolitan, she was unsure about its validity.

The same day Sam Antonio was buried, the motorcade bearing Saetta, Faraci, and King arrived at the front door of the Third Precinct. The talkative Saetta was now at a loss for words as Griggs escorted him up the six granite steps, past the columned archway, and toward the double oak doors. Once inside the two-story brick building, Saetta and Faraci were led past the booking desk and brought directly to the cell area at the rear of the building. Like their travel arrangements from Poughkeepsie, the two men were separated and placed in different cells. Gertrude King's placement presented a problem because there wasn't a jail matron assigned to the Third Precinct. Arrangements were made to accommodate her at the Second Precinct.

In direct contrast to the crestfallen Faraci and the bewildered Gertrude King, Vincent Saetta instantly regained his composure and self-confidence after passing through the doors of the Third Precinct. Saetta had mentally prepared himself for this moment. He knew that because he had been associated with Sam Antonio while working for the New York Central Railroad, there was a possibility that the authorities might question him. Adhering to the time-honored tradition of "simple is best," Saetta quickly concocted a story that was easy and straightforward. If questioned by the police, he would claim that they left Albany for New York City between the early morning hours of 5 A.M. and 6 A.M. This time frame, he assured his partner, would put plenty of distance between them and the discovery of Sam Antonio's corpse. It was critical to their own survival that both men repeat the *same* story with no variations. In this they were almost successful.

Since Saetta had been such a good conversationalist during his ride from Poughkeepsie, the detectives agreed that he should be interviewed first. Griggs knew that many officers would participate in the interview and that the detention room with its long table and straight-backed chairs near the cell would be ill suited for a small crowd. A more relaxed atmosphere, thought Griggs, might put Saetta at ease. At about 2:00 P.M. Saetta was brought from his cell to the front of the building by several officers who then led him up a brass-railed circular stairway to the second floor. At the top of the stairs was an immense room, a dormitory with twenty-four beds and just as many chairs. Saetta was asked to sit in one chair while Griggs and six other officers sat on the edge of the beds. The last one to arrive upstairs was Flubacher, having concluded another interview with Anna Antonio.

Griggs began the interview by asking Saetta a series of harmless questions designed to gain his trust and also to glean a few bits of new information. Saetta seemed perfectly at ease when asked about his activities the day before Easter. He had been at a pool room here, a restaurant there, and several other places. As to his trip to New York, he said that he had planned to take the train to the city to visit his parents for Easter, but at the last minute, he happened upon his pal Faraci at a lunchroom on Green Street. Faraci told him that he wanted to go home to Geneva but didn't have much money to make the trip. Saetta suggested that they go to New York and stay with his family and take in the sights of the city. Faraci liked the idea and liked it even more when Saetta said he could bring along his girlfriend, Gertrude King.

Saetta was adamant about the time he left Albany and so was Faraci when it was his turn to be questioned in the upstairs dormitory. "They all professed to know nothing of the crime and attempted to explain their movements the day preceding and the day after the crime," said an exasperated John T. Delaney, adding, "their plan was so well-conceived that it looked hopeless to solve." With no eyewitness to the murder and scant physical evidence, Delaney was prepared to release both men. What changed his mind, he later recalled, was Flubacher's "dogged tenacity."[1] The state policeman implored Delaney to hold both men. He was convinced that they were lying and just needed more time to get to the truth. Tired of hearing the same story of how they left Albany down "Broadway to Clinton, then down Pearl Street," Flubacher abruptly changed the subject.[2]

"So Vince, where did you get the new shoes?"

Surprised, Saetta told everyone that they were a gift from his mother. Flubacher shook his head in disbelief. You hadn't seen your mother in over six or seven months and when you suddenly appear at her house, she presents you with new shoes? Sure, said Vincent. The other shoes were old and worn, not much good, so he told his mother to throw them away.

Well, queried Flubacher, since you didn't have to pay for the new shoes, how much money did you have to make the trip to New York? Saetta told Griggs and Flubacher that he and Faraci had seven dollars apiece. The free pair of shoes was perhaps possible, but seven dollars each to spend in New York was simply unbelievable. Saetta was returned to his cell and Faraci was taken from his cell and asked the same questions.

Upstairs in the dormitory, surrounded by detectives, Faraci gave essentially the same answers to the questions that had been posed to Saetta moments earlier. Specific details regarding where he was in Albany and how he decided to go to New York with Saetta matched perfectly. As he had done with Saetta, Flubacher complimented Faraci on his new shoes and then asked him where he had purchased them.

"I got them at the same place Vincent bought his," said Faraci.

When asked what became of his old shoes, Faraci said that since they were so old and worn, the shoes were of little value to him, and he tossed them in the trash can outside the store. Faraci added that although the new shoes cost $3.25, he didn't pay for them; Vincent did.

Obviously, somebody wasn't telling the truth about their new shoes. Faraci was brought back to his cell, and Saetta was once again escorted back to the dormitory. Saetta insisted that his mother bought him the shoes. When Flubacher told him what Faraci said, Saetta had an explanation. "Well," he said in a haltering tone, "my mother didn't buy them, but my mother gave me $5 to buy them. Among Italian people, when they give you the money to buy them, that is just the same as if they bought them, and I thought that is what you wanted to know."[3]

Flubacher was not amused and gave Saetta a quick lesson in finances. The money his mother supposedly gave him, plus the money he had, came to only $12. "You paid $2 for gas, and you paid $1 for bridge fare, and you paid $2.50 for the room for Sam and his girl the first night, and you paid $1.50 for a room for yourself, you paid for getting the automobile washed, which was another dollar. . . . count that up and see how much that amounts to."[4]

Flubacher and Griggs weren't convinced by his first explanation and didn't believe his second. Both suspected that Saetta had a lot more money on his person when he made the trip to New York and that money could be traced to the wallet of Sam Antonio. Flubacher recalled in his interview with Anna Antonio that she believed her husband had a sizable amount of money when he left home that night, perhaps as much as $400.

When pressing the issue of money yielded no tangible results, the questions shifted to Saetta's movements in the city and the phone call he had placed to his landlady. Saetta calmly fielded each question with an innocent air until Flubacher stopped him cold and began asking about his relationship with Sam Antonio. Saetta remained calm and told the officers that he was acquainted with Sam Antonio as they had worked on the railroad together in Hudson. Flubacher then asked him about an altercation he and Antonio had on Division Street. At this point, Saetta became concerned. How did the police know about this fight?

"Yes," said Saetta, trying to downplay the incident, "but that is a long time ago."

"Who got the worst of the fight?"

"I did," said Saetta, trying not to laugh, "he was too strong for me, he nearly broke my arm, twisted my arm, nearly broke it."

"Couldn't you lick him?" asked Flubacher.

"No," said Saetta with a chuckle, "he is a bigger man than I am."

Saetta told the story that he and Sam Antonio argued about money. He claimed that Antonio refused to repay a seventy-five-dollar loan. What Saetta conveniently omitted—and what Flubacher already knew from his conversation with Richard Kelly—was that Saetta started the fight when he sucker punched Antonio. He also didn't mention the fact that Antonio landed one punch to the eye that sent Saetta sprawling across the sidewalk. Sam Antonio did twist his arm like he said, but only to disarm him. After Saetta recovered from being punched in the eye, he drew a knife on Sam Antonio.[5]

"What happened after that?"

"I met Sam on Green Street," said Saetta, "and I said to him, 'it's no use of us being bad friends,' and we shook hands and that was all there was to it."[6]

Flubacher pressed him further to tell the truth about what he knew of Sam Antonio to no avail. Saetta confessed to know nothing. They knew each other, but they were not really close friends. When the detectives told Saetta that Sam Antonio had been viciously attacked and later died at Memorial Hospital, Saetta expressed his complete surprise.

"I didn't know that Antonio was taken to the hospital," said Saetta. "It is too bad, too bad, he was a nice man."[7]

The fake sincerity didn't fool anyone in the dormitory. Saetta knew something and was now guarding his answers carefully. He still held firm to his alibi that he was in New York visiting his family when Antonio was killed. When Faraci returned to the dormitory for questioning, he repeated the story of how he came by a pair of new shoes but categorically denied knowing anyone by the name of Sam Antonio. "I don't even know who he is even," he told Griggs, "I don't know if Vincent knew him or not, I don't know him."[8]

And so it went for the rest of the afternoon. Back and forth the two were brought to the dormitory for questioning. Saetta continued to act as if his being at the precinct was a total misunderstanding. He sidestepped questions, gave vague answers, and admitted to nothing. In direct contrast was Sam Faraci. Lacking Saetta's confidence, the sullen and gloomy Sam Faraci stumbled over questions, giving vague responses. Agitated and restless, his eyes darted about the dormitory room as if his thoughts were elsewhere.

"What's the matter Sam," asked one detective, "you got something on your mind?"

"I ain't got nothing on my mind."

"Yes, you have," said the detective, "why don't you tell us the truth and get this off your mind?"

"Na," said Faraci, shaking his head, "I ain't got nothing on my mind."[9]

Several of the detectives present in the dormitory wondered if Faraci had any idea of the seriousness of his situation. They needn't have concerned themselves. Faraci was well aware of his current predicament. He knew he was in trouble, but right now his mind was preoccupied with trying to find a way out of his current situation. Like his friend Saetta, Faraci had run afoul of the law before and knew that he had rights. What worried Faraci now was that the detectives were ignoring his constant pleas to provide him with an attorney.

Throughout the afternoon the detectives did their best to wear down each of them and in the process became fairly worn down themselves. It had been an exceptionally long day for those who had made the trip to Poughkeepsie, and by early evening, they were tired. All they had to show for their efforts were a few inconsistencies of money and arrival times in New York, not enough to charge them with any crime. They resolved to try again the next day, but Delaney had different plans.

Griggs was home, having just finished his supper, when he received a telephone call informing him to report immediately to the Third Precinct. He wasn't sure what was taking place but interpreted the call as an urgent directive. He arrived at the precinct at 8 P.M. and proceeded directly to the captain's office. Delaney was talking with another detective, while several other policemen were inspecting Faraci's overcoat and another was examining the contents of Gertrude King's suitcase. Griggs looked across the hall and noticed that King had been brought from the Second Precinct and was sitting near the sergeant's desk. He glanced at her belongings and found nothing unusual. There were a few dresses, three neckties, no doubt belonging to Faraci, a toothbrush, and a powder puff, typical items one might pack for a weekend trip.

The chatter in the office subsided briefly when Anna Antonio was escorted into the room and was seated by the captain's desk. Now Griggs knew why Delaney wanted him and everyone else to be present. Delaney wanted a room full of witnesses for what he had planned. Nodding to a detective standing in the doorway, Delaney turned to Anna Antonio. "We are going to bring some men in here," he said, "and I want you to look at them and see if you know them."[10]

Det. James "Jimmie" Hynes walked into the room with Saetta.

"What is your name?" asked Delaney.

"Vincent Saetta"

"Where do you live?"

"Columbia Street."

"Where are you from?"

"I am from New York."

"All right."

With a simple nod, Delaney motioned Hynes to remove Saetta from the room and return with his companion.

"What is your name?"

"Sam Faraci."

"Where do you live?"

"Geneva."

"That's all, Sam."

Delaney paused for a moment to give Hynes enough time to return Faraci to his cell before questioning Anna Antonio. When Hynes returned, Delaney asked her if she had ever seen any of these men before. Anna shook her head and in a voice just above a whisper, said, "No."

"You are not helping the police any in this case," said Delaney with a deep, frustrated sigh, "those are the men who murdered your husband."[11]

Saetta and Faraci refused to talk, and Anna Antonio denied knowing either of them. Delaney sensed that something was wrong and after the impromptu lineup began to suspect Anna Antonio of complicity in her husband's murder. Her earlier refusal to cooperate, stating that if he wanted to find out anything regarding the murder, he would have to discover it on his own was the most incredible statement he had ever heard from a widow of a brutally murdered man. This, together with the calm demeanor she had displayed this evening, bothered him. There were no shrieks, no hysterics, not even a tear of grief on her cheek. She was too emotionless or, as he liked to say, "too cool." She never asked him any questions and just didn't behave like a woman faced with this terrible calamity.[12] He had hoped for some sort of reaction from her and when he received none, turned to a detective and said in disgust, "Let her go home."[13]

Delaney didn't have enough physical evidence to charge Saetta or Faraci, but at the same time he couldn't risk letting them out of jail. He was sure that if he did, they would disappear. Faraci's car wasn't in the best shape, but it did get them to New York. For now, the two, who had not been fingerprinted or charged with any crime, could sit in their cells. During the next several days, while some detectives continued to interrogate the two, others scoured the Gut district looking for any clues that might tie them to Sam Antonio. Griggs knew the speakeasies at the south end of Abany better than most of the detectives and sought out patrons of Paul's Restaurant, the Musician's Club, Devil's Cave, and Green Cave. He didn't have to go to 21 Hamilton Street because the terrified proprietor, Phil Harris, showed up at the Third Precinct. Anxious to distance himself from Faraci after reading of his arrest in the newspapers, Harris spoke to Griggs and told all he knew about Faraci and his girlfriend, Gertrude King. Unlike his pal Saetta, Griggs saw Faraci as a quiet, somewhat subdued individual who appeared to be overly worried about being in jail. Of the two, Griggs believed that he was the weaker one. Given time, he believed that the detectives would be able to get him to talk before Saetta. As it turned out, the one who got Faraci to talk was not a detective but a woman.

If John T. Delaney thought that his impromptu lineup or face-to-face encounter between Anna Antonio and the accused was unsuccessful, he was mistaken. It was effective in a way he least expected. If Anna Antonio wasn't moved by the words "Those men are the murderers of your husband," then Gertrude King certainly was. Up to this point she had absolutely no idea why Saetta, Faraci, and herself had been whisked from Poughkeepsie to Albany in police cars. The word *murder* resonated in her ears. She had been in trouble with the law before, but nothing on a scale such as this.

Returned to the Second Precinct, King spent a restless night worried that she would be implicated in a crime she knew nothing about. The next morning, she steadfastly proclaimed her innocence to the detectives at the precinct. She told them that not only did she know nothing about a murder, she had never heard of Sam Antonio. Gertrude King told the detectives that she may have seen him, perhaps once in the company of Sam Faraci, and the only time she had ever seen Anna Antonio was the previous evening at the Third Precinct.

On the other side of the cell bars, detectives told King that her situation was not hopeless. She wasn't under arrest, but they told her that she was not going to be released until they got what they were after. They knew all about her checkered past and were not interested in her recent arrest for prostitution in Newburgh. What they wanted to know from her was where she and Sam Faraci were early Saturday evening before the murder of Sam Antonio and the circumstances involving her trip to New York City with Saetta and Faraci.

The detectives didn't have to prod Gertrude King into cooperating. With complete candor she told all about her relationship with Sam Faraci. Originally from Oswego, New York, King told how she hooked up with Sam Faraci when he managed a roadhouse speakeasy called Far View Inn, south of Geneva. She freely admitted being a prostitute, conceding that it was a nomadic, unlucrative existence. She said that it was Sam Faraci who drove her all over central New York to ply her avocation. Binghamton, Penn Yan, and the notorious Diamond Street section of Hudson were only a few of the places he took her, and yes, she said they had been to Newburgh. King said that when they arrived in Albany, they were penniless. They had the car, the clothes on their backs, and a few suitcases. She said that Faraci sought out an old friend, Phil Harris, a proprietor of a speakeasy at 21 Hamilton Street. Harris fixed up a place in the back of his establishment for them.

Everything Gertrude King recalled about that Saturday night and the trip to New York contradicted what Faraci had told them. Whereas Sam Faraci had said that he was in Schenectady the evening of the murder, King flatly denied that she ever went there with him on that night. After dinner, she left Faraci with Saetta and returned to the apartment.

She said she didn't see Faraci until early in the morning on Easter Sunday. It was he who suggested that they accompany Saetta to New York and spend Easter with his family. King said at first, she protested. She wanted to go home to Oswego, but she later relented when Faraci told her that she would enjoy the trip. They would cross Bear Mountain Bridge, one of the largest suspension bridges in the world, and take in other sites once they got to the city. She told of meeting Saetta's family and the fair amount of whining it took on her part to get Faraci to buy her a new dress.

What interested the detectives the most about their interview with King was the time frame involved in the trip and the amount of money expended. The times King gave for departing Albany and arriving in the city were far different from what Saetta and Faraci had claimed. As for the dress, she told them that Saetta had given the money to Faraci to purchase her dress. In fact, she said, it was Saetta who handled the money for gas, tolls, food, hotel bills, two pairs of new shoes, and her dress.

With the information provided by King, the detectives were now ready to confront Sam Faraci. Back at the Third Precinct, Faraci was brought up to the dormitory, and he knew right away that he was in trouble. When Flubacher asked him why he claimed to have been in Schenectady and Gertrude King said he wasn't, his suspicions were confirmed. King was telling the police all she knew. Faraci, realizing that he was boxed into a corner, asked Flubacher for a favor.

"What is it?"

"Will you bring my girl up to see me?"

"When?"

"At the first chance you get."[14]

7

"AT LAST, A BREAK"

After spending several days in the conference room and dormitory questioning Saetta and Faraci, the detectives assigned to the Antonio murder case were making little progress. They were so frustrated that on one occasion, they moved Saetta and Faraci to adjoining cells and installed a Dictaphone to eavesdrop on their conversations. Even with this technology, they were unable to get any new leads, clues, or incriminating evidence to aid them in their investigation. It was only when Faraci asked to see his girlfriend that Flubacher, Hynes, and Griggs believed that they were making some progress. The detectives assigned to the case didn't look on this as a big break but a big opportunity to crack Sam Faraci.

On Saturday, April 9, Flubacher and Hynes drove to the Second Precinct and met with Gertrude King. They told her that Sam Faraci had been asking for her and if she wished, they had made arrangements for her to meet him at the Third Precinct. King was absolutely elated and would have sprinted down the hall and out the precinct door to the waiting patrol car if she could. She was desperate to have this entire affair cleared up so she could get out of jail. When they arrived at the Third Precinct, Flubacher escorted her to the captain's office and Hynes went to collect Sam Faraci.

In a moment Hynes appeared in the doorway with Faraci. Anticipating another round of questioning at the hands of the detectives, Faraci was awestruck when he saw King. "You asked us to bring her up," said Hynes, "come on in and see her now."

"Now, Sam," said Flubacher, "we will straighten out—"

"How are you?" said Faraci softly.

He threw his arms around King in a tender embrace and passionately kissed her. They hugged each other again and kissed one more time. A surprised Hynes looked at Flubacher and shook his head in disbelief. He hadn't realized that the two were this close. Flubacher, too, was just as surprised. In his notepad he wrote, "Lots of love."[1] After the two sat down, hand in hand, Flubacher tried once again to ask his initial question.

"Now, Sam, we are going to straighten out the story you told us about being around Green Street and Madison Avenue and the one you told us about being in Schenectady."

Flubacher's comment brought concern from Faraci and a scowl from Gertrude King. From the beginning, Faraci had claimed that he had been at pool halls and speakeasies on these streets early in the evening of the murder and had been with King in Schenectady when Antonio was killed.

"If I told my girl that I was in Schenectady," said Faraci apologetically, "I was wrong. I was down where I told you men I was."

"Sam, for God's sake," implored King, "why do you make a liar out of me? If you know anything about this why don't you tell the truth?"

Faraci turned to her and asked, "Do you think I do it?"

"No, I don't think you did it, Sam, but for God's sake if you do know anything tell those men the truth and have it over with."

"I don't know anything," said Faraci in a halfhearted way, "and I can't say anything."

With this, Hynes walked over to Faraci and, taking him by the arm, said, "Well, there is no need of sitting here any further, come on, we will go back to the detention room."

Faraci hadn't picked himself up from the chair when King suddenly threw her arms about his neck, kissed him, and said, "Sam, for God's sake why don't you tell the truth? Tell the truth if you know anything. Tell it, and if you don't know anything you cannot tell it."

Hynes led him out of the captain's office and down the corridor that led to the detention room and asked the same question King had asked: "Why don't you tell the truth, Sam, for the girl's sake?"

Faraci, visibly shaken from the encounter with King, replied sheepishly, "I don't know anything, how can I tell the truth?"

In the detention room, Hynes asked Faraci why he didn't mention anything about the dress he had purchased for King while in New York and, more importantly, how he was able to pay for it. "You know a woman wants a dress," said Faraci, "and she kept bothering me, and I got the money off Vincent and got the dress." Hynes wanted to continue to ask a few more questions about the amount of money he and his partner had when Faraci suddenly interrupted him.[2]

"Will you bring my girl up to see me again? I want to talk to my girl," said Faraci with a big sigh. "I want to talk to her alone."

"I cannot bring her up this afternoon," promised Hynes, "but I will bring her up in the morning sometime."

"All right, please do."[3]

Hynes reasoned, as did Flubacher, that the first reunion between Faraci and King was not a waste of time. The emotional attachment between the two was obvious. For days detectives had interrogated Sam Faraci and not one of them came close to eliciting the emotion from him that King had done in a twenty-minute encounter. If anyone was going to get Faraci to talk, it would be Gertrude King. After all, she needed Faraci to talk so she could be exonerated and released from jail, and Faraci needed to talk for the same reason. After Hynes brought him back to his cell, Faraci had the entire weekend to come up with a convincing story that would exonerate him as well. Ten years earlier he had turned informant in a successful bid to gain an early release from Auburn State Prison. Now, sitting in a Third Precinct cell, Faraci made up his mind to do the same thing.

On Monday, April 11, Flubacher and Hynes brought Gertrude King to the Third Precinct. Both men were hopeful that the next meeting between the two would be more productive than the first. When they brought her in to meet with Faraci, both men noticed that the reunion was not as tender as before. There were no smiles, no sparkle in the eyes, no embrace, and no kiss.

"Can I talk to my girl alone?"

Over Flubacher's objection, Hynes agreed to leave the two alone in the captain's office. Outside the office door, Hynes did his best to eavesdrop, but as the two spoke in a low whisper, he could make out only a word here and there or a phrase. An hour passed and suddenly Gertrude King came out in the hall and announced, "Sam wants to tell the truth about this thing."[4]

"I just told my girl what happened," said Faraci when Flubacher and Hynes reentered the captain's office, "and I want to tell you the truth. I was with Vince when he done it, but I didn't do it."[5]

For a brief moment there was silence. Not wishing to appear excited, Flubacher scribbled in his notepad "At last, a break."[6] He and Hynes looked at Faraci, hoping that more details of his supposed innocence would be forthcoming than just a simple sentence. When it didn't appear so, a visibly upset Gertrude King began asking the questions. "For God's sake Sam, tell them all you know." When Faraci attempted to repeat his "that's all I know" excuse, an extremely frustrated Gertrude King shot back, "Were you in the car with Vince? Where did you go?"[7]

In his attempt to tell what had occurred the day before the murder, Faraci drifted back and forth telling a myriad of details that occurred. Some were trivial, a few were important, but all were designed to separate him from Saetta. According to Faraci, Sam Antonio was a friend who had done him no wrong. True, he drove him around Albany when asked, but Antonio always reciprocated with a tank of gas for his efforts. "I don't see that man treat me bad," said Faraci in a hackneyed Italian-English accent. Faraci claimed that he was lured into the plot to kill Antonio by a vengeful Saetta. It was his idea to go to Hudson.[8]

"We all three were in the car," said Faraci hesitantly, "Vincent was driving the car. I was sitting in the middle; Antonio was sitting near the door. We were going down the road and I tell Vincent a couple of times I got to take a piss. He don't stop. We go to Hudson and come back and half ways between Hudson and Albany I tell Vincent to stop, I got to go to the toilet."

Hynes and Flubacher had been scribbling in their notepads when Faraci paused for a moment. "You know," he said, "I take pills, and they make me go in a hurry. So I got out and I go across the road. I am taking a crap, and all of a sudden I hear shooting. Bang, bang, bang. I jump up run over, hold my pants, and Vincent is on top of Antonio and stabbing him. I grab Vincent and I pull him away and I get blood on my hands. I come over and say, 'Vince, what did you do?' Vince says, 'That son of a bitch double-crossed me. It was either him or me and I gave it to him.' Then I say, 'Now I am in trouble, this is my automobile, and they know the number of my automobile and I get picked up and I get blamed.' Vince said, 'Never mind. Don't say anything to anybody about this. Get in the car.' Then we get in the car and we drive to Albany."[9]

Faraci had rehearsed his story for the entire weekend, trying his best not to incriminate himself. It was Vincent who used the knife and it was Vincent who tossed away the gun. From the blood on his hands and shirt from wrestling with Saetta to the muddy shoes, Faraci even included his aggravated stomach condition. He admitted that he was there, but was a witness to, not a participant in, the murder. "I never do anything like this before," he pleaded.[10]

Questioned about money, Faraci said that he had only a few dollars and that it was Saetta who arranged to get money so they could leave Albany. Did he recognize Anna Antonio when they drove to Broadway Street? Faraci said that he couldn't be absolutely certain that it was her. In his final bid to separate himself from the crime, Faraci suggested that Saetta was involved with Anna Antonio. "Vincent, now tell me the truth," said Faraci, "are you been having something to do with his wife. ... you been up to something with her?"

When he was through, Hynes asked him if he was telling the truth about all he knew about the murder of Sam Antonio. "Sure it is the truth," said a confident Faraci. "I will say it to Vincent's face."[11] As the first to cooperate with the authorities, Faraci believed that he was in a better position to strike a deal for a light sentence or, hopefully, a release from jail. He signed the confession and said good-bye to Gertrude King. King was returned to the Second Precinct and later released. Sam Faraci's confession was her get-out-of-jail ticket. She never saw him again.

Faraci's boast of reciting his confession in the presence of his partner wasn't too far-fetched. It was exactly what Hynes had planned to do. The next day he, in the company of Flubacher, brought Faraci into the corridor within earshot of Saetta's cell and had asked him to repeat his confession. When Faraci finished his version of the crime, Hynes casually walked toward Saetta's cell.

"Hey, Vince," said Hynes, "you heard what Faraci said?"

"Yes," grumbled Saetta, "I heard what he say. That man is a yellow dog. He is trying to rat out of it. That man is just as guilty of this as I am. I shoot the man, but he knifed him."

But why, asked Flubacher, was Antonio killed?

"There was a question of my life or his anyway," said Saetta in a firm, loud voice. "He was going to bump me off, so I had to kill him. Bring Faraci here in my presence and I will tell you that he, Faraci, told me that Antonio was going to kill me some day. Right in his house, you will find a gun, and you will find knives that he bought to kill me with."

After being questioned countless times by different detectives, Saetta never lost his temper. He had remained calm and unflustered. Although he refrained from offering specific details to any questions posed to him, Saetta never got agitated until now. Observing the marked change in his behavior, Hynes and Flubacher saw their chance and prodded Saetta for more information.

"That man done me plenty of dirt," said Saetta. "He double-crossed me on many deals. He was going to kill me sure some day or other . . . I had to do it."

Hynes, recalling how Anna Antonio reacted in front of Delaney when Saetta and Faraci were brought before her, asked if there was anyone else involved.

"Yes," said Saetta in a matter-of-fact way, "I was going to get some money out of this; his wife didn't like him anyway; he was dirty to everybody, even to his own children and his own wife, but I was going to kill him anyway because of the dirty deal he pulled on me."[12]

Finally, after more than two weeks and countless hours of interrogation, Saetta and Faraci were talking. Now, the only question that remained was who was telling the truth and who was lying to save himself. Flubacher and Hynes were fairly certain what had occurred on Castleton Road on Easter Sunday morning and were convinced Faraci was lying. What better way to prove their point than to put both men together? Later that same day on the evening of April 15, Hynes arranged to have both men brought together for a face-to-face confrontation in

the captain's office at the Third Precinct. It was the first time Saetta and
Faraci had seen each other since they were picked up in Poughkeepsie
with Gertrude King. As it turned out, it wasn't a pleasant reunion between two old friends.

"There is just a few points we want to straighten out about this thing,"
said Flubacher. "Vincent says that he shot Antonio and that Faraci
stabbed him and Faraci says that Vincent shot and stabbed him. Now we
want to get this thing straightened out."[13]

"I am telling the truth," shouted Saetta. He glared at Faraci and in the
same tone of voice declared, "Sam, I am man enough to stand for and
tell the truth and take my medicine. You had the guts to go down there
with me and help kill this man. Why don't you have the guts to tell these
men the truth about the thing. Don't make a liar out of me. I know I am
going to the electric chair, but Sam, I don't want you to make a liar out
of me in front of these men. I shoot the man and you stabbed the man.
You are not yellow?"

"No, I am not yellow, I will take my part," said Faraci, "I was in it just
the same as you were, but you know I got nine kids."

Flubacher and Hynes turned to each other with a look of astonish-
ment. Both were stunned by this admission. They knew that Sam Faraci
had been dodging child-support payments in Ontario County and running all over the state with Gertrude King, but they had no idea that he
had abandoned a family of nine children.

Saetta, however, was unimpressed with Faraci's sympathetic over-
tone. He wasn't the only one with a family. "Well, you don't think of my
mother. My mother loves me just as much as you love your children.
I am taking the blame but I don't want you to lie. Tell them just what
happened."

Faraci paused for a moment. "We were both in it," he said. "We might
as well tell the truth."[14]

THREE CONFESSIONS

Telling the truth never came easy to Sam Faraci. Since the first time he had run afoul of the law in Geneva, Faraci had always tried to lie his way out of things. He lacked finesse and style, and, above all, he wasn't a very convincing liar. This was made clear when he made his first confession and two days later made a second. Desperate to distance himself from his accomplice, Faraci recanted most of what he said in his second confession.

As he had done previously, Faraci described himself as an unwilling participant. It was Saetta who was out to even a score, not him. Faraci got along with Sam Antonio and insisted, "He's done nothing to me." In fact, Faraci said, he had been trying to talk Saetta out of going through with the murder partly because he had misgivings about Sam Antonio's wife. "Listen, Vincent, now be careful," he warned, "never go up to that house because probably his wife will double-cross you."[1] Vincent Saetta, according to Faraci, became obsessed with doing away with a man who had cheated him. Faraci told the police that once Saetta's mind was made up, there was no stopping him. Saetta arranged to get the knife, planned the trip to Hudson, and came up with the idea of how everyone was to be seated in the car.

It was only after Saetta had confessed to his part in the crime to Hynes and Flubacher that Faraci had to admit his part in the death of Sam Antonio. He avoided giving specifics, but admitted that he had perhaps stabbed Sam Antonio "five or ten" times. Since he never removed the wrapping paper from the knife to fully expose the entire blade, Faraci assumed that he never delivered a fatal stab wound to Sam Antonio.[2] In Faraci's mind, the real killer of Sam Antonio was the shooter, Vincent Saetta. Surely one of his bullets found its mark.

As in the first confession he made, Faraci rambled on stressing trivial details. However, there was one similarity in both confessions when it came to Anna Antonio. Faraci said he still wasn't quite sure if the woman he saw pass forty dollars to Saetta at the corner of Broadway and Columbia was Sam Antonio's wife. "I don't know if it was her or not," he said.[3] If he could not or would not tie Anna Antonio to the murder, the police soon discovered that Vincent Saetta was more than willing to make that connection for them.

When it came to his turn to be interviewed and sign a confession, the cunning Saetta changed his tune. He wasn't about to accept all the blame for the murder and wasted little time in passing himself off as a sympathetic friend to Anna Antonio. Of their initial meeting at the Leland Theater, Saetta claimed that it was Anna who propositioned him.

"Well," he recalled Anna as saying, "Vince, I want my husband out of this world."

"Don't talk like that, what do you want to do that for?"

"Vince," she said, "if you don't do it I will have to do it."

A week later after the murder of her husband, Saetta said it was a cold, businesslike Anna he met at the corner of Columbia and Broadway.

"Vince," she said, "are you sure you done it right? If you didn't he kills me, and also if you double-cross me, Vincent don't forget I know where you live and I will kill you."[4] After she gave him forty dollars, Anna said that the balance of the money would be forthcoming. "When I get the insurance money I will get in touch with you and give you the rest. You don't have to worry. You know I am as good as gold."[5]

After Saetta signed his confession and was led back to his cell, Flubacher thought about what Saetta claimed that Anna Antonio had said. Saetta made her out to be a tough, stereotypical gangster moll. This certainly didn't sound like the little woman he had spoken to at Memorial Hospital and later at 3 Teunis Street on the day of her husband's funeral. Something was amiss. But, as Anna was clearly implicated by Saetta's sworn statement, Flubacher had no other recourse but to bring her to the station to be questioned.

Despite the late hour—it was 11:30 P.M.—Hynes and Flubacher drove to Anna's apartment and told her that she was needed for questioning at the precinct. Over her protests, officers told her that this could not wait until morning. Anna got dressed and went next door to rouse a neighbor to watch her children.

At midnight Flubacher brought Anna into the captain's office of the precinct. Walking into the building, Hynes abruptly excused himself, leaving Flubacher and Anna Antonio alone in the captain's office. Seated near the desk, Flubacher asked Anna how she was getting along these past few days and how her children were doing. She replied that for the moment, things were good, but she wasn't really sure if she was going to move in with her brother for a short while or try to find an apartment closer to the school her daughters attended. Their conversation was cut short by voices outside the captain's office door. Flubacher noticed that the look on Anna's face suddenly changed when she recognized the voice of Vincent Saetta.

Employing the same tactic that had served him well in having Faraci break Saetta, Hynes did the same thing to Anna Antonio. Positioning Saetta near the captain's door, Hynes had Saetta repeat his question-and-answer-style confession aloud.[6] Saetta spoke for a couple of minutes and that was all Hynes needed. Saetta was escorted back to his cell by another officer, and Hynes walked into the captain's office to face a dejected and forlorn Anna Antonio.

It was Flubacher who spoke first. Shaking his head in disbelief, he looked at Anna and asked, "How did you ever come to get in a thing like this with two mugs like them?"

"Oh, I don't know," replied Anna.

"Who raised the money to a thousand dollars, was it you or them?"

Anna denied that she had ever offered Saetta that much money, but Flubacher persisted, asking her several more times the exact amount of money that was decided upon. Physically exhausted due to the late hour and emotionally drained after hearing Saetta speak about the murder and payoff, Anna simply gave up.

"Oh, what's the use," she said, "call Mr. Delaney, I will talk to him."[7]

Twenty minutes later, after receiving Flubacher's telephone call, John T. Delaney arrived at the precinct with the assistant district attorney, Joseph Casey. Briefed by Flubacher on the phone that Mrs. Antonio was ready to speak, Delaney strode into the office with an air of authority. Glancing quickly about the room, he recognized Flubacher, Hynes, plus several other officers and a stenographer. Delaney looked at the only woman in the room and brusquely remarked, "Mrs. Antonio, what is there to this?"

She paused for a moment, removed her veiled hat, and placed it on the desk before Delaney. Leaning back in the wooden office chair, she let out a deep sigh. She looked at Delaney and bared her soul.

"Mr. Delaney," she said, "I done it and I am not a bit sorry. I done it. I would do it all over again if I had the chance. He is the cause of somebody that is six feet under this earth."

"How did you get into a terrible thing like that?"

"Mr. Delaney," replied Anna, "when they brought my husband home and I see the terrible condition of his body I was going to come up that Sunday night and tell you all about it."

"Why didn't you?"

Anna sat still for a moment, starred ahead, and shrugged her shoulders in resignation. Breaking the silence Delaney asked her if it wouldn't be best to start right from the beginning.

In a soft voice filled with little emotion, Anna told her audience that she was no stranger to Vincent Saetta. He had met with her husband on several occasions at their apartment. She, too, had met with Saetta, not once as he had claimed but twice at the Leland Theater. "I told him I wanted him to do something," she said. "I promised him I would give him $500 for it." It was at their second meeting at the Leland that Vincent upped the ante to $800 because he needed to bring in extra help from New York City to complete the job.[8]

When $500 suddenly became $800, Delaney interrupted her and asked where she thought she could possibly obtain such a large sum of money. Would this money come from a life insurance settlement? Anna paused, thought for a moment, and replied, "Well, I suppose so." The statement sealed her fate in Delaney's mind. If she was planning to pay off Vincent Saetta with insurance money, then she was fully aware that her husband was going to be killed at his hands.

In the course of the interview Anna made it perfectly clear that she didn't believe Vincent would go through with it. She said that she was dumbfounded when he met with her at the corner of Columbia and Broadway on Easter morning. "Vince," she explained to Delaney and all the others present, "he talks a lot, he blows, but I didn't think that he would go that far with it." On this point she remained firm. On seven separate occasions in the course of the interview she expressed her doubts that Saetta would in fact kill her husband. She believed that her husband would receive "a darn good beating" at the hands of Saetta and his help from New York.[9] "I didn't think they would kill him that way, like a dog, leave him in the road to die."[10]

Finally, when Delaney accused her of trying to cover up the crime by refusing to cooperate with the police, Anna's response was terse. After the savage murder of her husband at the hands of Saetta, she feared for her life and that of her children. It was because of that fear that she maintained her silence. "I was afraid I would get the same medicine."[11] She wasn't about to identify Saetta or accuse him of anything because, as she explained, although he was in custody, she wasn't sure if he had another accomplice on the loose. "No," said Anna, "I didn't try to cover up anybody. I said I didn't know anything. In other words, I didn't try to cover him or anybody else. I said I don't know. I said if you find out anything you would find it of your own accord and not by me telling you, that is all."[12]

Without a tear in her eye, she offered no apologies and expressed no regrets. With a nod from Delaney, the stenographer left the room, his cue that the interview had concluded. While detectives whispered among themselves, Anna sat still and stared at the floor. The only other sound was the clicking of keys on a manual typewriter. It was 3 A.M. when the stenographer reappeared and handed Delaney a typed transcript of Anna's confession. He quickly glanced at it and asked Anna if she wanted him to read it aloud. She shook her head and took it from his hand. Anna read it carefully and offered only a few revisions before signing her name at the bottom.

When she was finished, she asked Delaney if she could now go home. Delaney took the confession, looked at the signature, and had the document notarized immediately. Ignoring her request, Delaney turned to the detectives present and announced that Anna was under arrest. At 5:30 A.M. Anna was brought to the Second Precinct, the same precinct that had been the recent home of Gertrude King, and locked up for the remainder of the morning. The next day she was brought to the Albany County Jail. Her world at Teunis Street with her children had come to an end, and her life as part of the legal system had just begun.

The same could almost be said for Vincent Saetta and Sam Faraci, except that their lives changed when they were picked up in Poughkeepsie. On April 14, Anna Antonio was charged with murder and transferred to the county jail. Saetta and Faraci were likewise charged and transferred. That evening, at Delaney's behest, the two men were taken from the county jail to retrace their movements on Castleton Road on the night of the murder.

It was almost 11 P.M. when the two Albany patrol cars arrived at the Park Restaurant in Hudson. Hynes had to admit that after his confession, Saetta had been cooperative to the point of assisting in the investigation. As they approached the horseshoe-shaped counter, Flubacher asked Saetta if he recognized any of the staff who served him that night.

"That is the fellow that waited on me," said Faraci.

"No," replied Saetta, "it was the other fellow."

Flubacher motioned to both men to step forward. Before he had a chance to ask a question, Saetta blurted out, "Don't you remember giving me coffee and crullers?"[13]

When one of them said they didn't quite recall this, Saetta tried to refresh his memory. Raising both arms, as he was handcuffed, Saetta motioned across the counter. "Don't you remember, there were three of us sitting over there." When this wasn't enough to jog the man's memory, Saetta motioned to another employee. "This was the fellow that was the cashier. Don't you remember us paying our bill and giving you some nickels?"[14]

When they retraced the route from Hudson to Albany on Castleton Road, Flubacher asked Saetta if he recognized any landmarks that might assist them in the investigation. Flanked by two officers in the backseat of the squad car, Saetta looked about and confessed that as it was dark now and certainly was dark on the night of the murder, he couldn't be sure. "You go over a little bridge," he recalled, "and just beyond there is a billboard on the left, and that is the spot." Flubacher was just making small talk. He knew where the murder took place, having visited the location the following day. After passing the billboard, Saetta peered out the window and said, "It is some where's near here."[15]

In the other squad car, the same sort of conversation was taking place with Faraci. Avoiding details, he gave a hazy description of the spot where the murder took place. Unlike his associate, Faraci wasn't as talkative or cooperative. When Griggs asked him what had become of the gun, Faraci glanced out the window into total darkness and said, "I don't know, some where's along the road. It was broke and then thrown out."

Saetta, too, could not be sure where the parts of the gun were. Hynes found a little humor in this grim situation and remarked, "I will have nice job down there looking around in all that mud for the next couple days trying to find that gun."

"Jimmie," said Saetta in an apologetic tone, "I would like to help you find that gun. If I could find it I would go and help you find it now. I want to make it easy for you fellows because you have been so nice to me."[16] Saetta had to admit that he didn't think anyone would be able to locate the parts to his gun. However, he did say that he had a second gun if they were interested. It was at the New York Loan, a pawnshop. The next day Hynes went to the New York Loan, but was disappointed when the pistol Saetta had mention wasn't there. This didn't stop Saetta from offering to help Hynes one more time.

"Did you go to my room and look over my room?"

"No," replied Hynes.

"If you do," said Saetta, "you will find a half bottle of whiskey up there I drank before we went on the ride to Hudson."

Intrigued by this admission, Hynes asked if there was anything else in the room that could be useful to their investigation.

"There is an old torn shirt belongs to me, that Sam [Faraci] wiped the mud off his shoes and I wiped the little bit that was on mine off, and I helped to wipe the mud off Sam's pants. You will find that in my room."[17]

It didn't escape Hynes, Flubacher, Griggs, or anyone else for that matter that Saetta was being overly cooperative for a reason. Saetta had only one chance to save himself. He believed that if he cooperated fully and did not impede the investigation, there was a chance the district attorney might set the death penalty aside in his case. Faraci did not share his optimism. Sitting in the backseat of the squad car on the way back from Hudson, an officer placed a blanket around Faraci's shoulders. When asked if that helped, Faraci replied, "Only God can help me now."[18]

Part II

THE TRIAL

THE GATHERING OF LEGALS

Following the grand jury indictment of Anna Antonio, Vincent Saetta, and Sam Faraci in April 1932, members of the Saetta family secured the services of attorney Henry A. Lowenberg. As the Antonio murder had not been reported in any of the New York City newspapers, the family could provide Lowenberg only with vague details as to Vincent's latest scrape with the law. The Manhattan attorney knew the Saetta family, having represented Vincent on a previous occasion in a New York City court. He accepted the case and traveled to Albany to meet with his client.

The Saetta family was desperately in need of the services of Lowenberg. Cocky, arrogant, and aggressive, the Fordham Law School graduate had been a practicing attorney in the boroughs of New York for over a dozen years. Honing his skills in the city courts, Lowenberg defended a variety of small-time thugs, career criminals, and assorted underworld figures. "If someone comes to me with a domestic problem," he brazenly said, "I will recommend him or her to another attorney. I do not handle anything except criminal cases."[1]

His first stop was the county courthouse on Eagle Street. A relatively new building, having been completed a year prior to America's entry in the First World War, the courthouse, with its limestone and granite exterior, offered an imposing yet conservative exterior. It was only after one passed through the front doors that one could behold the magnificence of the building. Massive columns in the main hall rose up to the center of the ceiling and supported a vaulted stained-glass window. The amber glow of the interior lights bathed the deep-red woodwork, gold leaf trim, and brass elevator doors. The building, thought Lowenberg, was in great contrast to the archaically worded indictment that was given to him by a court clerk.

> And the said Vincent Saetta and the said Sam Faraci . . . willfully, feloniously, inexcusably, unjustifiably, unlawfully, designedly and with premeditation make an assault in and upon the body of said Salvatore Antonio and with a certain dangerous weapon, commonly known as a pistol, the same being then and there loaded with gunpowder and bullets, and with a certain knife, dagger, poniard, did then and there shoot, cut, stab, and wound in and upon the head, breast, back thighs, abdomen and upon divers other parts of the body of him the said Salvatore Antonio.[2]

After reading the indictment and the accompanying confession signed by Saetta, Lowenberg realized how precarious the situation was for his client.

Setting the indictment aside, Lowenberg made his way north of Albany to the county jail on Shaker Road to meet with his client. The fact that bail was never offered to Saetta or any of the others was of no concern to Lowenberg. He surmised that all of them had limited means at their disposal. However, he was extremely angry when he discovered that his client had been held incommunicado for sixteen days by the Albany police and denied the use of a telephone to contact an attorney. Saetta, and this went for Faraci as well, was denied the basic rights of the accused as outlined in the state and federal constitutions.

Lowenberg's advice to Saetta was short and simple—keep quiet. Saetta had already talked too much, all without the benefit of counsel. From this moment on, said Lowenberg, he was to speak to no one but his attorney. Lowenberg, who once boasted that he never asked clients he defended if they had committed the crime they were accused of, told Saetta that his signed confession made his job all the more difficult. Lowenberg discussed the charge of first-degree murder, which was serious, and the options available to him, which were few. At this moment the only thing he could think of was to ask the district attorney to reduce the charge.

Lowenberg arrived at Delaney's office and wasted little time in making his pitch. He had read the indictment, met with Saetta, and was prepared to plead guilty to second-degree murder in exchange for a life sentence. The district attorney shook his head. "Much as I would like to entertain, I cannot," said Delaney. Before Lowenberg could interject, he added, "because it would weaken my case in the other defendants."[3]

Delaney surmised, and rightly so, that Lowenberg would next speak with the attorneys representing the other defendants. Whereas Lowenberg had been unsuccessful in his attempt to reduce the charge against his client, the most logical move would be for him to join forces to formulate a defensive strategy beneficial to all their clients. The district attorney didn't know Lowenberg personally or by reputation, but the fact that he entered his office and tried to trade the electric chair for a life sentence was significant. The case against his client didn't look good, and he knew it. Still, Delaney wasn't about to take Lowenberg for granted. Saetta may have lived day to day, one drug deal after another in the Gut, but his family had gone to considerable expense to hire a lawyer to defend him.

Delaney wasn't worried when he learned that Charles J. Duncan had been assigned to represent the penniless Faraci. Capable and methodical, Duncan was a well-respected lawyer in the capital region. What did concern him was the attorney for Anna Antonio—Daniel H. Prior. The district attorney wasn't quite sure how she was able to secure his services, but having Prior in the courtroom demanded his utmost attention. Delaney knew that if he made a mistake in the trial, no matter how trivial it might appear, Prior would move quickly to exploit it to his own advantage.

The last installment of Lowenberg's Albany itinerary was under way when he arrived at 63 State Street. He had called Prior earlier to arrange this meeting and hoped that it would result in a genial, productive discussion. The New York City attorney came on strong and did his best to impress both attorneys, especially Prior, with his résumé. He dropped the names of several underworld characters he had represented in the city courts, including one familiar to Prior—Legs Diamond. However, this ice-breaker statement fell flat. Prior couldn't care less about Lowenberg's association with Diamond. After all, he had successfully defended Diamond not once as Lowenberg had claimed, but on two separate occasions.

When his accomplishments in the courtroom and list of clients failed to impress Prior, Lowenberg got to the point of his visit. He suggested that each attorney lay his cards on the table and thus coordinate their general strategies for the upcoming trial. Duncan and Prior remained silent while the New York City attorney justified this proposal. Lowenberg wanted to ensure that when the trial began, it would not come to finger-pointing among the three defendants as to who was responsible for the murder of Sam Antonio. Adamant on the subject, Lowenberg ended with a stern warning. If the three of them were not in agreement on this subject, then "all three [defendants] are going to be in worse trouble than they already are . . . I want defenses for all defendants revealed to see whether we're all going to get along."[4]

Prior hesitated for a brief moment, not to consider the offer but to study the man who had proposed it. How much more "worse trouble" could there be? All three were facing death in the electric chair. Could he possibly be that naive? Of course it was going to come down to Anna Antonio's word against Vincent Saetta as it was going to come down to Sam Faraci's word against Saetta's.

"Henry," said Prior, "I don't think we are going to get along on this case."[5]

"All right, Dan, the conference is ended. I'll see you in court."[6]

Having failed in his attempt to establish an alliance with Prior and Duncan, Lowenberg moved ahead, filing a motion to dismiss the charges against Saetta. On June 14, 1932, he traveled to Albany and appeared before county judge Earl H. Gallup and argued that his client's constitutional rights had been violated. He charged that the methods used by the Albany police and Delaney in obtaining a confession from Saetta were questionable. Lowenberg maintained that Saetta was held for sixteen days, "far in excess of the legal time limit—that extortion was used to obtain an alleged confession or statement and that his client was deprived of the right of testifying or presenting witnesses in his own behalf." Judge Gallup deemed the motion papers unacceptable due to "a lack of facts"[7] as Lowenberg presented no evidence to back up his claims of the police using strong-armed methods to obtain his client's confession.

The following year, Lowenberg again appeared before Judge Gallup, only this time he wasn't alone. Standing next to him were Dan Prior and Charles Duncan. The date was March 22, 1933, the first day of jury selection for the trial for Anna Antonio, Vincent Saetta, and Sam Faraci. Proceedings had hardly begun when, after the court had just been called to order, Lowenberg rose from his chair and announced to the judge that he had several motions to introduce.

"And counsel prefer to make them in chambers in the absence of the jury," said Judge Gallup. "Is that true of all of you?"[8]

The trio of defense attorneys were in agreement and followed Judge Gallup to his chambers, along with the district attorney, John T. Delaney. Lowenberg spoke first by illustrating the obvious. This case involved three different defendants with three different attorneys. How could a jury not be confused with discerning the testimony of any of the defendants? Lowenberg explained, "Assuming that my client had made a statement involving Anna Antonio or Sam Faraci, or assuming that Sam Faraci made a statement mentioning the identity of my client or Mrs. Antonio, these twelve men sitting there will not be able to establish between the competency of that confession."[9] In light of this, Lowenberg believed his client was entitled to a separate trial.

Lowenberg's confusing rhetoric in his example did not sway Gallup. A precedent had been set in other cases involving multiple defendants, and he denied the motion for a separate trial. He cited the celebrated Snyder-Gray case and the little-known Doran-Harrington case to justify his decision.

In 1927, Ruth Snyder and Judd Gray went on trial, charged together with the murder of Ruth's husband, Albert Snyder. Driven in part by passion and a $48,000 life insurance policy with a double indemnity clause, paramour Judd Gray became a willing accomplice of Ruth Snyder. When the two star-crossed lovers went on trial at the Long Island City courthouse, the case was widely covered by the press, culminating with the sensational *New York Daily News* photograph of Ruth Snyder strapped into the electric chair at Sing Sing prison receiving a fatal jolt of electricity.

"I am familiar with the Snyder-Gray case," said an unimpressed Dan Prior, who was also asking for a separate trial for his client. "I do not know that it is a precedent for a denial of a motion." Prior reminded the judge that in the Snyder-Gray case, both of the defendants took part in the bludgeoning death of Albert Snyder. This was not the same scenario with his client. "You have not got the same situation in this case," declared Prior, "the District Attorney won't contend that Anna Antonio was present; that she ever laid hands on the man who is alleged to have been murdered."[10] Prior contended that the same was true in the Doran-Harrington case.

The same year Snyder and Gray went to trial, Charles Doran, Floyd Damp, and Theodore "Chickie" Harrington stood accused of a gas station murder on New Scotland Avenue in Albany. The owner of the gas station, Raymond E. Jackson, was gunned down, and the trio fled with twenty-nine dollars. The three were eventually arrested, charged with felony murder, and went on trial at the same time. In the course of the trial, which, incidentally, was presided over by Judge Gallup, the driver of the getaway car, Floyd Damp, was acquitted. Then the district attorney, together with his able assistant, John T. Delaney, obtained the cooperation of Chickie Harrington. He turned state's evidence, and Charles Doran went to the electric chair.[11]

As Prior saw it, these were hardly definitive examples in establishing a precedent for multiple defendants in a trial. Instead, they were perfect examples of why a separate trial for Anna Antonio should be granted. Whereas Judd Gray assisted in the actual murder of Albert Snyder, the same could not be said of his client. Anna Antonio was miles away from the crime scene, at home in bed. Prior told Gallup that his client should be acquitted as a nonparticipant in the crime, just the way he had acquitted Floyd Damp six years earlier.

"I look at it as a question of doing justice here," said Prior. "This is serious. Human lives are at stake."[12] Not only was a separate trial in order, but the charges against his client should be dropped to reflect what really happened. The indictment charged her with murder when in fact, alleged Prior, she should have been charged with conspiracy.

Denied a separate trial, just as Lowenberg had been, Prior turned to Charles Duncan. Not wishing to repeat what the others had already expounded upon before Judge Gallup, Duncan expressed his concern for a fair trial for not only his client but the others as well. Could twelve men differentiate one confession from another and another? "I don't see how it is humanly possible," said Duncan, "for all three to be fairly tried, in view of the fact that confessions for all three will be introduced . . . there is no human being, it is my contention, that can hear the confession of the other two defendants and not consider it against the other two."[13]

Tired of the delays and anxious to get the trial started, Gallup denied Duncan's motion, reiterating that in his estimation, based on the facts of this case, a fair trial would take place for all three and separate trials were not necessary. Believing he had heard the last of these requests, Judge Gallup was preparing to leave his chambers when he was suddenly interrupted by Dan Prior.

"May I call your Honor's attention to the fact that nobody opposes our motion? You made your decision without any opposition."

Momentarily caught off guard, Gallup looked directly at John Delaney and asked if anyone in the room opposed his decision. As if on cue, Delaney reaffirmed what Gallup had decided.

"We feel they can get a fair trial," said Delaney, "they are represented by able attorneys; we assume that they will select intelligent jurors . . . there is absolutely no reason why the County should be put to the expense and delay of separate trials."[14]

Prior made a mental note of the district attorney's statement. When the opportunity presented itself, possibly during the trial, he would remind him, as well as Judge Gallup, that this trial had nothing to do with saving money and everything to do with people's lives. But for the time being, Prior knew that any further arguments before Judge Gallup would be futile. The trial had been postponed once, having been on the docket in November 1932. It was now March, and Gallup was determined to get jury selection under way and move the trial forward without any additional delays.

The three days it took to choose twelve men from seventy potential jurors received only a passing glance from the Albany and Schenectady newspapers. A few candidates were dismissed immediately due to preconceived notions about the guilt of the suspects after having read these very same newspapers. As expected, the attorneys listened to a variety of excuses from those attempting to opt out of their civic duty. Asking an assortment of questions regarding their thoughts on capital punishment and their understanding of felony murder—if one was guilty, all were guilty—the attorneys were a little taken aback by the comments of Mosher Ames. A farmer from the nearby town of Feura Bush, Ames was dismissed when he readily admitted that he saw nothing wrong with police brutality "to a certain extent" when seeking information from alleged suspects.[15] Of the twelve men drawn for the jury, nine were from the city of Albany. One of them, Charles Chapman, a salesman, lived on the same street as Saetta. All were married men, and none of them were Italian.

Throughout the proceedings, Anna Antonio, attired in black, remained still, often with her gaze fixed on the floor. She seldom made eye contact with any of the potential jurors. In sharp contrast, Saetta and Faraci seemed to be enjoying themselves, taking, as one reporter mused, a "lively interest" in the judicial process. They smiled, smirked, and casually looked about the courtroom. Their behavior quickly changed when the last juror was chosen. It was late Friday afternoon, and both of them knew that the following Monday would be no cause for levity.

Shortly after 9 A.M. on March 27, 1933, the motorcade bearing Anna Antonio, Vincent Saetta, and Sam Faraci left Albany County Jail and traveled south to the courthouse on Eagle Street. The courtroom they entered was markedly different from the last time they were brought there. Jury selection hadn't attracted a fraction of the crowd that gawked at them when court officers escorted them to their seats. Reporters from all the capital region newspapers, as well as spectators, occupied every seat in the courtroom. An array of family members were also on hand to support the three defendants. Mary Ferugia was there with five of her nine children. She could ill afford the train ticket to Albany to see the husband who had abandoned her, but she found a way to be there. Sitting by Vincent Saetta was his mother and several of his sisters. Anna Antonio's brother, Pasquale "Patsy" Cappello was there with his wife. And there was Mary DeSisto. Recently arrived from Brooklyn, her icy stare was fixed on those she deemed responsible for the brutal murder of her brother, Sam Antonio.

When Judge Gallup entered the courtroom, he eased himself into his seat, grasped his gavel, and struck his desk firmly. The sharp echo of the gavel resonated throughout the crowded courtroom. He was preparing to ask all the attorneys present if they were prepared to present their opening remarks to the jury when Henry Lowenberg rose from his chair and asked the court to provide him with the names and addresses of the participants in the murder, an opportunity to inspect the pistol used in the crime, as well as the knife and what part his client played in, as he put it, "this alleged murder."[16]

"I make these requests," said Lowenberg, "not for the purpose of prying into the State's case, but I make it at this time to enable me to adequately prepare this case for trial."[17] Lowenberg was aware of the fact and wanted the district attorney's office to admit that the murder weapon used in the crime had never been recovered and as such could not be traced to his client.

The assistant district attorney, Joseph J. Casey, shook his head in disbelief. A round-faced man with round glasses, it would be a mistake to confuse Casey's youthful appearance with inexperience. He had been with the district attorney's office for a number of years and, as Dan Prior admitted, was a formidable opponent.[18] Casey reminded everyone that what Lowenberg was asking for had already been discussed at length and decided upon ten months earlier. He was free to inspect any physical evidence held by the district attorney's office, and this included the signed confessions. Casey didn't believe for one moment that Lowenberg needed additional time to prepare for the trial. This was a ploy on his part to stall the trial. He didn't like it, and neither did Judge Gallup. The ruling handed down ten months earlier remained unchanged.

With Lowenberg temporarily at bay and the precedent for interruptions having been firmly established, Delaney rose from his chair and slowly walked toward the jury box. Although it was not necessary for him to make an opening statement to the jury, he felt it necessary, given the severity of the crime. In a calm, businesslike fashion, he told the dozen men seated before him that he would dispense with reading the indictment lodged against the defendants. Instead, he would take the jury step-by-step through the crime. Delaney began his lengthy dissertation by informing the jury that it was his firm belief that the crime originated with an agreement between Anna Antonio and Vincent Saetta. With the promise of monetary compensation, Saetta was able to persuade Sam Faraci to assist him in the murder of Sam Antonio. Delaney gave an account of the murder, the flight of the killers, their capture, their incarceration, and their eventual confessions. Each of the defendants seated in the courtroom that day had made statements while in police custody as to the role he or she had in this sordid affair. Given the evidence, Delaney was confident the jury would see fit to declare each of them guilty.

Well, said Prior with a charismatic smile, that's one side of the story. Delaney was entitled to make all the accusations he wanted, but in the end, Prior told the jury, it was the evidence that would decide the outcome of this case. Evidence, he said, that Delaney had conveniently omitted. "The District Attorney has not told you all the facts," said Prior. "I don't like that."

Although Prior said it was not prudent to speak ill of the dead, in this instance he could not help but do so. Delaney informed the jury that Sam Antonio was a brakeman on the railroad, but he neglected to mention his other activities. "Antonio was in the narcotics business, the vilest kind of nefarious traffic that ever existed on the face of the earth . . . Antonio was a seller of cocaine, morphine and heroin to dope addicts in the Tenderloin section of Albany." Prior maintained that it was Antonio's decision to sell dope that ultimately transformed his client's life and that of her three small children into an existence of "terror and misery." There was only one way for the jury to fully comprehend what had actually happened and that was to hear it from the lips of Anna Antonio. "She will be a witness here. You will judge her as you find her on the witness stand."[19]

Charles Duncan was far less dramatic than either Prior or Delaney in his remarks to the jury, but what he had to say was just as important. In a brief twelve-sentence speech, Duncan stressed the seriousness of the oral testimony each member of the jury was about to hear. Although he never mentioned his client by name, Duncan implored the jury to consider the lives of all the defendants in this case. "I ask you not to miss a word of testimony anywhere in the case," he said, "I ask you to give it your undivided attention. . . . You have never been called upon for such a task as is before you now. . . . You are going to decide whether they live or whether they die. . . . In the name of God, gentlemen, make no mistake."[20]

Lowenberg, too, stressed the importance of the evidence while at the same time cautioning the jury not to be hasty in their decisions regarding the fate of the accused. The very worst thing they could do would be to accept the evidence at face value. "Well, if that man has been murdered," said Lowenberg as an example, "then the defendants must have been the people who did it, otherwise they would not be on trial."[21] No, insisted Lowenberg, the evidence must be carefully considered and must reflect the guilt or innocence of the defendants beyond a reasonable doubt.

As the first witnesses were called to the stand and sworn to testify, the *Albany Evening News* had gone to print. A photograph of the principals of the case—Delaney, the three defendants, Duncan, and Lowenberg—appeared in the center of the front page with the title, "Albany Mother and Two Men Facing Joint Battle for Lives in County Court."[22] The headlines were correct; the "battle" was about to begin.

10

FLUBACHER AND THE
ITALIAN DETECTIVE

John T. Delaney's strategy for prosecuting the three defendants was nothing out of the ordinary, his plan being twofold. In an effort to make it easier for the jury to comprehend what had occurred on Castleton Road that Easter Sunday morning, he would use a chronological time frame of witnesses. Law students John Crary Jr. and William McDermott described how they came upon Sam Antonio with an outstretched arm lying across Castleton Road early Sunday morning. After loading the grievously wounded Antonio into the back of Crary's car, McDermott said that at times it was difficult to understand what the wounded man was trying to convey to his rescuers. Groaning and gasping for breath, McDermott recalled that Antonio pleaded for a doctor and begged for help. He said his name and address several times but, much to the relief of Lowenberg and Duncan, never named his assailants.

Next, Delaney called everyone, with the exception of the switchboard operator (who was on duty in the emergency room at Memorial Hospital), to testify. The most important testimony gleaned from this group came from the physicians. Dr. Irvin Gage briefly described the condition of Sam Antonio when he was brought to the emergency room, but it was Dr. Orvis A. Brenenstuhl who gave the postmortem account. Using as little medical jargon as possible, Dr. Brenenstuhl described the knife wounds inflicted upon Sam Antonio as anywhere from severe stab wounds to slight lacerations. Although there were multiple stab wounds, none were fatal. Dr. Brenenstuhl said that in his opinion, the fatal wound came from the one bullet that severed the right iliac vein. When Delaney presented him with Exhibit 1, he asked Dr. Brenenstuhl if he could identify it. "Yes," he said, "I removed it from the body of Antonio."[1]

Still holding firm to his chronological method of relating the crime to the jury, Delaney began his second phase. With three people on trial simultaneously, Delaney wasn't about to take any chances. Anyone who had a badge who came in contact with any of the defendants would be subpoenaed. To this end, he had nine police officers representing four separate law enforcement agencies ready to testify. The first one to the witness stand was the first who greeted Anna Antonio at Memorial Hospital.

Helping solve the Antonio murder turned out to be a career booster for William H. Flubacher. On July 18, 1932, he was promoted to sergeant, due in part "for his work in solving the murder of Salvatore Antonio."[2] Delaney looked to Flubacher as his chief witness, his testimony being absolutely critical to achieve a triple conviction. From the morning he arrived at Memorial Hospital to the evening he heard Anna Antonio's confession, Flubacher had been a constant presence. On the first day of the trial, Delaney would lead his chief witness through a series of questions designed to be corroborated by other law enforcement officials. In almost every instance, Delaney asked questions of Flubacher while at the same time trying to ensure his credibility as a witness. With rumors afloat about alleged strong-armed methods used by the police to achieve confessions, Delaney made sure that almost every question he asked of Flubacher was followed by another question: Who was with you when you interviewed Saetta or Faraci? Flubacher testified time after time that there was always another officer present when he interviewed any of the suspects, including Anna Antonio. Later in the trial, when it came his turn to testify, each detective assigned to the case offered testimony that supported Flubacher.

Under the precise and carefully worded questions of Delaney, Flubacher told the court everything he did in connection to the case. On the

witness stand for what amounted to almost three days, Flubacher's testimony was all inclusive. He mentioned dates, times, and entire conversations he had with all three of the defendants. The only thing Delaney
was worried about was how the sergeant would hold up against the
other three attorneys. The attorneys for Saetta and Faraci concentrated
most of their cross-examination on how their clients were treated while
in police custody at the Third Precinct. Asking about everything from
soundproof walls and windowless rooms to the use of bats and clubs,
they did their best to suggest to the jury that this was a medieval torture chamber rather than a police dormitory. Flubacher testified that
he never witnessed any of the beatings Lowenberg and Duncan had alluded to in their cross-examination. He stood his ground and was neither intimidated nor caught off guard with this line of questioning. This
would not be the case when he came up against Dan Prior.

For hours Prior had listened intently to Flubacher's testimony. What
impressed him most was not so much the clarity and detail expressed by
the state trooper on the witness stand but his ability to recite day after
day such a vast amount of information without the benefit of referring
to any notes.

"Now may I see any memorandum or notes that you made of the happenings to which you testified during the last couple days?"

"I haven't any," replied Flubacher.

"Did you ever have any?"

"I did."

"And what did you do with them?"

"I don't know," said Flubacher, "I may have thrown them away."

"Oh, no," remarked Prior, in a tone of voice mixed with shock and
sarcasm.[3]

Although this line of questioning was objected to by the assistant
district attorney, Joseph Casey, Prior could only hope that the jury understood what had just transpired. Previously, this nine-and-a-half-year
veteran of the New York State Police had testified under oath that in his
career he had made close to two thousand arrests or approximately two
hundred arrests per year. With no notes to rely on, Flubacher seemed
extremely confident in recalling specific details in this particular case.
This confidence eroded when Prior pressed him further about the miss-

ing notes. Flubacher may have had experience in the field making arrests, but Prior sensed his inexperience sitting at the witness stand and continued to hammer him about the missing notes.

"You do not mean to tell me that you remember distinctly the happenings day by day, hour by hour and minute by minute of what transpired a year ago from the 27th of March to and including the 15th of April, and, yet you do not remember what you did with the notes and memorandum that you made up?"[4]

For the first time, Flubacher hesitated in answering, finally admitting that the testimony he had presented in court had been, as he said, "To the best of my knowledge."

"You knew that a written memorandum was much more reliable than your naked memory, didn't you?"

"Yes, sir."

"You knew that you were about to testify in a case where human life was at stake for the penalty of conviction, didn't you?"

"I did."

"And you knew that it was very important that your testimony be accurate, didn't you?"

"I did."

"And with that knowledge you deliberately destroyed that means of making your testimony accurate, didn't you?"

"I did."[5]

What Delaney had feared—a relentless Dan Prior cross-examination of his star witness—was unfolding. Over and over again, Prior assailed Flubacher's memory in hopes of chiseling away at his credibility as a witness. Flubacher's frequent responses of "I don't know" or "I don't recall" in time resulted in Prior condescendingly asking him at one point, "Now Sergeant, is there anything I can do to refresh your memory. Is there any memorandum I can give you, anything I can suggest to you; can you think of anything?"[6]

After a sound thrashing at the hands of Prior over not having any notes or memorandum to base his testimony on, Flubacher had to redeem himself. On his return to the witness stand after a brief recess, the state policeman casually tossed a set of papers on Prior's desk. When Prior asked what the papers were and if they had anything to do with the case, Flubacher replied, "It is my official report."[7] Prior glanced at the report and set it aside. There would be no more questioning of Flubacher about missing notes or memorandum. Not only was the report detailed, it was typed on "Police Court: City of Albany" letterhead, which meant that the state police, the Albany police, and the district attorney's office had copies.

Prior was also highly critical of Flubacher not fully investigating the narcotic activity of Sam Antonio. He maintained that peddling dope throughout the Gut was a motive for murder. Without accusing Saetta or Faraci, Prior said that others—enemies or friends of Sam Antonio—might be responsible for his murder.

"We are not trying the deceased," interrupted Judge Gallup.

"Of course we are not trying the deceased," replied Prior.

"It does not matter whether he was a good man or a bad man."

"Not so far as the killing is concerned," said Prior. "As far the motive for killing is concerned it is very important. . . . I will prove it. I cannot do it all at once. I will do it step-by-step."[8]

Prior maintained that the lead investigator in the case was somewhat negligent when following up certain leads in the case that could firmly establish a revenge motive for murder. Didn't the incident involving John Gonyea, accosted in the hallway of the Teunis Street apartment building by two unsavory characters, deserve further investigation? What of the numerous phone calls that Anna Antonio said her husband had received from Buffalo and New York City? Prior was highly critical of Flubacher and later Det. George Griggs for not looking into these phone calls. Why were these not investigated, especially after Anna Antonio had said that her husband was visibly shaken when he received these calls? Prior said that Flubacher and the other detectives had missed these opportunities to explore the double life of Sam Antonio.

If Prior was going to prove revenge for a dope deal gone bad as a possible motive for murder, he wasn't going to do it with Flubacher. After Saetta and Faraci had been brought in from Poughkeepsie, Flubacher and the other detectives concentrated their background investigations on them and not Sam Antonio. Flubacher admitted that he had been in communication with federal narcotics agent Richard Kelly on a few occasions and learned that Sam Antonio was an active dope peddler in the Gut. Again, after Saetta and Faraci were brought in, it seemed like a moot point to investigate the activities of the deceased.[9]

Prior believed that the character of the deceased—that of a dope peddler—was just as important as the character of his client. Flubacher had already testified that he had spoken with Anna Antonio at Memorial Hospital, at her apartment at 3 Teunis Street, and at the precinct station. Most of the conversations he had with her were in the presence of other police officers, except one. This conversation caused irreparable harm to his client.

No one found fault or criticized John Delaney for his efforts in shielding Saetta and Faraci from the press while the duo was incarcerated in the Third Precinct. The same could not be said of Anna Antonio. When she became a suspect and was shuttled back and forth from her apartment to the precinct, Delaney kept reporters at bay. Unfortunately, on the day she signed her confession, a newspaper reporter was present, overheard what Anna said, and eagerly printed it the following day.

When Flubacher asked her how she was able to control her emotions upon first viewing the body of her husband lying in the casket in their living room, Anna replied, "He forgave me. I know I talked to him while he was in his coffin. I put my face close to his and said, 'Sam forgive me. Do something to show that you forgive me and I will promise you that I will always take care of the children, just as good as you would have if you lived.' Then I saw a light around his face, and he smiled at me. I knew he had heard me and forgave me."[10]

Every newspaper in the capital region printed the "smiling face in the coffin" story. The fallout from this piece raised serious doubts as to her sanity at this moment and her complicity in the crime. Guilty individuals ask for forgiveness, not the innocent. Prior had to illustrate to the jury that this was a meaningless statement, an offhand remark made by his client under extreme emotional stress. To accomplish this, he set a trap and Flubacher obligingly walked into it.

Prior asked Flubacher if the statement Anna Antonio had made—that her husband had smiled at her while lying in the coffin—was, in his estimation, the reaction of a rational woman.

"What do you mean?"

"Well," said Prior, endeavoring to explain, "one that has full use of her powers of reason and is not hysterical and who has not lost the mental ability to reason. Do you understand it now?"

"Yes, sir," replied Flubacher, adding that she impressed him as someone who indeed appeared to possess all the qualities that he had just mentioned. At that moment, Prior sprung the trap.

"You've seen dead people smile in coffins, haven't you?"

Prior's question didn't prompt an uproar of laughter from the courtroom, but a few snickers were audible as Casey leapt from his chair to voice his stern objection to this "highly improper" remark. Judge Gallup, however, seemed somewhat intrigued by this line of questioning. "Let him answer."

"I am asking you," said Prior, "have you seen dead people smile in coffins?"

"No," replied Flubacher.

"And you think people that do see them smile are rational when they see them smile, do you?"

"Yes."

"All right. So that impressed you that night as a woman in full possession of all her reasoning powers and perfectly rational?"

Flubacher paused for a moment, and in a halfhearted admission quietly said, "Yes, sir."[11]

It was a minor victory for Prior early during a trial in which he hoped would swing a jury to his side. Flubacher may have been an inexperienced witness on the stand, but as it turned out, he wasn't totally naive due in part to the planning of John T. Delaney. The district attorney wasn't about to let his star witness be discredited. Instead of calling an Albany police detective to reinforce Flubacher's testimony, in a deft move, Delaney opted to bring in an outsider.

On April 1, 1932, the day after Saetta, Faraci, and Gertrude King were brought to Albany, Delaney secured the services of a police detective from another type of police agency. Since Sam Antonio was a railroad brakeman at the time of his death and Vincent Saetta had at one time been employed by the railroad, Delaney enlisted the services of Lt. Joseph Genova of the New York Central Railroad Police.

For twenty-seven years, Genova had been assisting local authorities in solving crimes associated with the railroad from Albany to Buffalo. The *Utica Dispatch* called him the "Italian Detective" for good reason.[12] Used primarily for his translating skills when interviewing Italian railroad workers, Genova's interrogation techniques should not be underrated. He had a smooth, easygoing manner about him that made suspects feel comfortable. As an Italian, he immediately put Italian suspects at ease, thus gaining their trust. On one occasion, he closed a murder investigation by simple guile and bluff. "Tony, the jig is up," declared Genova confidently, "we know all about it. We've got everything, how, where and when it was done." With that, Tony opened up, confessed, and later revealed many new details of the murder previously unknown to the authorities.[13]

By 1931, Genova's reputation was well established in the law enforcement community. A recent issue of *Popular Science* magazine lauded him as "industrious . . . so accomplished in tracking murders that his services are often loaned to small towns bewildered by a mysterious crime."[14] His hometown newspaper, the *Amsterdam Evening Recorder*, was equally generous in its plaudits. "Genova seems to be regarded by some pretty big police authorities, as a valued cog in one of the most efficient police machines in the nation."[15] The qualities Genova possessed his translating skills, knowledge of the customs of his native country, plus his interrogation style—were exactly what Delaney needed in the Antonio murder investigation.

The first time Genova met Anna Antonio was when Flubacher and Detective Hynes brought her to the precinct station shortly after midnight on April 14, 1932. Anna was sitting in an interview room with Flubacher when Genova arrived and asked the state policeman if he might be able to talk with Mrs. Antonio alone. Flubacher nodded and left the room, and Genova seated himself across the table from Anna. In a calm, reassuring voice, he introduced himself as a railroad detective and a fellow countryman. What Genova had hoped for—a pleasant conversation—was not what he received. Confronted with yet another police officer, Anna Antonio went immediately on the defensive the minute Genova implicated her in Saetta's confession. "Now," he explained to her, "it is up to you to make up your mind what to say and what to do in this case." Anna's eyes turned wild with excitement as she quickly denounced Saetta's claims.

"What that man say is a lie! I don't know nothing about my husband's death. I had nothing to do with it."[16]

Genova struck a nerve at the mere mention of Saetta's name. Instead of pursuing this line of questioning, thus further antagonizing an obviously distraught woman, Genova did what he did best. He changed the subject and warmed to her by asking about her past. Was she born here or in Italy?

"No," replied Anna, "in Italy. I came here when I was a little bit of a girl."

The story she related of her childhood in America came as no surprise to Genova. Anna said she had attended public school for a brief time but went to work as a domestic and eventually got a job in her sister's restaurant in Colonie. It was here that she first met Sam Antonio.

"They married me to this man when I was a little bit of a girl then. I didn't know anything at all then," and with a big sigh added, "he made my life miserable."[17]

Genova listened quietly as Anna told of her life at 3 Teunis Street. She blamed the death of her daughter Anita on her husband, hinted at his underworld connections, his activities in the south end of Albany, and, not surprisingly, expressed little remorse regarding his death. "Any woman in Italy who had to kill a man who had done it to her after so much harm as he done me," she concluded, "would have a medal, but I didn't kill him."

"That is all right, Mrs. Antonio," said Genova, "but Italy is Italy and we are here."[18]

Anna paused for a moment and asked how much longer she would have to stay at the precinct. Genova told her that it really wasn't up to him. "Now," said Genova, "I am not boss here. Mr. Delaney is the one who is running this thing. If Mr. Delaney says that you can go home, why, I will take you home to your family and your children."[19]

"Suppose I make a statement," said Anna, "will you let me go home to my children and to my family?"[20] Once more, Genova told her that it was up to Delaney and that if he released her, she could go home.

When Lieutenant Genova appeared as a witness in the trial, Dan Prior was well aware of the fact that his testimony could be deemed helpful or detrimental to the case against his client. Throughout several conversations Genova had with Anna Antonio, the railroad detective had lent a sympathetic ear to her. If Prior was careful in his cross-examination, Genova might echo these same sentiments for the jury.

Recalling the conversation Genova had with Anna at the Third Precinct, Prior asked if the conversation was in Italian. "I speak Italian and I speak English," said Genova, "but she understood very good English. She talks better English than I do."[21]

Genova recalled that after Flubacher had left the room at the Third Precinct, he tried to put Anna Antonio at ease by conversing in Italian. Anna told him that her marriage was arranged by her family, and in time the marriage was in trouble. What concerned Prior the most was Anna's inference that any abused woman who had her husband killed in Italy would have received a medal. "Well," said Genova, "I think it was a mutual expression, hers and mine; say if it had been in Italy any woman that would kill him would get a medal, but I said, 'This is not Italy.'"[22]

Prior breathed a small sigh of relief that the medal story was a "mutual expression" and nothing more. His only hope now was that the jury would accept this in the same way he hoped they had accepted the "smiling in the coffin" story.

Encouraged by Genova's response, Prior forged ahead and asked him to tell the court more details of his conversation with Anna Antonio. What Genova recalled caught everyone off guard. "She told me Mr. Prior that she had been abused by her husband and that she was miserable; that her husband was going around with other women; that her husband was responsible for the death of one of her children; that he was diseased, her husband was diseased."

Prior was stunned and to make sure the courtroom understood the ramifications of this statement, he innocently asked what kind of disease.

"Well," said Genova, "venereal disease."

"Venereal disease?" exclaimed Prior in a voice that filled the courtroom.

"Yes."

"All right," said Prior, "go ahead."

"She caught him treating himself in the basement with medicines."[23]

Unwittingly, Genova had introduced to everyone present in the court yet another major flaw in the character of Sam Antonio. The small-time dope peddler was also a womanizer. For dramatic effect, Prior acted startled by this claim. But Delaney was fully aware of this aspect of Sam Antonio's life and chose to ignore it. A year earlier, when Anna was first interviewed at the Third Precinct by Flubacher, Griggs, and Delaney, she said that she suspected "another girl." Flubacher never discarded his notes from the time he interviewed Anna Antonio. "She thought he had another girl somewhere," recorded Flubacher in his notepad, "as she found cundrums [condoms] in the house after he was dead. She also thought that he had [a] social disease as she had found a syringe and some medicine in the cellar."[24]

Unfortunately for Prior, what Genova had testified to could not be proved or disproved. The autopsy report entered into evidence on Sam Antonio was focused on bullet holes and knife wounds. It didn't mention venereal disease, but Dr. Brenenstuhl wasn't looking for the disease when he performed the autopsy.

When Prior asked him to relate more of the conversation that took place at the precinct, Genova was extremely cooperative. Unlike Flubacher before him, Genova was perfectly at ease on the witness stand. Relaxed and confident, he candidly answered every question put to him, especially those regarding Sam Antonio's other activities.

"She said her husband associated with the underworld, with criminals, that her husband was in the dope, in the drugs racket. Why, Mr. Prior," said Genova with a sigh, "she told me many things."

Not wishing to appear anxious, Prior encouraged Genova to elaborate on what he had just said. The railroad detective recalled how Anna had said her husband had "double crossed some people in some dealings." When Prior asked if some of these "double crosses" had to do with a certain arson that had occurred in the western part of the state, Genova, for the first time, hesitated.

"Must I answer that?"

Prior told him that he was obligated, under oath, to tell what he knew. When no one objected, Genova went on to tell Anna's version of the Steamburg arson. Unaware of Saetta's involvement in the arson, Genova concluded his story with, "But this had nothing to do with this murder case."

"I know," said Prior masking a grin, "I will get to that, I will get to that."[25]

Prior knew a good thing when he saw it. Genova's testimony was for the most part favorable to his client. With few objections from Delaney or Casey, Prior was able to turn a state witness into a character witness for Anna Antonio. This would not be the case when it came to Henry Lowenberg. From the onset, Genova and the city attorney clashed. The aggressive, sarcastic interrogating style of Lowenberg directly contrasted with Genova's old-world charm and manners.

After briefly explaining for the third time, once for Prior and once for Casey, why he was brought into the Antonio case, Lowenberg asked if he was being compensated. Genova replied that when he arrived at the Third Precinct on April 1, compensation wasn't initially discussed, but later on he did submit a pay voucher.

"Without being personal, Lieutenant, may I inquire as to how much that bill was?"

It was personal, but Genova fielded the question on his own terms. Instead of giving Lowenberg a total amount for his services, Genova said that he was paid at the rate of twenty dollars per day.

"You would consider that pretty good pay wouldn't you?"

"No, sir," replied Genova. If the railroad detective had said that it was adequate compensation for his services, Lowenberg could turn on him and declare that Genova was performing this service because of the money. Genova perhaps sensed this and quickly added that he wasn't receiving any money or submitting any pay voucher for his appearance on the witness stand.[26]

What set Genova apart from some of the other witnesses in the trial who were questioned—almost interrogated—by Lowenberg was the simple fact that he was more adept at answering questions than the man asking them. Never missing a chance to berate Genova, Lowenberg tried on countless occasions to question his usefulness to the investigation. When asked if he was brought into the Antonio investigation simply because he and the defendants were of Italian descent, Genova grinned. "You want me to tell you why? Because they felt I was more able and capable to do the job than they were."

Lowenberg could not believe what he had just heard and demanded to know how he felt he was more capable than an Albany police detective with ten years of experience. Genova smiled and said, "I spent 28."

Almost at the point of frustration, Lowenberg asked him how many times he had been called to testify in a murder case.[27] "That is a big one," said Genova, "I cannot tell you, quite a few." Pressed by Lowenberg for an exact number, Genova said that in his career, he had testified in close to twenty murder cases. With that, Lowenberg backed down. Even he, in his brashness, had to realize that Genova had participated in more murder trials than he had in his brief legal career.[28]

Having failed to publicly embarrass Genova regarding his paid services to the Antonio investigation and his years of service as a detective with the railroad, Lowenberg questioned his usefulness to the Albany police.

"You were told in substance," said Lowenberg, "that it would be your job to get these defendants to talk."

"No, sir."

"Well, you were told were you not, that you would talk to these defendants?"

"I wasn't told anything of the kind."[29]

And so it went, back and forth. Each time Lowenberg attempted to set a trap or back Genova into a corner, it failed. Attempting to discredit Genova another time, Lowenberg suggested, in questions laced with innuendo, that the railroad detective had acted improperly when interviewing Vincent Saetta's mother and searching their home in Queens, New York. Genova categorically denied that this had taken place. His services were necessary in Queens because Mrs. Saetta couldn't speak English. As for searching the home for a gun and knife the way Lowenberg had suggested, not only did it not take place, it wasn't necessary. He and Hynes didn't have a search warrant when they went to Queens. The knife had already been recovered at the scene of the crime, and Vincent Saetta had already told them that pistol had been tossed away.

In his final attempt to discredit Genova, Lowenberg assailed the railroad detective with questions regarding the Steamburg arson. As the arson was way beyond the jurisdiction of the Albany Police Department, Lowenberg set his sights on finding fault with Genova's detective skills in this investigation. In a volley of sarcastic repartee, Genova had the last word.

When Lowenberg asked him to supply details of his knowledge of the arson, details that were supplied to him by his client, Genova raised his arm and pointed directly to Saetta. "Ask him, I don't know." Aware of the Steamburg arson, Genova said he wasn't really interested in the crime. He looked at it as a separate crime, unrelated to the murder of Sam Antonio. He did recall in his conversation with Saetta that the job was supposed to have netted $2,500 instead of the $1,000 split between the two of them. This revelation raised a few eyebrows in the courtroom. Suddenly $2,500 looked like a much better motive for revenge. Realizing that this line of questioning was detrimental to his client, Lowenberg quickly distanced himself from the payoff money and concentrated on the details of the torching of the creamery. Pressed by Lowenberg to reveal details of the arson and the owner of the creamery, Genova leaned forward in the witness chair, smiled at Lowenberg, and said, "Just subpoena me."[30]

Genova really didn't know the owner of the creamery and, what's more, the only details of the crime he received came from Saetta. This was a crime that Saetta claimed he, a former employee of the New York Central Railroad, and the deceased, at the time employed by the railroad, committed. As to the investigation that took place at the creamery, Genova said that the report was on file with his superior and if Lowenberg wanted to know the details of the arson, he should subpoena him as well.[31]

Overall, Genova's testimony at the trial had the effect of a double-edged sword. Although the railroad detective spoke with all three of the defendants, not once did he speak of them in pairs. Testimony he offered for Anna Antonio was just that—about her and only her. Never once did he try to tie in Saetta. This and the sympathetic tone he expressed on the witness stand for her pleased Dan Prior. However, Lowenberg viewed Genova with scorn. He was nothing more than a paid informant of the Albany police, one who weaseled himself into the good graces of an aged Mrs. Saetta to obtain information about her son. For Charles Duncan, Genova's testimony about his client, Sam Faraci, was inconsequential. Other than visiting and conversing with Faraci in his cell, Genova was unable to collect any pertinent information from him that could assist in the investigation.

11

JIMMY HYNES, THE ICE CREAM BOY

On April 6, 1933, James J. "Jimmy" Hynes became the ninth member of the law enforcement community to testify in the Antonio trial. On the witness stand, Hynes said that he was a patrolman with the Albany Police Department, which was true, and that he served in no official capacity with the district attorney's office, which was subject to debate.

Hynes was a First World War Marine Corps veteran who joined the police force on December 27, 1922. Assigned to the south end of Albany, the uniformed officer was a familiar sight near speakeasies, pool halls, and Italian restaurants. In time, his knowledge of the south end and some of its inhabitants, who were only a whisker away from breaking the law, came to the attention of the district attorney's office. Delaney plucked Hynes from the Gut and had him reassigned to his office. For the past three years Hynes served in an unofficial capacity as a liaison between the Albany police and the district attorney's office. Assuming the responsibilities of an investigator or detective, Hynes reported directly to Delaney any current developments or progress in any ongoing investigation.[1] Although Flubacher was the lead investigator in the Antonio murder case, he was, after all, a state policeman who had other cases that demanded his attention. Hynes, however, was involved with the Antonio murder from start to finish, with no interruptions.

No other Albany police officer or detective spent more time with the defendants than Jimmy Hynes.

On the witness stand, Hynes echoed the testimony presented by Flubacher. Slowly and methodically he retraced his steps with the state policeman. From interviewing each suspect to accompanying Saetta and Faraci to the scene of the crime to combing the Gut for clues, Hynes offered few new details to what was already entered into the court record. Questioned by Delaney, someone he knew, Hynes seemed confidant and relaxed as he recalled times, places, and entire conversations that took place with all three of the defendants. Like Flubacher, Hynes readily admitted that he took no notes and relied on his memory. "My memory was pretty clear," he said of events that occurred a year earlier, "and it is clear yet."[2] That memory would be put to the test.

Prior came on strong and went after Hynes in much the same way he had gone after Flubacher. In an attempt to trip up the patrolman's memory, Prior asked him several times to recall entire conversations he had with Anna Antonio. In particular, Prior was trying to establish whether it was his client or Vincent Saetta who had supplied the phone number of the Quarter Cab to John Delaney. This was the second time Prior tried to throw suspicion on the Quarter Cab that Anna took to the corner of Broadway and Columbia when she made her forty-dollar rendezvous with Saetta after the murder. Earlier in the trial, Prior ruthlessly destroyed the credibility of one-time taxi driver Joseph DiJullio.

Delaney sat by and allowed his assistant Joseph Casey to question DiJullio. The former employee of the Quarter Cab said he received a phone call at their Lark Street office at about 4:55 A.M. on Easter Sunday. He went on to say that he picked up a woman on the corner of Clinton Street and Fourth Avenue, about two blocks from Teunis Street. Casey then asked if that woman was in the courtroom.

"This is not fair, and I object," cried Prior. "The three people contain one woman and he knows it. He looked around the courtroom and could not identify her."[3]

After that, it was all over as far as Joseph DiJullio was concerned. Moving restlessly in the witness chair and with facial expressions that bordered on sheer terror, Prior sensed his weakness and moved to exploit it. How could he be sure that the only woman in the courtroom was his cab fare at that hour of the morning? He couldn't describe the dress she was wearing and couldn't remember if she met with anyone after she exited his cab. Casey tried to salvage what he could from the witness by reminding him of their April 20 meeting in the district attorney's office, when he was presented with a photograph of Anna Antonio. In doing so, Casey had made himself an unsworn witness by reminding DiJullio of this meeting. The question was improper, and Prior should have objected.

Prior did object, but not to the question Carey posed. He objected to the use of a photograph. A lone photograph. Was this the best the district attorney's office could do? What about a lineup of, say, a half-dozen pictures to choose from? And as far April 20 was concerned, Prior reminded everyone that this was twenty-five days after Easter. Could this cab driver recall the details of a lone fare from such a long time ago? In rapid succession, Prior shot off the names of streets and directions to the hapless cab driver. In a confusing gamut, Prior asked DiJullio if he recognized streets in the Gut that ran north and south when in reality they ran east and west. He then questioned him about the various locations of businesses in that area. A totally befuddled DiJullio misidentified some establishments on one side of the street and a few on the wrong street.[4]

"You don't know whether this is the woman or not, do you?"

"I don't know at all," replied DiJullio.[5]

Judge Gallup ruled that the testimony offered by DiJullio was inadmissible, prompting Delaney to damn Prior with faint praise. "I do not say that any of us would want to be questioned by Prior."[6]

However, Hynes was no DiJullio. Using the same tactics he had used to trip up DiJullio, Prior asked a series of questions and eventually asked if the number Anna Antonio called for the Quarter Cab was 4-1977. Here Prior was in for a surprise. Hynes wasn't fooled by this ruse and quickly corrected Prior. The phone number Anna Antonio gave to Delaney while in his presence was 4-9177.[7]

On several occasions, Hynes paused for a moment while the court stenographer repeated the question. In this way, he gave carefully worded answers instead of an ill-prepared hasty reply. The verbal sparring that took place with Prior was tame compared to what was to follow.

Straddling the fence of being sarcastic and obnoxious, Henry Lowenberg questioned the methods and motives of the only uniformed policeman assigned to the Antonio murder investigation.

"You and Vincent were pretty chummy, were you not?"

For the most part, Hynes said that he had always been on friendly terms with Saetta. Even before he had run afoul of the law, Hynes had been acquainted with Saetta when he walked a beat in the south end. Now that Saetta was behind bars facing the possibility of death in the electric chair, he admitted to Lowenberg that he sort of felt sorry for him.

"You took a liking to him?"

"Well," said Hynes, sensing a trap, "not more than any other fellow."

"I mean well enough to buy him ice cream and cigars and call him Vince and go to sleep on his shoulder. Took quite a liking to him, didn't you?"[8]

In a trial with very few, if any, lighthearted moments, Lowenberg attempted to assail Hynes's professionalism, recalling an incident he had testified to earlier. Hynes was seated in the back of a police squad car with Saetta, after leaving Hudson and the scene of the crime. Delaney asked Hynes what conversations took place in the car. Hynes said he couldn't recall any conversation that took place with Saetta because he had fallen asleep on his shoulder and didn't wake up until the car hit a bump in the road in Albany. "Gee," said Delaney, shaking his head, "I thought the police never slept."[9]

Much to Lowenberg's rancor, Hynes came across as a hospitable host to Saetta as well as Faraci while they were being held by the police prior to their confessions. On several occasions, Hynes went to several local stores to get ice cream, cigars, and fruit, especially oranges, for both men. Friendly gestures like this were a ruse, claimed Lowenberg, designed to make up for the maltreatment his client had received at the hands of the police. Hynes maintained that the exact opposite was true.

Hynes testified that he had gone out of his way multiple times to make both men comfortable. "I asked Vincent how the eats were," said Hynes. Lowenberg's client told him that the food was fair, but he really missed having fruit, especially oranges "on account of my stomach." Hynes offered to go to the A and P store on the corner of Wilson and North Pearl and as an afterthought went to Faraci's cell and asked if there was anything he could get him. Hynes said he returned with a dozen oranges and two packs of cigarettes to split between the two.[10] When Hynes brought Saetta oranges, Lowenberg said, "Of course, you didn't go to work on him after he ate the oranges to get the return [a confession], did you?" And when Saetta was interviewed in the upstairs dormitory, "You didn't strike a blow, did you?" When Hynes emphatically denied that "no blows" took place, Lowenberg sarcastically remarked, "You were too chummy with him to do anything like that, were you not?"[11]

Hynes held his temper and went on to say that he periodically called on both Saetta and Faraci. The jail wasn't a restaurant, but he told both men he would do what he could to make their stay more comfortable and, yes, this included ice cream for Saetta. When Faraci complained that soup wasn't included with the meals, Hynes went to the store and bought a carton of chicken soup and crackers. For good measure, he brought them each a few nickel cigars. In the course of his testimony, Lowenberg discovered that Hynes's civil nature extended beyond that of oranges and ice cream. As both men neared the time of their arraignment, Saetta asked for a special favor. "Is there any chance," he asked Hynes and Genova, "of getting me some clean socks and a handkerchief and some underwear and a suit or a shirt? I would like to look kind of decent when I go to court."[12] Hynes made sure that both men were provided with clean clothes.

Lowenberg just could not accept the fact that Hynes was this good to both men. The city attorney tried to suggest that a conspiracy of sorts existed between Flubacher and Hynes. The details of their individual testimonies matched exactly in so many instances that the two must have rehearsed their testimony prior to the trial. Nothing of this sort took place, said Hynes, reminding Lowenberg that he wasn't present in court on the days that Flubacher had testified. Besides, he said, on the few occasions they had met outside the courtroom, they never discussed the case.

"Now I believe you testified yesterday that you brought for Vincent Saetta some cigars and some ice cream and what else . . . got him blankets, and what else did you get him?"

"Got him some spaghetti."

"You do that for everyone that you come in contact that is under arrest?"

Hynes attempted to explain that his duty, as he perceived it, was to fulfill any reasonable request made by a prisoner while in his care. Oranges, cigars, and even ice cream were not unusual or difficult items to obtain for anyone.

"In other words," said Lowenberg, "outside of being a patrolman you are also an errand boy for any and all prisoners who might make requests of you?"

Hynes chafed at the insult. "No," he replied in a firm voice, "not an errand boy." Unabated, Lowenberg pressed on in his attempt to belittle any kindness Hynes demonstrated to his client. When Lowenberg insinuated that Hynes was instructed to provide any prisoner he came in contact with certain creature comforts, it drew a sharp retort.

"No," said a visibly angry Hynes, "I am not told to do it."

"You are just a kindly soul who would like to help other people along; that is right, isn't it?"

"Well," said Hynes, "yes."

"Well, you are that good natured to take care of a man in distress?"

Hynes seized the moment. Leaning forward in the witness chair, he stared at Lowenberg and with a firm voice replied, "No more than I would want to be taken care of under the same circumstances."[13] Hynes walked away from the witness stand virtually unscathed by the incessant verbal attacks launched by Lowenberg. He came across as a decent person, and nothing Lowenberg insinuated changed that. Still, "little Jimmy Hynes, the ice cream boy" was held in contempt by the New York City attorney. Lowenberg was firmly convinced that Hynes's seemingly endless acts of kindness were orchestrated to mask the ill treatment Vincent Saetta had received at the hands of others. Ice cream, oranges, cigars, and clean clothes were welcome gratuities, but something was missing. Lowenberg never asked specifically when all this took place. Was this jailhouse hospitality extended to Saetta on the first day he was incarcerated, or the fifth, tenth, or the fifteenth? Or did all this take place after he and Faraci confessed? The most important thing to be provided to his client, incarcerated for sixteen days, said Lowenberg, was an attorney, and this was flatly denied.[14]

Equally unimpressed with Jimmy Hynes was Dan Prior. "Hynes," Prior later said, "failed miserably on the witness stand."[15] Actually, the only witness who testified to the extent of Flubacher did quite well in fielding answers to Dan Prior—save one. A week before the trial, Hynes admitted that he had gone to the evidence locker in the district attorney's office and in an effort to refresh his memory, reread Anna Antonio's confession. He no doubt took the liberty of rereading the confessions of Saetta and Faraci as well, but none of this sat well with Prior, especially when Hynes justified it with as "part of my work."[16] Earlier, the district attorney's secretary testified that it certainly wasn't in Hynes's job description to inspect trial evidence.

12

THE FIFTY-CENT KNIFE

The autopsy report filed by Dr. Orvis A. Brenenstuhl concluded that although the victim, Sam Antonio, had suffered five bullet wounds, only one proved to be fatal. The lone .38-caliber slug removed from the body was the first piece of evidence entered into the court record. Delaney was fully aware that it would have been a much more compelling piece of evidence if he had the gun that it was fired from. The absence of the pistol meant there was no sense of shock or repugnance that was always associated with an execution-style murder. However, he did have a hunting knife discovered near a pool of blood on Castleton Road.

It really didn't matter to Delaney that the autopsy report stated that the dozen or so stab wounds inflicted upon Sam Antonio were not fatal. The district attorney wanted to prove that Sam Faraci was a willing participant, just as anxious to do harm to Antonio with a knife as Saetta had done with a pistol. Saetta and Faraci may have been inconsistent in some details of the crime in their signed confessions, but they agreed on one point—where they purchased the knife. On Saturday, April 2, 1932, Delaney sent Jimmy Hynes to Uncle Jack's Pawn Shop and Jeweler.[1]

The arrival of Hynes at the secondhand store came as no surprise to the proprietor. Ever since he learned of the arrest of Saetta and Faraci, Julius Kommit had been expecting a visit from the Albany police.

Hynes walked into his establishment and immediately presented him with the bone-handled hunting knife for identification. The forty-five-year-old store owner gave the knife a cursory glance before returning it to Hynes. "The district attorney wants you," said Hynes. Kommit nodded his head to Hynes and before leaving his store, turned to a clerk and did the same.[2]

Kommit didn't engage in any small talk or light conversation with Hynes during their fifteen-minute ride to the Third Precinct. Escorted into the station house, he never once asked any of the several officers present why he was being detained. Led to a small room, Kommit continued to maintain his silence for another twenty minutes while Hynes went for Delaney. The silence was broken when an excitable Delaney flung open the door and began asking questions. When did he last see Saetta? Faraci? Did he sell them this knife?

An unruffled Kommit said that yes, both of the men in question had been to his store and purchased a knife. Poised to ask more detailed questions, Delaney's efforts were thwarted by the sudden appearance of Albany attorney David Belkin. It was only then that Jimmy Hynes fully understood the meaning of Kommit's final nod to the store clerk. It was the signal to contact his attorney. Belkin informed Delaney that the interview was concluded and that if he required any more cooperation from his client, he could do so with a subpoena.

When called to testify at the trial, the pawnshop owner was not a hostile witness, but he wasn't exactly a helpful one either. In the ten years he had operated Uncle Jack's, Kommit had come to know quite a few Albany detectives. They sometimes frequented his store, but not as customers. In almost every instance, the detectives sought information regarding stolen property or suspiciously pawned items. With his own lawyer only a phone call away, Kommit cautiously answered their questions. On the witness stand, he saw no reason to deviate from this method.

Kommit testified that he had known Saetta and Faraci for about eight months, perhaps a year, but only as patrons of his store. As to the purchase of the knife, he was equally vague. He recalled that they entered his store late in the afternoon but couldn't recall the exact date. Kommit told the court that it was a simple business transaction. "Mr. Saetta asked me to show him a knife in the showcase," said Kommit.

"It was sort of a hunting knife. I picked out the knife, and I gave it to Mr. Saetta, and he looked at it and bought it. He paid me and I wrapped up the knife, and that's about all."[3] The two men were in and out of his store in about ten minutes.

Delaney walked toward the evidence table, lifting the knife high in the air for all to see, and asked, "I show you People's Exhibit 5 and ask you if you recall a knife of this nature?"

Kommit paused for a moment, stared at the knife, and turned to Delaney. "Well, it was a knife, something like that," he said.[4]

Taken aback by this response, Delaney rephrased the question and asked Kommit if this was not the same knife he had sold to Saetta. Kommit said that he couldn't be absolutely certain. "I sell all kinds," he said, "I got knives, dozens of them." No, said Kommit later, he would not swear that the knife marked Exhibit 5 was the knife purchased at his store.[5] Disappointed at this response, Delaney asked Kommit if he could recall any conversation he had with Saetta or, more importantly, any conversation between Saetta and Faraci. Once more, Kommit was not a great help. This was a fifty-cent business transaction that didn't require a lot of conversation or eavesdropping on his part.

By now, Delaney's disappointment with Kommit as a witness turned to disgust. The pawnshop owner offered little in the way of valuable testimony and avoided commitment at every turn. He remembered selling the knife, couldn't recall the day it was sold, and couldn't describe the transaction. He couldn't recognize the knife on the evidence table, nor could he recall any of the conversation between himself, Saetta, and Faraci. The only thing Delaney had was a knife found at the scene of the crime that only he could vouch for. From the moment Flubacher picked up the knife after its discovery on Castleton Road, Delaney made sure he knew exactly how many people had possession of this critical piece of evidence. When he arrived at his office, he instructed his secretary, Sara Mara, to place the knife in the evidence locker.

Every lawyer and judge in the capital region knew the secretary with the rhyming name. A graduate of Albany Business College, Sara Mara became on January 1, 1923, the first woman to hold the position of stenographer to the grand jury and secretary to the district attorney's office. Respected by the law community, she was admired outside the district attorney's office as well. Although she never married, she had many children—all of them girls. Living two doors down from the St. Vincent Female Orphan Asylum, "Aunt Sate" was known for her tireless volunteer work and charitable contributions to the orphanage.[6]

Sara Mara was seemingly unimpressed with the knife Delaney presented to her the day it was discovered on Castleton Road. In the ten years she had served as secretary to the district attorney, she had made a record of a variety of guns, knives, and other bludgeoning devices used in Albany County felonies. The bone-handled knife simply didn't pique her curiosity. "It was a dirty looking knife," she recalled.[7]

On April 8, Sara Mara was called to the witness stand in the trial. Pleasant and cheerful, she was completely at ease on the witness stand, for every lawyer present except Lowenberg knew her. In a trial that was already in its fifteenth day, marked by frequent outbursts and flared tempers, Sara Mara came on like a breath of fresh air. Before answering any questions, she turned and gently smiled at Anna Antonio. Unbeknownst to Anna, Sara Mara periodically looked in on her two daughters at St. Vincent Female Orphan Asylum.

Mara testified that when any evidence was presented to her by the district attorney, it was her job to store it in the evidence locker in her office. The evidence locker was an imposing seven-foot-tall steel safe. She opened the safe each morning when she came to work and closed it whenever she left her desk. Inside the safe was a separate drawer for evidence for which only she and her boss, John T. Delaney, had a key. Interestingly, Sara Mara said that although Delaney had a key, he always asked her to open the drawer and personally hand him any particular piece of evidence he asked for. What he did with that piece of evidence was not her concern. The only thing that concerned her was that the evidence be returned, as she said, "and kept in its proper place."[8]

When asked if the knife on the evidence table was in the same condition as it was when she first took custody of it, Sara Mara quipped, "Why wouldn't it be? It hasn't been taken out." It had been secured in the evidence locker for almost a year.

It may have surprised some people in the courtroom that the attorney who had the most to gain from the testimony of Julius Kommit and Sara Mara asked the fewest questions. Charles J. Duncan, representing

Sam Faraci, was fairly conservative in his questioning of Kommit. It was Saetta who purchased the knife and carried it out the door of his establishment. At no time did he ever say that Sam Faraci had the knife in his possession. After its discovery on Castleton Road, the knife was passed from one person to the next. From Flubacher to Smurl to Delaney to Mara to Hynes. The only other person to have the knife in his possession was fingerprint man Thomas Straney. "If Faraci had blood on his hands and had that knife," concluded Duncan, "could you get a more perfect set of fingerprints?"[9] Straney couldn't lift a single print from the knife. Who wielded the knife in the attack on Sam Antonio was simply Saetta's word against Faraci's. "As far as Sam Faraci is concerned," said Duncan, "the evidence in this case is not much."[10]

Delaney thought otherwise. Regardless of the fact that he had a bullet with no gun and a knife with no fingerprints, he believed that he had more than enough evidence to send all three defendants to the electric chair. Over the objections of all three defense attorneys, Delaney was able to enter into evidence the three signed confessions he obtained from each of the accused—confessions that he conveniently did not mention were obtained without the benefit of legal counsel. The signed confessions that Delaney had entered into evidence were confusing, somewhat fanciful, and in many instances lacked solid facts. Saetta said he shot Sam Antonio but did not act alone. He implicated Sam Faraci and later Anna Antonio. Faraci claimed he didn't know Anna Antonio but was present when Saetta shot and stabbed Sam Antonio. None of this mattered to Delaney, who viewed each of their confessions as their suicide notes. What's more, Saetta's confession clearly implicated Anna Antonio, thus sealing her fate. After a parade of thirty-seven witnesses, he believed that he had built a formidable case against the defendants.

Charles Duncan couldn't believe that a confession obtained from his client was admissible as evidence. Why did it take the police sixteen days to get a confession? Didn't any of the police officers and detectives take into account that Sam Faraci was illiterate? Delaney assured Duncan that this was taken into account. After Faraci's confession was prepared for his signature, it was read aloud to him. As for the delay of sixteen days, several detectives testified that this prolonged delay was necessary. They simply did not have enough evidence to charge him and his partner with murder. As expected, this did not sit well with Saetta's attorney. "I will say," said Lowenberg later, "I would have confessed to the murder of [gangster] Arnold Rothstein if I had been in there sixteen days."[11] Prior concurred. Brought to the precinct at midnight and then questioned for five hours, Anna Antonio would sign anything if she could return home.

The most vocal of the trio of defense attorneys was Dan Prior. Delaney hadn't settled into his seat when the charismatic Prior rose from his and asked for a new trial for his client. "The People have failed to prove any case," he explained, "there is no evidence in this case to sustain the allegations in the indictment . . . there is no evidence to show that she was guilty of the crime of murder in the first degree, or any other crime."

Holding the indictment in one hand and slapping it with the other, Prior denounced the indictment as one of the most poorly written and confusing he had ever read. "In fact," he added, "it is different from any other indictment I have seen, and I have seen a great many of them."[12] Line by line Prior disputed the charges leveled against Anna Antonio. Had a conspiracy existed to kill Sam Antonio? That depended upon which confession you were referring to. "There is not anything," he said with regard to a conspiracy on the part of his client, except "the statements of Flubacher and Hynes and some other officers."[13] Not even People's Exhibit 14, Anna Antonio's signed confession, proved that she had entered into a conspiracy with Saetta and Faraci to kill her husband. Although the evidence Delaney presented indicated that both men, as the indictment read, "did willfully . . . make an assault in and upon the body" of Sam Antonio, Prior stressed that his client was not present.[14] If the trial thus far had proved anything, it clearly revealed that the district attorney lacked physical evidence to charge Anna Antonio with first-degree murder.

Prior, Lowenberg, and Delaney clashed, argued, and disagreed on many themes throughout the trial with one exception. All three desired and asked for separate trials for their clients. Now, after Delaney had called his last witness, Prior maintained that the confusion in the proceedings thus far was a perfect illustration of why separate trials were needed. Which Sam are we referring to? There was the deceased, Sam Antonio, and one of the defendants, Sam Faraci. Added to this, there were several instances where Dan Prior was addressed as "Judge," as he had once been an Albany city judge, by John T. Delaney as well as Judge Gallup. The entire trial was a myriad of stories pitting one defendant against the other. "This is worse than a jig saw puzzle," said Prior.[15]

The real confusion began immediately when the first witness testified. From that moment on, each witness was met by a chorus of frequent objections from all three defense attorneys: "I ask that this not be allowed in the Antonio case" and "I assume this is not being accepted in the Saetta case," or "I move that this not be included in the Faraci case." Conservatively, Prior estimated that these "exceptions" were voiced by the defense attorneys over a hundred times. How could any jury disseminate the vast amount of material presented thus far in this trial?

"Now we might as well be honest with ourselves here," said Prior. "Nobody can believe, I think, that any jury could remember all these things. They are not lawyers, they are layman. They are not accustomed to the reasons for the exclusions of certain statements of certain defendants. I may be able to remember them, and your Honor might be able to remember them, because we are supposed to be, at least supposed to be trained in the law, and we know the reasons for the exclusion of the statements of one against the other, but here we have a carpenter and a farmer and other men sitting there, and we are to presume he knows it because your honor says as a statement of law you won't consider that. How can he remember back two weeks ago as to what he was told?"[16]

"It would require a jury with the intelligence of God," contended Prior, "to deliberate and give justice in this case with the hodgepodge of testimony directed at only one or two of the various defendants."[17]

Last, Prior brought up how unconscionable it was to consider how the cost of three trials would burden the taxpayers of Albany County when three lives were at stake. Previously, while in Judge Gallup's chambers, John T. Delaney expressed his confidence that a fair trial for all three was possible, seeing no need to expend taxpayers' money when one trial was sufficient. The remark didn't sit well with Prior, and now was the time to tell everyone in the courtroom how he felt on this subject. "Money?" charged Prior in a voice that filled every corner of the courtroom. "Suppose it costs the County of Albany thousands and thousands of dollars for separate trial for this defendant but that it insured justice. That is the purpose of the law. You do not balance any justice against dollars."[18]

As Prior returned to his seat, Charles J. Duncan rose from his to add a postscript. "I have just one more thought on the matter," he said. Duncan took issue with Judge Gallup's repeated claim that the celebrated Snyder-Gray case and the lesser-known Doran case served as precedents for having multiple suspects tried together. Diplomatically, Duncan calmly reminded the judge that the Court of Appeals ruling in the Snyder-Gray case was fairly explicit. "Each case," said Duncan paraphrasing the appeals decision, "must be decided according to the facts of that case and whether or not they shall have separate trials must be decided according to the circumstances of that particular case." In other words, the court ruled, said Duncan, "that it never laid down a hard and fast rule that they will be tried together."

In a rare moment of solidarity, the outspoken Henry Lowenberg was reticent. "I join in the motion. I won't argue it at length."[19]

Regardless of how persuasive an argument Prior presented or the insight provided by Duncan on the Snyder-Gray case, Judge Gallup wasn't about to grant a motion for a separate trial for any of the defendants. With the last of Delaney's witnesses called to testify, Gallup saw the trial as being half over. Completely ignoring the impact of the cost of three separate trials to the taxpayers, Gallup denied the motions while at the same time lauding the efforts of a jury where "every juror sworn was carefully examined." In a ruling as confusing as the testimony that Prior had criticized, Judge Gallup declared that the responsibility of the jurors was not daunting. "They have not got to recall and remember each individual ruling throughout this trial. All they have to do is follow the one basic rule, everything said by each and every one of the defendants, or which it is alleged they have said is to be regarded as to everyone else, and that goes for every bit of evidence that has been received in the case. They just have to follow that rule and they said they would do it and I believe the defendants will obtain a fair trial and justice being tried together as they are being tried. For these reasons I deny each and all of your motions for separate trials at this time."[20]

With the failure of the motion for a separate trial, Prior knew that the only way Anna Antonio could be saved was to take the witness stand in her own defense. In essence, she had to save herself.

13

ANNA ANTONIO

By 1929, the Albany County Board of Supervisors came to the conclusion that they were in desperate need of a new county jail. The current facility, which predated the Civil War, was overcrowded and literally falling apart, prompting the *Albany Evening News* to dub the old jail an "ancient Delaware Avenue Bastille."[1] After a fair amount of discussion and debate, the board accepted the low bid from the Marinello and Stanzo construction firm. The estimated cost of $2 million was a hefty sum for the taxpayers of Albany County on the eve of the Great Depression. The board's decision was to move the jail outside the city of Albany to the site of an old Shaker farm. The Shakers, a pacifist sect, would have been no doubt horrified at the prospect of their former home as the site of a multistoried brick colossus that could house as many as four hundred of Albany's worst felons.

Masons hadn't finished tapping the mortar on the remaining bricks when in September 1931 sheriff deputies began ferrying thieves, drunks, drug users, and brawlers northward on old Shaker Road to their new home. Some were serving light sentences, a few were awaiting court appearances, and then there were those who were awaiting transfer to other facilities after the courts had decided their fate. Women, too, ran afoul of the law and sometimes found themselves in jail. When they did, they became the responsibility of the matrons. One such matron was fifty-eight-year-old Mrs. Elizabeth Fox.

A jail matron since the late 1920s, Mrs. Fox had been assigned to monitor her fair share of prostitutes and embezzlers, as well as a few drug users. On April 14, 1932, she was introduced to her latest prisoner, a young mother of three children charged with murder. Elizabeth Fox became her constant companion, and the two formed a unique friendship. It was Mrs. Fox who listened to Anna Antonio, visited with her, and above all told her when she was about to receive a visitor.

Throughout the summer months and well into the fall, a constant presence at the jail was her brother Patsy Cappello. Since the day of her incarceration, Patsy had taken it upon himself to look after Phyllis, Marie, and Frankie. This was an arrangement that for now suited Patsy, but in time it did not sit well with his wife, Concetta. As the couple had no children of their own, Patsy had promised his sister that he could and would care for all three. As his work schedule with General Electric often alternated between part-time and full-time employment, Patsy endeavored to keep his promise. Concetta, however, was not bound by this oath. She chafed under the responsibilities of this instant family she inherited from her sister-in-law. Concetta had a social life. She enjoyed parties, the movies, and her friends. Caring for three children while her husband was away at work didn't fit into her lifestyle. One-year-old Frankie was easy to care for as he was still in a crib. But the girls proved to be a handful. Phyllis was a headstrong, rebellious seven-year-old while Marie, at age three, was constantly wetting her bed. Under pressure from his wife, Patsy made arrangements to have the girls placed in St. Vincent Female Orphan Asylum.

In addition to Patsy and Concetta, several of her cousins and a few Teunis Street neighbors visited Anna, but it is unclear if her father ever came to see her at the Albany County lockup. Ferdinando Cappello remains a shadowy figure. Little is known of her widowed father with the wooden leg except that after Anna's elopement with Sam Antonio, the relationship between father and daughter became strained. She never spoke of him, and he never spoke of her to the press. Family and friends may have provided comfort and encouragement at this time, but it was one visitor, Daniel H. Prior, whom she looked forward to seeing.

One could only imagine what went through the mind of Anna Antonio when the most famous attorney in Albany stepped forward to take
her case. Surely, if Prior could successfully defend Legs Diamond, he
would do right by her. Upbeat, confident, and slightly cocky, Dan Prior
gave hope. He visited her on numerous occasions. Prior delved into
her past and questioned her about husband's activities in the Gut while
carefully laying out his blueprint for her defense. On one point Prior
remained firm: it was absolutely imperative for him to know every detail of her conversations with Vincent Saetta. Prior knew all too well
that the information obtained from these conversations could carry
the weight of a conviction or the veil of acquittal to a jury.

On April 10, 1933, Anna Antonio was roused from her bed by one
of the matrons. She washed, dressed herself, and sat down to a light
breakfast. After having been in the county jail for a year, she became
accustomed to routine. Everyone rose at the same time, ate at the same
time, and if they were fortunate, received visitors during the hours des-
ignated by the jail. The only time this regimen was broken was when
an inmate had a court date. On this particular morning, it was the six-
teenth time Anna Antonio had been escorted from her cell to the front
door of the county jail. Here a sheriff's car had been assigned to take her
on the nine-mile drive southward on Shaker Road to the courthouse on
Eagle Street.

There were no crowds to greet her when she arrived at the back
entrance to the courthouse. Only after she was brought into the courtroom did she realize that something was amiss. There wasn't an empty
space or seat to be had. Nervous, her big black eyes darted about the
room, searching every face. Who were all these people? Prior, sensing
her fear, rose from his chair and motioned her forward. The people she
hadn't recognized, he told her, were reporters from every newspaper
in the tri-county area.

Press coverage of the trial thus far had been what one might have expected. The Albany and Schenectady papers did a fair job of reporting
the trial, finding good copy in the friction that had developed between
five attorneys and an unwavering judge. But April 10 would be different. The previous day, which was a Sunday, Prior had visited Anna
at the county jail and told her that unless a witness he called to testify

was the subject of a lengthy cross-examination by Delaney or Casey, she should expect to be called as a witness. After rehearsing the questions he intended to ask and how she should answer, Prior instructed Anna to be on her guard when being questioned by Delaney and Casey. Both prosecutors were not to be taken lightly. Charles Duncan, Faraci's attorney, however, was not perceived as a great threat, but Lowenberg was a different matter. After twelve days of testimony, the city attorney had proven himself a driven, formidable opponent.

Prior was correct in his assumption that at least one of the witnesses he called to testify would cause some controversy. William J. Dempsey, forty-nine-year-old proprietor of Dempsey's News Room in Schenectady, had at one time been a morphine addict. Few eyebrows were raised in the courtroom when he said that his supplier was Sam Antonio. Dempsey, who now claimed that he had recovered from his addiction, said that the last time he attempted to purchase morphine from Antonio was in December 1931. According to Dempsey, the seventy-five-dollar transaction took place at his newsstand on 136 Jay Street. Dempsey said that Antonio took his money with the promise that he would soon return with the morphine. Days passed, and when Antonio failed to appear, Dempsey became concerned. He eventually confronted his errant drug supplier near his Teunis Street apartment. The two exchanged words, and Dempsey left for Schenectady without his money or his morphine.

"Are you seeking to show that this witness had motive?" inquired Judge Gallup, reminding him once more that the character of the deceased was not on trial.

"In answer to your Honor's inquiry," replied Prior, "I propose to show by this witness that the deceased Antonio was engaged in the narcotic traffic."[2] Despite the continued objections and arguments presented by Delaney and Casey and an occasional rebuke from an exasperated judge, Prior did his best to portray Sam Antonio as a dope peddler who had enemies. It was quite possible that Sam Antonio had cheated others out of their money. A few may not have been as forgiving as Dempsey and instead sought revenge.

Lowenberg never questioned the recovered morphine addict, perhaps with good reason. Unlike Prior, who hoped to keep the image of Antonio as dope peddler forefront in the minds of the jury, Lowenberg hoped they would forget it all together. Clearly, Dempsey's testimony did not implicate Vincent Saetta in drug trafficking. There was, however, the possibility of the jury accepting Saetta as one who was capable of the revenge Prior alluded to.

After more witnesses were sworn in and testified, Prior nodded in the direction of his client. Dull whispers were audible, together with a rustling of spectators in their seats, craning for a better view of the woman who strode to the front of the courtroom and placed her left hand on the Bible.

Dan Prior may have coached her on how to behave in the courtroom, but no one had to tell Anna Antonio how to dress for the occasion. Unlike the stylish Ruth Snyder, Anna Antonio arrived in court each day in the plain clothes one would associate with a typical lower-middle-class Italian homemaker. She wore no makeup, jewelry, nail polish, or fancy dress. She did not dress this way at the behest of her attorney in hopes of giving the jury the impression that she was an ordinary woman. She dressed this way because that was who she was. Anna Antonio was a petite, Italian American woman with short black hair and piercing black eyes. Like the other two defendants, she, too, passed through Ellis Island. Hard times in Italy, followed by hard times during the Great Depression, were etched into the lines under her big eyes. She had a tired and worn look about her that made her look older than her twenty-six years. The apartment she lived in with her three children was her world. She did not go out at night, did not attend parties, and expressed no regrets at not having done so. She was timid, shy, and, above all, extremely nervous as she sat down in the witness chair.

"Now, Mrs. Antonio," said Prior, waving his outstretched arm in the direction of the back of the room, "I want you to talk up so the last man can hear you."[3]

For the next hour Prior gently walked Anna Antonio through a series of questions regarding her past. Her answers, interrupted only by requests from Delaney and Casey to speak louder, were precise and clear. She told of her marriage to Sam Antonio at the age of sixteen and the time spent in Wayne County, the miscarriage of one child and the birth of another. She then went on to tell the court of the gypsy-like life she led raising her children while being constantly shuffled about Albany.

Anna testified that the relationship between her and her husband became strained shortly after they moved to 3 Teunis Street. Anita was gravely ill, and after her death, Sam ceased to keep regular hours working as a brakeman for the railroad and seemed to be spending more and more time away from the apartment in the company of Vincent Saetta. Over the strenuous objections of Lowenberg, Anna proceeded to describe in detail how, on one occasion in December 1931, her husband, in the company of several other men, which included Saetta, left the apartment and got into a black car that awaited them in front of the apartment. Before he left the apartment, her husband had told her to expect a phone call from New York City and told her how to respond to it. She didn't know where they were going, but she noticed they had burlap bags and pistols when they left the apartment.

Anna told the court that she was fairly certain that whatever her husband was doing involved big money. Without ever mentioning by name the Steamburg arson, Anna said that after this affair, the relationship between her husband and Vincent Saetta soured as the latter claimed he had been cheated out of money.

Constantly cautioned about "leading the witness"—that is, asking questions to get a desired response—Prior tried time and again to let Anna Antonio tell her story. Specifically, he wanted Anna to clarify certain statements attributed to her while being questioned by the authorities. Many of these statements, according to Prior, were taken out of context.

First, Sam Antonio didn't come home from work and abruptly leave the apartment. Anna said that she gave him a cool reception when he suddenly appeared early Saturday afternoon from work. She cooked his supper and asked if she could have some money to buy one of her friends an Easter plant. It was only after peeling off a ten-dollar bill from a sizable wad of money did Sam announce that he was leaving and would not be home until early morning. Telling her to hurry back as he was going out for the evening, Anna told the court that she became disgusted. "That is not very nice going out the day before Easter," she said, "my family is coming down for Easter." None of this seemed to concern him. Her husband simply got up from the kitchen table and went to take a bath.[4]

It was the meeting at the Leland Theater, however, that called for clarification. Anna said that she agreed to meet Saetta at the theater for the sole purpose of putting an end to his incessant phone calls to the apartment, demanding money. The last phone call she received from Saetta was in the early morning hours of Easter Sunday. Once more, he was demanding money with his promise of leaving town. Eager to rid herself of him, Anna testified that she took a taxi and met him at the corner of Columbia and Broadway. "I got out of the cab," said Anna, "and I didn't see anyone and I started to walk up the street and I seen Vincent standing in a doorway."[5] Anna said she was in disbelief when Saetta claimed to have killed her husband. Taken aback by what Saetta had told her, Anna said that she immediately hailed a cab and returned to Teunis Street. She claimed that she no sooner opened the door when the phone rang. It was Memorial Hospital informing her that her husband had been in an accident.

Led by Prior's questions, Anna said that after the phone call, events quickened. She went to the hospital and was interviewed by then Corporal Flubacher. She then went home and arranged to have her children taken to her brother's home in Schenectady and afterward made arrangements with the undertakers. After that she was brought by police to the Third Precinct on two occasions, all in the course of a day. "I was in a daze," she said.[6]

It was at this juncture that Prior took the dual opportunity to review some of the statements his client purportedly made to the authorities along with their less than professional treatment of her. He minced few words while telling the court how he detested the methods and motives of the police in obtaining her confession. She hadn't spoken to authorities in ten days, and then suddenly, at the stroke of midnight, she is literally dragged from her bed to the precinct. This could only be construed as the police wanting her to be in a weakened state—dazed—to get what they wanted.

"Have anybody with you," he asked, "any friend, relative or a lawyer?"[7] Like the other defense attorneys, Prior wanted to underscore the fact that Flubacher, Hynes, Genova, and a host of others had ample time to question Anna Antonio but just didn't see fit to tell her that she was entitled to legal representation.

On the same night she was brought to the precinct, Anna said that she heard voices in the hall outside the room she was being held in for questioning. The one voice she recognized immediately was that of Vincent Saetta. The other voice belonged to the man who walked into the room and introduced himself.

"Who was that?" asked Prior.[8]

"Mr. Genova."

Here, Prior exercised a certain degree of caution. Earlier in the trial Lieutenant Genova's testimony helped portray Anna Antonio in a sympathetic light. Now, with a few carefully asked questions, Prior wanted to maintain this image for the jury, while at the same time letting Anna clear up any misconceptions or confusion that may have come about during Genova's interview.

"The things I said to him," said Anna, "was that I wanted Sam to do was go to work and be a good father, that is the only thing. I didn't say all the things he said I did."[9]

As for Genova suggesting that Sam Antonio had been cruel or in some way mistreated his children, Anna set the record straight. "Them children had everything they could wish for." The only fault she found with her husband was his continued absence from home. "I didn't like his running around," she said.[10] Prior stalled for a moment in hopes the jury could take in her last statement. Did "running around" mean with other women or "running around" the Gut peddling narcotics, or both?

Still, the most damning piece of evidence against all three defendants were their signed confessions. Whereas Faraci and Saetta would claim that they were physically coerced, beaten to obtain their confessions, Prior said his client was mentally abused. He emphasized the fact that Anna had been taken from her home at midnight, grilled by the police, and given her confession to sign. True, Anna read her confession, pointed out a few errors, and signed it believing she could return home to her children. Instead of being allowed to return home, she was treated as if she were a flight risk. Within hours she was whisked away to the county jail. She was never given the opportunity to make any arrangements for her children.

Setting her confession on the exhibit table, Prior then picked up another set of papers. With his glasses perched on the tip of his nose, he turned a few pages and then paused.

"Now, I notice that in People's Exhibit 14 in evidence, this question appears: there is a question and answer on that paper I want you to tell these men about it. Somebody, apparently Mr. Delaney said to you, according to this, 'Q. Did you say where you were going to get the money from, or did he say something about where you were going to get the money from?' and the answer is, 'Yes, he told me he knew he had insurance and if I get rid of him and I would give him $800, and I said yes.'"

Prior removed his glasses and asked Anna if she ever made such a statement to Vincent Saetta. She replied with an emphatic, "No, I did not."[11]

It was impossible for anyone to deny that insurance was a major issue in the trial. From the moment all three defendants were placed in custody, the press wasted little ink in characterizing the murder as one motivated by a large insurance settlement. The fact that Sam Antonio signed up for a Metropolitan Life insurance policy on February 29, weeks before his murder, was suspicious. The real challenge facing Prior was trying to convince a jury that as far as life insurance was concerned, the little Italian housewife on the witness stand had not the slightest idea what insurance policies her husband had.

Selling life insurance during the Great Depression was difficult, and attempting to sell policies in the poorest section of Albany was next to impossible. For three years, Samuel Weidman of the Metropolitan Life Insurance Company had been trying to win over Sam Antonio. Rebuffed at every turn due to the high monthly premiums, Weidman was suddenly taken aback when Sam invited him to 3 Teunis Street to discuss the possibility of purchasing a new policy. Earlier in the trial, Weidman testified that as Sam Antonio was a brakeman on the railroad, his company deemed this position a "hazardous" job, hence the high premiums. After looking over the figures, Weidman recalled that Sam nodded, telling him that he would take the policy. At the last minute, Sam added, "I would like to have some insurance on the misses; she hasn't got any insurance."[12]

Weidman explained to the court that compared to the $4.75 per month premium Sam Antonio was already paying on the Brotherhood of Railroad Trainmen policy, the Metropolitan premium of $8.55 a month was a considerable increase. According to Weidman, the deciding factor was when Sam Antonio learned that unlike the Brotherhood policy, he could borrow against the Metropolitan policy.[13] Weidman said that once

Sam signed the Metropolitan policy, he intended to drop the Brother-hood policy.

Prior explained to the jury that obtaining this policy on the last day of February wasn't as suspicious as the press made it out to be. Anna tes-tified that she was aware of the Metropolitan policy but that she didn't believe it was an active policy. Sam Antonio never contacted the Broth-erhood to cancel the policy, and at the time of his death, unbeknownst to his wife, Sam Antonio had two active life insurance policies. When un-dertaker John M. Zwack arrived at her Teunis Street apartment to make the funeral arrangements for her husband, Anna said that she went to the desk drawer where her husband kept all his papers and retrieved both policies, not knowing that both were active. It was only after Zwack returned to the apartment and had her sign them that she realized the Metropolitan policy became active the day her husband had signed the contract. Did Vincent Saetta know of the existence of an additional life insurance policy? Perhaps not, for if he had, he would have no doubt tried to extort more money from Anna Antonio.

The only thing remaining for Prior in his defense of Anna Antonio was to convince the court that she was not party to the murder of her husband. She didn't deny that she knew Vincent Saetta. Anna testified that he had been to the Teunis Street apartment on numerous occasions and that she had spoken to him on the phone countless times. When she came face-to-face with him at the precinct, Prior said that his client had good reason to deny knowing him.

"I told Mr. Delaney I was afraid," she said, being quick to add, "I was afraid to tell him."[14]

This caught Delaney's attention. How could she possibly be afraid of a man who was already being held by the police?

"Well," replied Anna, "Saetta told me he had two men up from New York. As I told Mr. Delaney when I made that statement, even if they had him arrested, I was still afraid."

It was a piece of testimony that could not be easily dismissed. Could these men from New York that Saetta threatened her with be the same men who accosted John Gonyea in the hallway of her Teunis Street apartment? If they were, Prior argued, she had reason to fear.

"What were you afraid would happen?" asked Prior.

"Get the same medicine myself," she replied.[15]

Prior had no more questions to ask of Anna Antonio, having done his best to portray her as a young Italian immigrant trapped in a hopeless marriage, attempting to raise three small children on her own. Vincent Saetta was not her friend or partner. If he could lure a defenseless man to a lonely back road and shoot him in cold blood, he was perfectly capable of blackmailing a timid mother.

Prior returned to his seat and braced himself. The second part of his defense of Anna Antonio wasn't going to be easy. Like a shepherd watching over a single sheep, Prior knew he would have to be diligent. The wolves were waiting. Could Anna Antonio withstand the cross-examinations of Duncan, Lowenberg, Delaney, and Casey?

14

HENRY LOWENBERG

Decades after the trial, racked with cancer and near death, Henry Lowenberg dictated his memoirs, recalling the Antonio case as one of the most challenging in his legal career. It presented to him a unique challenge, one that he had never before encountered. "I found myself playing what was for me a strange part. I was required for a time to assume the unaccustomed role of prosecutor." Essentially, Lowenberg would have everyone believe that he was singled out for this particular role when in reality, each of the defense attorneys had done the same thing. One statement he did make was succinct. "The star attraction of the trial, of course, was Anna Antonio."[1] If she was the star of the show, then he was the villain.

When Judge Gallup entered the courtroom the following day, April 11, and with a bang of his gavel called the court to order, Lowenberg leaned toward Dan Prior and whispered, "Now Dan, I'm forced to become the district attorney for a few hours." This didn't bother Prior so much as the veiled threat that followed. "Your client's next stop is the death house. That's where she is going to be travelling next."[2] With this, the gauntlet was tossed. For thirteen days, Prior had studied Lowenberg's every move in court. He was aggressive, which, under the circumstances, was good, but he possessed a wide streak of vanity that bordered on belligerence. Simply put, if Saetta was headed for the electric chair, Lowenberg was going to make sure that Anna Antonio joined him. The battle to save Anna Antonio was about to begin, and Prior could not afford to have Lowenberg win the slightest skirmish.

"With some witnesses on cross examination," recalled Lowenberg in his memoirs, "you must take it easy in the beginning. You must first size up the person. My interrogation of Mrs. Antonio began in an easy-going manner."[3] Apparently the passage of time clouded his memory as the trial transcripts revealed a nasty exchange between him and Prior within minutes of the cross-examination.

Lowenberg began by asking Anna Antonio if her attorney had visited her at the jail and if they had discussed previous days' testimony. Additionally, Lowenberg wanted to know if Prior had coached her in what sort of questions she might anticipate being asked by him. Prior was on his feet in an instant. He loudly objected to these questions being asked of his client. "You cannot do that to me Brother, like you did with them," cried Prior, "I object to his question calling for an improper conclusion."[4] In the heated exchange that followed, which now included Judge Gallup, the question was raised. Did Lowenberg have the legal right to question Anna Antonio about any confidential conversations she had with her attorney? Didn't this violate the most sacred trust between a client and his or her attorney?

"She has taken the stand voluntarily in her own behalf," ruled Judge Gallup. "Now she is under cross examination and I think on the question of credibility he [Lowenberg] has the right to ask her whether she talked with anyone and whether they have given her any advice or made suggestions."[5]

The ruling was a minor victory for Lowenberg, but it was one that came with caution. In his effort to "size up" Anna Antonio, Lowenberg had inadvertently "sized up" her attorney. Dan Prior was not about to sit idly by and let any statement by Lowenberg go unchallenged. What Lowenberg did next caught everyone by surprise.

"I had wondered," Lowenberg later recalled, "what reasons a woman in Mrs. Antonio's circumstances would have for arranging her husband's murder." In formulating his strategy for the cross-examination of Anna Antonio, Lowenberg immediately discarded Sam Antonio's cruelty toward his wife. On the witness stand, Anna never said that she was mistreated or gave any indication that her husband had been cruel in any way toward her. As for money, Lowenberg assumed that the Antonios were, as he said, "modestly well off financially and did not seem to lack material security." This was an odd statement to make when one considers that earlier in the trial, two railroad men, one of them a timekeeper, testified to Sam Antonio's sporadic work schedule. Maintaining a small apartment and raising three children in the poorest section of Albany could hardly be construed as fine living. So, if lack money and physical cruelty were ruled out, what was her motive? "The answer, I concluded," said Lowenberg, "had to be another man."[6] To Lowenberg and, to some degree, the reporters who had been following the story, another man was a plausible explanation. If Ruth Snyder could enter into a romantic liaison and have her husband murdered for insurance money, then why couldn't Anna Antonio?

"At the time you married Sam Antonio, you did not really love him, did you?"

"Yes, I did," replied Anna.

"Were you not keeping company with another man at that time?"

Usually soft-spoken, Anna Antonio had to be prodded by the judge and defense counsel to raise her voice on several occasions, but not this time. She answered with a resounding "No!" that could be heard in the far corners of the courtroom. Dan Prior's "Objection!" was just as loud. Lowenberg turned on his heels, looked directly at Prior, and shouted, "I am going to prove a motive for this woman in hiring two men other than the defendant to kill that man!"

Prior could hardly contain himself from not bursting out loud in laughter. "Yes, that is nice."

"And that is not a smiling matter, either," shot back Lowenberg.

"Go ahead," shouted Prior in return, "I object to the question."[7]

Surely, thought Prior, Lowenberg couldn't be serious. Attempting to prove that Anna Antonio was motivated to do away with her husband because of her involvement in an illicit affair was one thing, but was he really going to try and prove that two other men killed Sam Antonio and not the defendants? If he could, it would be a plot twist worthy of a Raymond Chandler mystery novel. Gallup, too, was intrigued by this idea and allowed Lowenberg to continue.

Bolstered by the court's ruling against Prior a second time, the confident Lowenberg went on the attack and hammered away at Anna's marriage. When she said that before her marriage at the age of sixteen, she had other suitors, Lowenberg wanted to know if she was still keeping company with any of them after her marriage. Anna said that this would have been impossible as she resided in Wayne County.

"Are some of these suitors to your knowledge, unmarried?"

"They are all married and have families."

"Every one of them?"

"Large families."

"Are you absolutely sure?"

"Absolutely."[8]

In an effort to pass off Anna Antonio as a sixteen-year-old juggling boyfriend relationships, Lowenberg asked if she had eloped with Sam Antonio to spite a spurned lover. Anna became angry. She insisted that this wasn't the case. There was no "spurned lover," adding that the only one who was upset about her marriage at that time was her father.

"Well," charged Lowenberg, "you lived with Salvatore Antonio—you lived with him out of fear, didn't you?"

"Towards the last," she said.

"And when you say 'Towards the last,' how many months did you live with him prior to his death that you lived with him out of fear rather than love and respect?"

"I loved him," admitted Anna, "and feared him."

"You were afraid," said Lowenberg, "and how long was that fear carried in your breast as far as Salvatore Antonio was concerned?"

"When he started keeping company with your defendant!"[9]

Her response was a combination of sarcasm, wit, and perfect timing. Prior, sitting a short distance from her, beamed with pride as Anna held her ground. In an instant, the little woman on the witness stand turned Lowenberg's entire cross-examination from an extramarital affair to focusing on his client. Now Lowenberg was stuck. Having failed to prove that there was not another man in her life, he had no other choice but to revert to his original premise—that someone other than his client killed Sam Antonio. He began by asking her questions regarding the two mysterious strangers who had been in her Teunis Street apartment.

Delaney and Casey may have been wondering where Lowenberg was going with these questions. The John Gonyea episode had been thoroughly checked out by Albany detectives. They located Gonyea and asked him if what Anna Antonio had said was true. Her version of what had happened and his were a perfect match. Both said that the hallway of the apartment building was dark and that they could not identify the two men in question. Why, then, did Lowenberg act surprised when Anna Antonio said that as it was dark, she couldn't properly identify Saetta and Faraci as the two mysterious strangers? She told her husband of the incident and not the police.

"Did you," said Lowenberg in his usual condescending tone, "as a loving and respected wife, one who claims that she held Sam Antonio to breast and heart, did you get in touch with the police authorities with a view of trying to get them to protect your husband from possible death?"

"I couldn't very well do that," replied Anna.

"Why couldn't you do it?"

"Well, the first thing is I would be giving my own husband away."[10]

She was right. If she or her husband had gone to the authorities, what possible explanation could they offer as to why two suspicious-looking characters had been lurking about the hallway of their apartment house? Lowenberg guessed that the reason these two men were there was to settle some business with Sam, business that perhaps involved narcotics. Since the Albany detectives could not locate the two men in question, Lowenberg gently dropped his strategy that they could have been the murderers of Sam Antonio and changed his line of questions. "How long was your husband dealing in the narcotic traffic?"

The question didn't surprise Anna—or anyone else in the courtroom for that matter. Dan Prior had said this since the trial began. Federal narcotics agent Richard Kelly, as well as several Albany detectives, had been following Sam Antonio. Anna Antonio said that she believed her husband was actively dealing, as she called it, "dope," since August 1931. Soon it became clear to all that Lowenberg wasn't so much interested in the narcotics trade as he was in the money it generated for the Antonio household.

"You took that money," sneered Lowenberg, "that *filthy* money from him, and used it, didn't you?"

"We had to live," pleaded Anna, "I had four children to think about."

"I didn't ask you that," shot back Lowenberg, "You took some of that *filthy* money and used it, didn't you?"

That was about enough for Dan Prior. He objected to how the question was presented to his client only to have Lowenberg say, "Isn't it *filthy* money?"[11]

Of course, it was filthy money. What bothered Dan Prior was the double standard that existed. When Prior met Lowenberg for the first time in his State Street law office, the city attorney brazenly stated that he had once defended racketeer Legs Diamond. Did Lowenberg believe for one instance that the money he received for his fee came from Diamond's first communion money? It was all money from the rackets, and it was all filthy. Apparently, it was acceptable for a lawyer to take this kind of money, but not a housewife raising three children.

It didn't matter to Lowenberg that Anna had testified that at the time she was unaware of how and where Sam obtained the money he gave her to maintain the apartment. When given the money, she used it and never questioned its source. It was only after Christmas of 1931 that she began to suspect that a lot of the money Sam received was not legitimate. As to the money Sam received for his part in the Steamburg arson, Anna surprised her inquisitor by telling him that she purposely kept her own attorney in ignorance of the story.

"He didn't know nothing about it from me," said Anna, indicating that Prior heard about it when railroad detective Joseph Genova testified.[12]

By now a megalomaniac on the subject of money, Lowenberg still found it difficult to believe that Anna had withheld crucial information regarding the arson and its payoff from her attorney. "Here is a man," said Lowenberg, while pointing to Prior, "who was engaged to represent you, a man who is being paid to be your lawyer—."

"Are you sure he is being paid?" interrupted Prior.

"I assume so."[13]

For a brief moment, the barrister from New York City was caught off guard. Not only could Lowenberg not believe that she hadn't told her attorney any details surrounding the Steamburg arson, he was surprised to discover that Dan Prior was defending his client pro bono. Now it became obvious that the "filthy money" he accused Anna Antonio of accepting was not making its way to Dan Prior's legal fees. Instead of badgering Anna about the $1,000 her husband reputedly made from the arson and the subsequent rift it caused with Saetta, Lowenberg wisely dropped the issue altogether. A smaller sum would be much easier to question her about as it was already in her signed confession.

"I ask you," said Lowenberg, "whether your husband's life was worth more or less to you than $100?"

Earlier Anna had testified that Vincent Saetta had demanded $100 from her. Saetta, she claimed, threatened to kill her husband if she didn't come up with the money. Now, sensing a trap set by Lowenberg, she responded to his question with the utmost care.

"You cannot value a life with money, Mr. Lowenberg. . . . I am not stating a price on my husband's life."[14]

Her response didn't stop Lowenberg, and the trap was sprung. If his life was worth more to you than $100, why did you give $40 to Saetta, a man you professed to have not liked after he had told you that he had just killed your husband? When Anna fumbled with her response to this accusation, Lowenberg repeated himself again and again, his voice getting louder each time.

"You gave $40 to a man," said Lowenberg loudly for the fifth time, "whose company you didn't approve of to help him, you testified to on direct examination, to leave town, is that right?"

"I didn't have no other choice."

"I didn't ask you that. Please answer my questions. Did you, yes or no?"

"I had to, yes."

"Did you yes or no," screamed Lowenberg, "don't fence with me, answer the question!"

This was about all Dan Prior could take. "The witness is not deaf and she does not come from the Bronx!"

"Neither do I," shouted Lowenberg in return, "I will yell if I don't get the answers to the questions!"[15]

The shouting match continued with no intervention from Judge Gallup. With no immediate censure from the judge, Lowenberg bore down just as hard as he could on Anna Antonio, hoping that she would break down and confess to planning the murder of her husband. To Anna's credit, she, too, in her own way could be just as stubborn. Several times she told Lowenberg that although she gave Saetta the forty dollars, she steadfastly believed that he was lying. She didn't believe that Saetta had killed her husband and gave the money to him only out of fear for her own safety. She was afraid of his threats, afraid of the two men from New York, afraid of him when he was arrested, and still afraid of him while he was in jail. Lowenberg remained unconvinced. Toward the end of his questioning of Anna, he began to repeat himself in the hope that the exhausted witness might change her testimony. Prior recognized this technique and spoke out against it, reminding the court that her previous answers were recorded in the court minutes. Judge Gallup overruled Prior, and Lowenberg continued asking questions. Anna did her best to answer each of them, but when she hesitated once, Lowenberg cynically asked, "Is your memory so bad?"

"When you shoot questions every minute it is."[16]

Lowenberg grilled Anna Antonio on the witness stand for almost two and a half hours, punctuated by frequent outbursts from Dan Prior. In the midst of the numerous questions Lowenberg asked of Anna, many of which Prior objected to as being repetitious, Anna seldom changed her original testimony. On one point she remained firm. A short while before he concluded his cross-examination, Lowenberg interjected a scenario.

"Isn't it a fact that all of this is being conceived in your own mind to effect the death of these two men and pull yourself out so you can go back to the suitor that you had some years ago?"[17]

Her answer was a resounding "No."

The specter of another suitor had not disappeared.

15

"WHO IS TONY PINTO?"

Dan Prior stared intently at his client seated on the witness stand. Every so often he would gently nod his head in affirmation to the responses she provided to the sharp-tongued Lowenberg. Pleased with the way she had conducted herself, Prior was thankful that Anna hadn't been goaded into losing her temper while testifying. In fact, the press made more of the fact that Lowenberg had been quite dramatic with his temper tantrums than the little lady, who had to be constantly reminded to raise her voice. She had weathered a storm, but there was no safe harbor in sight. The Lowenberg tempest momentarily passed, and Prior was not naive enough to think that there would be a settled calm with the assistant district attorney, Joseph J. Casey.

Unlike Lowenberg, who could be sarcastic and theatrical in his court oratory, Casey was different. He shared the aggressiveness of Lowenberg but was far less abrasive. Polished, with a smooth, gentle manner, Casey was keenly aware that Anna Antonio had been through an ordeal with the previous cross-examiner. The slight woman sitting before him had just undergone a merciless interrogation at the hands of Lowenberg. He had questions to ask, but he would use a gentler approach. It was Prior's hope that she wouldn't be lulled into a false sense of security while being questioned by the soft-spoken, amicable Casey.

Joseph Casey began by asking Anna if she had been entirely truth-ful in answering the questions posed by Lowenberg. Anna nodded, remarking that everything she had said about Vincent Saetta was as she remembered it. As to Sam Faraci, Anna shrugged her shoulders. "I don't know the man." She reassured Casey that had she known Faraci, she would have certainly told him anything she knew.[1]

Satisfied for the moment, Casey made his way to the evidence table and retrieved a handwritten letter. He presented it to Anna and with-out asking her to read it, calmly asked her if she recognized the signa-ture at the bottom of the page. Years later, Lowenberg recalled the inci-dent: "For almost a full two minutes Anna sat in a state of shock staring at the letter fluttering in her hands. The [assistant] district attorney regarded her calmly, allowing the jury to observe the defendants re-action to this surprise piece of evidence. I too, watched her carefully. I had no idea what was in the letter."[2]

Lowenberg wasn't the only one watching Anna Antonio. John Del-aney noted that the letter instantly struck "a sore spot" as "a look of ag-ony came over her face," and she appeared to be "in a pitiful state."[3]

When Anna lifted her head and looked at Casey, she said in a weak, halting voice that the signature was hers. Removing the letter from her trembling hands, Casey once more asked her if what she had testified earlier—"I did not love any other man during my married life"—was true.[4] She shook her head and quietly said that everything she had said was the truth.

"Who is Tony Pinto?" asked Casey.[5]

As second- and third-generation Americans had been constantly in the habit of misspelling and mispronouncing Italian names, Anna should have told the court that she had no idea who "Tony Pinto" was and, furthermore, she didn't know anyone by the name of "Sal" or "Salvatore" Antonio. Her husband's name was Sam, and Tony Penta, not Pinto, was her husband's nephew.

Anna told the court that after her marriage to Sam, she lived with his parents on their farm in Wolcott. In addition to the newlyweds, there was a boarder, of sorts, Tony Penta. After his mother was committed to an asylum, Tony became a hired man on the Antonio farm. When Sam eventually sold the family farm in 1929 and moved to Albany, the entire family followed. Here, the two-bedroom apartment at 146 Clinton Street resembled a tenement apartment in the Little Italy section of New York City. Sam, Anna, and little Phyllis shared the flat with Mary and Peter DeSisto, Tony Penta, and the aged Frank and Felicia Antonio. In time, the DeSistos moved out on their own, taking Frank and Felicia with them, leaving only Tony. Anna testified that Tony Penta had been living intermittently with them for about ten years as they drifted from one apartment to the next in the capital region. This changed, however, in May 1931. After the death of Anita, followed by the birth of Frankie, Tony moved out permanently. "I wasn't able to take care of them all," she told Casey.[6]

"Now then," said Casey, glancing at the envelope clipped to the letter, "who is Mrs. Winters with particular reference to Tony?"[7]

With a deep sigh, Anna told him that Mrs. Winters was Anna Penta Winters and that she was Tony's sister. Anna Winters lived at 584 Masten Street in Buffalo, New York. The last time she had seen her was at Union Station in Albany in November 1931. When Casey questioned her about their meeting, Anna freely admitted that Tony accompanied her to the station. It was here, Anna said, that she confided in Anna Winters that her marriage to her uncle was unraveling and that she was seeking a divorce.

It was the first time she had mentioned a divorce during the trial, and it had a wildfire effect. Everyone in the court leaned forward in their seats, hoping to catch the gossipy details. Casey had already piqued their interests when, after a bit of prodding, he got Anna to admit that their on-again, off-again boarder Tony was close to her age. Sensing his sought-after infidelity motive, a jubilant Lowenberg sat by anxiously to hear all the particulars.

In August 1931, a short while after the death of Anita, Anna asked Albany attorney Lester Bolch to come to their Teunis Street apartment. Casey was about to ask what had transpired when Prior interrupted. This is dangerously close, claimed Prior in his objection, to violating a tenet held most sacred by the law community, that of attorney-client privilege. Casey argued that the conversation between Anna, her husband, and attorney Bolch was simply a conversation and should be admitted as evidence as Anna had not officially retained him as her lawyer. Prior

Anna and Sam Antonio in happier times (Antonio family)

New York Central Railroad brakeman, Sam Antonio (Antonio family)

Above: In spring 1931, Sam and Anna moved to the second floor at 3 Teunis Street in the south end of Albany. This image of the boarded-up building was taken in 1982. Since then, the building has been renovated and is currently occupied. (Historic Albany Foundation)

Left: The youngest of the Antonio children was Frankie, seen here in the living room at 3 Teunis Street. (Antonio family)

After several phone calls, Anna Antonio agreed to meet with Vincent Saetta at the Leland Theater on South Pearl Street. The conversation that took place in the ice cream parlor adjacent to the theater lobby was variously interpreted at the trial. (Albany Institute of History and Art)

The final meeting between Anna Antonio and Vincent Saetta took place on Easter Sunday morning at the intersection of Columbia and Broadway. After giving Saetta forty dollars, she went home, and Saetta, with Sam Faraci and Gertrude King, went to New York City. (Albany Institute of History and Art)

People's Exhibit Number 4, "Photograph showing scene of crime" (Trial Transcripts)

Above: An elegantly attired Vincent Saetta stares intently at the camera for his mug shot. (New York State Police, William H. Flubacher Papers)

Left: The lead investigator for the Antonio murder case was Corp. William H. Flubacher of the New York State Police. (New York State Police, William H. Flubacher Papers)

Above: As no photographer was present at the morgue, Flubacher obtained this image of Sam Antonio in his coffin from undertaker John M. Zwack and retained it for his records. (New York State Police, William H. Flubacher Papers)

Left: Dan Prior (*right*) with his most famous client, Jack "Legs" Diamond (Library of Congress)

Ever the opportunist, Sam Faraci signed his confession first in hopes of receiving leniency from the district attorney, John T. Delaney. (New York State Police, William H. Flubacher Papers)

The Third Precinct Station House on Pearl Street, where Vincent Saetta and Sam Faraci were held incommunicado for sixteen days while authorities attempted to piece together the murder of Sam Antonio and obtain their confessions. (Albany Institute of History and Art)

Constructed of granite and limestone, the neoclassical-style Albany County Supreme and County Courthouse on Eagle Street as it appeared at the time of the trial. The sheriff's motorcade that brought the three defendants to the courthouse routinely drove around the block and used a rear entrance to avoid spectators and the press. (Albany Public Library, Pruyn Collection)

Left: Judge Earl H. Gallup was firm in his belief that Anna Antonio, Vincent Saetta, and Sam Faraci would receive a fair trial in his court when tried together. (Acme Newspictures, Inc.; author's collection)

Below: The district attorney, John T. Delaney (*standing*), insisted that all three defendants were guilty of murder. Anna Antonio's attorney, Daniel H. Prior (*seated, middle*), disagreed. (International News Photo; author's collection)

At the insistence of their aunt Concetta Cappello, Anna's daughters, Phyllis and Marie, were sent to St. Vincent Female Orphan Asylum on Elm Street. After the execution of their mother, the girls were taken from the orphanage by another aunt, Mary DeSisto. (Albany Institute of History and Art)

Phyllis and Marie at St. Vincent Female Orphan Asylum (Antonio family)

Adjacent to the courthouse was the equally impressive State Court of Appeals building. One of the dissenting appellate judges was Irving Lehman, brother of Gov. Herbert Lehman. (Albany Public Library, Pruyn Collection)

While the Antonio children played in the hallway, Gov. Herbert Lehman listened as Dan Prior, Henry Lowenberg, and Charles Duncan pleaded for mercy for their clients. (Acme Newspictures, Inc.; author's collection)

An early view of the Death House at Sing Sing Correctional Facility. The last memory Phyllis Antonio has of her mother was Anna bouncing a red ball against the inside courtyard wall. (Ossining Historical Society Museum)

Outspoken critic of the death penalty, Sing Sing prison warden Lewis E. Lawes (Lewis Lawes Papers, Special Collections Lloyd Sealy Library, John Jay College of Criminal Justice/CUNY)

In the spring of 1934, Phyllis and Marie went to Sing Sing prison for what would be their final visit with their mother. Patsy Cappello took this photograph in front of the entrance to the Death House. (Antonio family)

Before each execution. Robert G. Elliott meticulously inspected each nut, bolt, screw, and leather strap of the electric chair. The chair was removed from Sing Sing Correctional Facility in 1971. (Ossining Historical Society Museum)

Above: The hearse bearing the remains of Anna Antonio leaves Sing Sing prison. (International News Photo; author's collection)

Left: The Antonio girls had fond memories of their uncle Peter. The same could not be said of his wife, the vindictive Mary DeSisto. (Antonio family)

vehemently disagreed. She contacted him, and their conversations were confidential. Lowenberg, however, was eager to hear any details of infidelity that could come to light and was just as eager to embarrass his nemesis. "I think Prior once said he wanted everything in the case," announced Lowenberg in a mocking tone, "and I am in favor of having everything in the case."[8]

Frustrated, Prior turned to Judge Gallup for a ruling on his objection. Incredibly, the judge seemed to waffle on the subject. Without delving into specifics, he said that some of the testimony could be accepted. Still, Prior objected, and Casey finally withdrew the question. It was far more important to keep Tony Penta in the minds of the jury than a divorce lawyer who had visited the Antonio apartment on just one occasion. It would be better to know how many times Tony Penta visited her while she was in the Albany County Jail.

Much to Casey's surprise, Anna said that Tony visited her twice, maybe three times the past year. This wasn't what Casey expected, but it was exactly what Prior needed. Three visits in one year could hardly be construed as the behavior of two people who were deeply in love and committed to each other.

Casey returned to the evidence table and retrieved another letter. Still shaken by the first letter, Anna's pallor dimmed even more with the prospect of another letter. Casey glanced at the letter and asked Anna if it was true what Mrs. Winters had written about her relationship with Tony. Did Mrs. Winters insist that she not wed Tony, "his uncle's wife because of his religion"? Not only did Anna categorically deny that this conversation took place, she insisted her husband had not driven Tony from their 3 Teunis Street apartment.[9]

Prior objected to this line of questioning and objected to having either letter introduced as evidence against his client. These letters were not sworn statements and should be regarded as nothing more than hearsay. In this he was partially successful. Casey set that letter aside, walked to the witness stand, and took the other letter from Anna's hand. Over Dan Prior's stern objection, Casey introduced People's Exhibit 36, Anna's letter to Mrs. Anna Winters, into evidence. As soon as Judge Gallup ruled it as admissible, Prior did an about-face and insisted that the letter be read aloud to the jury. He said his client had nothing to fear from its contents or what could be construed from the letter. In contrast, Lowenberg, too, wanted it read aloud—but for other reasons. Positive that this piece of evidence was literally the smoking gun that tied Tony and Anna together, he bellowed, "In fact, the earlier it is read the better I will like it."[10]

Casey paused for a moment, looked at Anna, and asked her again if what she had said to Lowenberg earlier was the truth, that there was no other man in her life. She assured him that what she had said was as it had happened. "Read all of it," said Prior, "I offer it."[11]

"Everything is here," said Casey, "People's Exhibit 36 in evidence, 4/11/33."

Albany, N.Y. January 7, 1932

Dear Anna,

I suppose you will be surprised to hear from me, but I have been so busy that I really haven't found time to write before. Also Anna I have seen the letter that you wrote Tony and I feel as if I ought to write and give you an explanation of what I started to tell you on the train. It is this Anna, I simply got tired of married life and I wanted a divorce. I do yet. Sam promised me I could have one after the holidays, but after waiting he has changed his mind. I have stopped caring for him and told him so. I am not blaming anyone. I heard things and also he done things to me that I can't like him anymore. I don't like to write what it is, he is your uncle. Maybe you know his ways and maybe you don't I could not stand for most things. Maybe he got away with it with his first wife, he can't with me. Also Anna don't think Tony would get in trouble through me because I think a lot of him and I know he does me. We have stuck together through a lot of fights and he didn't like to see me hurt. That's why he had to leave us and room among strangers. I know he would never tell you so that's why I am writing. We have been pals more than 10 years and I'll do anything for him and that's all there is to it. I am sorry you misunderstood. I thought you were different because that was what they all thought. Last time the kid was with me. Also I sent you Tony's address because he asked me to. Well Anna, it's too bad to live so far away. I think I can explain a lot better if I could talk to you. Also I went to New York alone for the funeral and I think Victoria looks awful bad I think, and so does the doctor that she is getting. Write soon and please don't mention anything. Also I'm coming to see you real soon.

Love to all, I remain as ever, Anna

"Now, Mrs. Antonio," said Casey, "do you still say that everything you told Mr. Lowenberg this morning was the absolute truth?"

"It was," said Anna.[12]

The letter Casey read aloud to the jury raised questions that were never addressed or answered. When Anna Antonio penned the lines that she and Tony "have stuck together through a lot of fights," someone—and this included Dan Prior—should have asked what these verbal or physical altercations were about. Any first-year law student knows that abuse of any form is grounds for a divorce. This passage and "he done things to me" opened up new insight into the troubled Antonio household.

More importantly, when Anna penned that "I just got tired of being married," it didn't sound like a woman who was anxious to obtain a divorce for the purpose of remarrying. She tried to straighten out the misunderstanding that her husband's niece may have had regarding her relationship with Tony. "We have been pals for 10 years, and I'll do anything for him and that's all there is to it." This expressed no desire, no passion, and no desire to marry Tony. They were friends who experienced difficult times under the roof of Sam Antonio's home.

Dan Prior never asked how the district attorney came into possession of the letter, but Anna Antonio knew the instant Casey placed it in her hands. The letter in evidence was a particularly hard blow for Anna, an indication that yet another member of the Antonio family had turned against her. First, it was Sam's sister, Mary Desisto, who testified against her at the trial, and now it was a niece, Anna Winters. Anna had confided in her, trusted her, and deemed her a friend. If the letter was that important as to be introduced as evidence, why didn't Casey contact the recipient? Why wasn't Anna Winters, living in Buffalo, brought in to testify? She could have told the court details of her conversation with Anna and Tony at Union Station. At the same time, if Tony was so important, call him in as well. He was closer yet, residing in Albany.

Casey returned the letter to the evidence table and resumed his cross-examination. His efforts would now be directed in trying to have Anna reverse or amend any statements she made when she became a "person of interest" or a viable suspect in the murder of her husband. What this involved was a lengthy recitation of testimony that had been previously obtained. In effect, the questions Delaney had asked the police and detectives were the same questions Casey would now ask Anna. This repetition of testimony was tedious and to some extent boring. From the Steamburg arson, to the falling out between Sam and Vincent Saetta, to her meeting at the Leland Theater, to the forty-dollar payoff and promise of insurance money—it all seemed like an incessant harping upon old testimony that yielded no new information.

When Casey confronted Anna with her initial meeting with sister-in-law Mary DeSisto when viewing Sam's body lying in the casket, Prior protested. "That has been gone over a least a half dozen times and I object."[13] And when Casey attempted to ask Anna about specific conversations she had had with Flubacher, he again protested. "I submit already gone over," said Prior, "This is a mere repetition and a waste of time."[14] Lowenberg, too, lost patience with Casey. "I submit that has been in five dozen times."[15]

Nevertheless, Casey continued questioning the defendant. He purposely asked Anna questions that were not in chronological order in an effort to confuse her. In this he was successful. When pinned down to exact times and places certain conversations took place, she replied, "I can't remember" or "I can't recall." Casey demanded specifics, especially those mentioned in her signed confession. Was her memory so poor that she could not recall what she had said?

"In the state of mind I was in that night," she said, "I was liable to say anything."

"You were dazed, is that right?"

"Wouldn't you be if you got taken out of your bed at 12 o'clock at night?"[16]

It was an understandable explanation, one that brought mild laughter to the courtroom but obviously not the answer Casey wanted. He asked her if she recalled signing her confession at 3 A.M. at the precinct.

"I don't know," she said, "I know you were all questioning me. You had me half crazy. That is the only thing I remember."

"Were you in a daze then?" asked Casey.

"I had not gotten over being frightened, if that is what you mean. I didn't know what I was being held for. They promised to take me home."[17]

The "hop-scotching around" method of questioning Casey employed paid off. Earlier in the trial, many recalled Anna had stated that she deemed her husband responsible for, as she said, putting little Anita "six feet under." Wishing to explore this as a mother's revenge motive, Casey began a series of questions concerning Anita. With questions that demanded yes or no responses, Anna tried desperately to explain the circumstances surrounding her daughter's death from lobar pneumonia.

Casey was about to question Anna about the diagnosis presented by Dr. Louis DeRusso when Prior suddenly cut him off. He not only objected to the way the question was presented, but he reminded everyone that Anna was not a medical expert. "That's only part of it," said Prior as he turned toward Judge Gallup. "She is entitled to tell all. He cannot bring out a bare statement without permitting the witness to tell the whole statement. . . . I submit that she is entitled to finish her answer."[18] For once, Gallup agreed.

"He told me," said Anna, recalling what Dr. DeRusso had told her, "that I ought to go down on my hands and knees and thank God he took her, because if the child had lived, she would not have been right, and he said the baby would have been—I can't explain it to you, she would not have been right."

Casey, seeing how shaken Anna was by recalling the death of her child, lowered his voice and softly asked, "Would not have been normal?"

"That's right," said Anna, "you could ask him."

"And you blame your husband?

"I do."[19]

Casey knew it was time to back off. To pursue this line of questioning any further could prove disastrous. To ask her, in the emotional state she was in, why she felt her husband should shoulder the responsibility of the death of a child could go either way. If she suddenly became hysterical, sobbing incessantly on the witness stand, it might draw a great deal of sympathy from a jury of married men with children. If she offered a fairly plausible explanation as to why her husband hastened the death of the child, it might help in her defense. This was a gamble Casey was unwilling to take.

Casey asked only a few more questions, and when he was finished, stepped aside. Prior took his cue, and it was his time to gamble. Having earlier failed to get a mistrial declared, Prior stood up, looked at Judge Gallup, and announced, "I am willing the jury be instructed by the court before the witness leaves the stand—"

A horrified Anna Antonio stared at Prior in disbelief, and, crying out, said, "You want the jury to think—"

"—to suggest," said Prior, trying his utmost to alleviate her fears, "any questions *they* would like to ask the witness."

"Do not volunteer anything," instructed Judge Gallup.

"But Judge Gallup," pleaded Anna, "he wanted the jury not to think something underhanded."

"Do not talk to me," said Gallup.

"I'm sorry."

Waving his long arm toward her and motioning with his hand, Prior said, "Come down near me. You are tired out."

John Delaney, who hadn't said one word in all the time Anna Antonio was on the witness stand, sprang to his feet and shouted, "I object to the remark and move to strike it from the record!"[20] Prior scornfully turned toward his adversary. Clearly, Delaney wanted no display of compassion for Anna Antonio to be part of the trial transcript. The court stenographer, however, not hearing a ruling by the judge, dutifully recorded the statement.

16

THE RAT

Charles Duncan could not have been more pleased with Anna Antonio's testimony. On two occasions she had steadfastly denied knowing his client. Except for the one instance when she had prepared a late-night meal for Faraci and her husband, Anna claimed to have not known him. Faraci, she said, had been to the apartment on that occasion and only that occasion. She also denied that Faraci was present in the apartment as a member of the Steamburg arson gang. Duncan realized that if he was going to be successful in his defense of Faraci, he would have to put as much distance as possible between his client and Vincent Saetta. Duncan believed that the only way to do this was to put Sam Faraci on the witness stand. This was a gamble as great as that of Prior's, but Duncan saw no other recourse. Faraci had made many conflicting statements and, as with the others, had signed a confession. Now it was time for Faraci to talk his way out of the corner he had backed himself into. From the day he set foot in America, Sam Faraci had been a self-preservationist. He wouldn't sell his soul to save himself, but he would sell yours. Friendships, family, and loyalty faded into the background when it came to saving himself.

Sam Faraci had the dubious distinction of being the only defendant with practical experience. This wasn't the first time he sat in a witness chair. Unlike Anna Antonio, who was visibly shaken and uncomfortable, Faraci had been there before and knew what to expect. Under the guidance of his attorney, Sam Faraci answered a series of questions that had only one end in sight and that was to elicit as much sympathy from the jury as possible. Here, he performed beautifully. In his broken English mixed with a thick Italian accent, Faraci recounted the hardships he endured in his first years in America. He worked on a small farm to save enough money to bring his wife and daughter from Sicily and was also employed at a canning factory, working long, hard hours to support a growing family. "I got nine [children]," he said, "four dead."[1]

Faraci admitted that he wasn't perfect. He had made mistakes. Faraci told the court that he had served time in prison and learned from the experience. After obtaining an early release from Auburn State Prison (being careful to omit that he went back to prison), Faraci said he was reunited with the family for whom he professed the deepest affections and immediately found employment in the only work that required his limited skills—that of a house painter in Geneva. As the economy in the 1930s faltered and painting jobs became scarce, Faraci said he had to look for work elsewhere to support his family. This is the reason, he told the court, that he relocated to Albany, in the company of Gertrude King.

Faraci, who had been married twenty-four years and claimed that he was loyal to his wife, said that his relationship with King was of a "friendly" nature. Duncan quietly brushed prostitute Gertrude King aside, focusing instead on the other "friends" Sam Faraci made in Albany, notably Sam Antonio and Vincent Saetta.

Needing little encouragement from his attorney, Faraci went to great lengths to tell everyone in the courtroom how accommodating he had been to both men. He was a talker. Faraci named the restaurants they dined at, the pool halls they frequented, and the speakeasies where they drank. He made himself out to be a good fellow and a friend to those in need. He didn't mind chauffeuring Sam Antonio to Schenectady in exchange for a few bucks or a tank of gas or Vincent Saetta to pool halls in the Gut. When Saetta told him about a job he had planned and needed a ride to Uncle Jack's Pawn Shop, Faraci, naturally, complied.

Faraci expressed bewilderment when Vincent Saetta presented him with the fifty-cent hunting knife and asked him to keep it for him in his car. "What are you going to do with it?" Saetta replied, "You mind too much. That is my business."[2]

For the most part, the prosecution team of Delaney and Casey let Faraci alone. Lowenberg, too, seemed unimpressed, at least for the moment. Riddled with half-truths, the pawnshop testimony Faraci offered paled in comparison to what he claimed had happened up to and including the attack on Sam Antonio. What Duncan needed—a believable alibi from his client—wasn't what he got. Faraci wove a fanciful tale of fact, fantasy, and pure fiction in a forlorn attempt to proclaim his innocence.

For the next hour, Sam Faraci retraced his movements on the night of the murder. Most of the early hours of that fateful Saturday night, he said, were spent chauffeuring Vincent Saetta from one place to the next in the Gut in an attempt to shake down those who owed him money. To reward him for this service, Saetta treated him and Gertrude King to a spaghetti dinner at Paul's Restaurant on Green Street. After dinner, Faraci drove Gertrude King home and then he and Saetta met up with Sam Antonio at Pete's Pool Hall on Madison Avenue. Now it was Sam Antonio's turn to be chauffeured around the Gut.

Throughout this recitation, Faraci maintained a naive air as to what was happening. When Saetta suggested they go to Hudson for a good time, Faraci claimed he spoke out against it. "I don't want to go any place because it is too late . . . I am leaving home for a few hours more. I promise the girl I take her home this morning. Two o'clock now. Too late to go anywhere to have a good time."

"You got lots of time," Saetta reportedly said, "only takes about a half hour to go to Hudson, come on, we go to Nigger Rose."[3]

For a moment, Duncan paused and asked where in Hudson was this "Nigger Rose." Faracci's reply of Diamond Street required no further explanation as this was the notorious red-light district of Hudson.

"Come on," he recalled Sam Antonio as saying, "I like to go down to Nigger Rose. For Christ sake, come on. I don't work in the morning. Come on, we go." Faraci insisted that he did not want to go and agreed to drive them there only when pressured by both men.[4]

Not wishing to hear any of the details concerning their visit to Hudson, Judge Gallup interrupted Faraci and asked how they were seated in his car while on Castleton Road. Faraci said, in a rare moment of truthfulness, that he sat in the middle and Vincent drove the car, leaving Sam on the passenger side. When it came time to tell his account of the murder, Faraci used a portion of his first confession, mixed in parts of his second confession, and, for good measure, added new material. Lured to darkened Castleton Road, Faraci wanted everyone to believe that he had no idea what Saetta had in store for Sam Antonio. After begging Saetta several times to stop the car because he had an upset stomach, Faraci said everything happened quickly the instant Saetta brought the car to a stop. Once outside, Faraci ran to the rear of the car. "My bowels was moving, and I thought I could take a crap. And at the time I try and put my pants down and take a crap. I hear a noise, bang, bang, bang, bang."[5]

"What was the next thing that happened?" asked Duncan.

"I raised my pants and I went to the car, but didn't button my pants, just put the belt up, and I saw Vincent . . . I see one on top of the other in a ditch, and I went to the car and Sam Antonio says 'Sam, help me,' and I don't do nothing, that's when I ran to the car. . . . I see one on top of the other. I pull one guy out, I don't know which one it was in the first place, and when I pull him out I know it was Vincent. I said 'Vincent, what have you done?' He said, 'You don't know anything about it. He done plenty a dirty trick on me. The less you know the better off you are.' I says, 'All right. You should have done things in your own car. Police in Albany know you drive my car. They going to come after my car.' He says, 'that's all right, nobody see you and keep your mouth shut.'"[6]

Faraci wanted everyone to believe that he was in the wrong place at the wrong time. It was Saetta, he said, who shot the unarmed Sam Antonio. And it was Saetta, he insisted, who slashed away at Antonio as he lay mortally wounded in a muddy ditch. As they sped away, leaving Sam Antonio in a muddy culvert, Faraci claimed that Saetta threatened to kill him if he didn't dispose of the pistol. When they arrived in Albany, it was Saetta, said Faraci, who needed to wash the mud and blood from his hands and clothes.

Sitting on almost the edge of his seat, Dan Prior braced himself for the next part of Faraci's story—the forty-dollar get-out-of-town money. After making a phone call, Saetta returned to his apartment and told Faraci to get Gertrude King and meet him at the corner of Broadway and Columbia. Still clinging to his innocent-bystander defense, Faraci said that after making his way to the corner, he and King saw Saetta talking to a woman. When Duncan asked if it was the defendant, Anna Antonio, Faraci shook his head. "I can't swear to that," he said, "I never seen that woman before. Only once, I was up at the house and had something to eat. I can't say she was her or not."[7] Prior was elated as Faraci once again denied knowing his client.

There was, however, someone who could identify her. If Faraci couldn't be sure it was Anna Antonio, why not ask the person who was sitting next to him in his car, Gertrude King? As the only other witness to the forty-dollar exchange, King was not called as a witness. Days before Faraci took the witness stand in his own defense, Charles Duncan asked John Delaney if the police were still in contact with King. Assured that she wasn't currently in police custody, Delaney informed him that she was still in the Albany area and could be easily located.

Delaney had no intention of issuing a subpoena to Gertrude King. As the one person responsible for influencing Sam Faraci to confess to his part in the murder, Delaney knew that Gertrude King could not identify Anna Antonio. In the impromptu lineup at the precinct after they were picked up in Poughkeepsie, Delaney asked Anna Antonio if she recognized Saetta and Faraci. Anna denied knowing them, which infuriated Delaney. Standing nearby was Gertrude King, who couldn't identify Anna Antonio. Having relied on a bevy of law enforcement, civil servants, and physicians to bolster his case against Anna Antonio, Delaney wasn't about to call on Gertrude King. Prostitute or not, he wanted only witnesses who could help him win his case to testify. This was a wise move on Delaney's part and a defense error on Dan Prior's part. He should have called Gertrude King to do just that—deny having ever seen Anna Antonio.

Duncan continued to let Faraci tell his side of the story by gently leading him with "What happened next?" style of questions. The trip to New York City was Saetta's idea. It was Vincent Saetta who paid for the gas and hotel rooms, bought him a new pair of shoes, and purchased a new dress for Gertrude King.

Having concentrated on presenting Sam Faraci as an unwilling or unwitting accomplice in this affair, Charles Duncan was now ready to begin the second phase of his defense. The testimony Faraci would now introduce would have nothing to do with the murder and everything to do with police brutality. It wasn't enough that his client had been held for sixteen days without being formally charged with any crime, but during that time Faraci maintained he was subjected to verbal harassment, physical abuse, and starvation at the hands of the police.

Unleashing a flood of obscenities, Faraci vividly recalled the ridicule and abuse he received at the hands of Jimmy Hynes and William Flubacher. "Jimmy Hynes says, 'You are a fucking liar!' and he slapped my face, he slapped mc on the face, and the trooper in the back hit me with the edge of the right hand back of the neck. He says 'If you dirty cocksucker don't tell the truth I will kill you and we will take you down the cellar.'"

"That was Flubacher?" cried Joseph Casey in disbelief.[8] Yes, claimed Faraci, noting that this was just the beginning of his ordeal.

"I done nothing wrong. He says, 'you did.' So Jimmy Hynes run, and he has a long club like this, and he start hitting me on my knees and my leg and say, 'If you don't tell me we will finish you up' now I says, 'I got nothing to tell you, because I done nothing' He says, 'you fucking liar, we will kill you if you don't tell the truth' I says 'I done nothing' they said, 'You are a pimp. You never was any good.'"[9]

Day after day, Faraci said he was dragged from his cell and brought to the dormitory of the Third Precinct, where he was at the mercy of Hynes and Flubacher. After drawing the shade down in the room, Jimmy Hynes began. "Listen, if you don't tell the truth nobody know you are in here. You dago wop. We are going to kill you. You no God Damn good. . . . a guy named Tom, I don't know his last name, so he grabbed my ear, stretch my ear, one in the back hit me with the edge of his hand and he says, 'What are you going to do, tell the truth or we give you the works?'"[10]

Faraci told the court that the "the works" was a blanket thrown over his head and tied about his torso. Unable to see, he told the court that he became a human punching bag, beaten about the chest and head. Knocked to the floor, he recalled being kicked about the ribs. After it was over, he recalled Hynes telling him that he would be killed "a little at a time" and that they would either stuff him in a bag and send him "back to the Old Country" or dump him in the Hudson River.[11] Speaking almost hysterically, Faraci described and repeated these beatings, indicating that he received "the works" almost every day, making the Third

Precinct look like a substation for the Spanish Inquisition. When he was through recalling these horrible events, few in the court believed that he was telling the truth. It was one thing to slightly embellish events, but what he claimed to have happened was unbelievable. John Delaney put it bluntly when he said, "No man can stand what he claimed he got."[12]

The timid lost-soul act that Faraci had played while being questioned by his attorney came to an abrupt end when Henry Lowenberg began his cross-examination. The New York City attorney wanted to make absolutely sure that everyone in the court clearly understood the character of the man sitting in the witness chair. This was no poor immigrant who had struggled to provide for his large family. The hard times Faraci had previously described were of his own doing, contended Lowenberg, and therefore did not deserve sympathy. A man who professed to love his wife and children, yet cavorted openly with a known prostitute as her pimp, deserved no respect. The only person Sam Faraci ever cared about was himself, and Lowenberg wasted no time in trying to prove it. "I want to show that this man has been a rat all his life," he announced to the court, "and I want to show that this man, in order to get himself out of difficulties involved other people in other crimes."[13]

The honest, hardworking persona Faraci attempted to convey was shattered under Lowenberg's withering cross-examination. In addition to farm work, factory work, and doing concrete work on a state road, Faraci said that he finally settled on house painting in Geneva. With prices ranging anywhere from $110 to $700, Faraci claimed that his total income for the year 1931 was "around $1,400 or $1,300."[14]

"And did you support the King girl on the side?"[15]

Employing the same "loving wife" sarcasm he had used when questioning Anna Antonio regarding her relationship with Tony Penta, Lowenberg now set his moral compass directly in the path of Sam Faraci. "So," he began, "you had this woman on the side, didn't you?"

When Lowenberg implied that Gertrude King was a "kept woman," Faraci hesitated, insisting that he didn't understand. "I kept her for company," he said, "but nothing else." Denying any knowledge of American slang, Faraci said the King girl was nothing more to him than a friend.

"You know, Sam," said Lowenberg, "don't you know that she is a street walker—you know what I mean by that?" Sure, replied Faraci, telling the court that as far as he knew, she walked the streets of Albany just like anyone else. Amid the smirks and snickers that were clearly audible in the court, a frustrated Lowenberg questioned him about King's particular occupation and if he had in fact received any of her income. "What she do for a living," responded Faraci, "that is none of my business what she is doing."[16]

Well, if that were true, how could he possibly exist in Albany? How could he afford to make a car payment, buy food, and pay rent? Faraci tried to convey the image that living in Albany was relatively inexpensive. With what little money he had saved from his last stint painting, he was able to pay his rent and put gas in his car. As for food, Faraci said, "I buy everything at once, I buy five or six bushels of potatoes, and I put a bushel of onions in the house and I put ten cases of spaghetti sauce and everything."[17]

The humble existence that Faraci claimed to enjoy in the capital city may have impressed some, but it didn't sit well with Lowenberg. The last honest dollar Sam Faraci made came from the last house he painted in Geneva. Lowenberg wanted to prove that any money he made in Albany was derived from illicit activities. Lowenberg drove his point home: "You are nothing but a small-time racketeer, aren't you?"[18]

Faraci had no difficulty comprehending this idiom and was quick to deny that he was a hoodlum. He had been in trouble once and since that time had reformed, working hard to provide for his family. Lowenberg scoffed at this and told the jury that his arrest in Geneva years ago should not be regarded lightly. Sam Faraci, he said, was part of an active criminal gang that terrorized the citizens of Geneva. He hadn't changed his stripes when he moved to Albany. There was no denying that he was capable of robbery, but could he commit murder?

"No, sir!" proclaimed Faraci, adding that he could not and did not commit any murder.

"You know," said Lowenberg, "that your testimony may be the means of bringing about the death of Vincent Saetta?"

It was a simple question that required a simple answer. As had been his standard routine throughout his session on the witness stand, Faraci carefully avoided giving a definitive answer. Everything he had said under oath, he said, was the truth. From the moment he first met Saetta, up to and including the murder of Sam Antonio and his subsequent journey to New York City, everything was as it happened. He swore that he was not spinning a tale to save himself from the electric chair.

"If anybody is to die for this crime," countered Lowenberg, "you would much rather see Vincent die than you, wouldn't you?"

"No, sir," replied Faraci.

"You would rather die than Vincent?"

"Absolutely."

"Is that right?"

"If I had done wrong."[19]

Over and over again Lowenberg leaned on Faraci in an effort to draw him in as an active participant in the murder, but it was no use. The wily Faraci fended off each accusation. When asked a second time if he or Saetta should go to the electric chair, Faraci answered like a seasoned debater. "I don't like to see anybody die." Every time Faraci proclaimed his innocence, he was in effect pointing to Saetta's guilt. "I don't want to take no rap for nothing I haven't done."[20]

Lowenberg never let up in his accusation of Sam Faraci being a lying narcissist. The great love he professed for the family he had abandoned was needed now, only because he was in trouble. He had turned on others in the past to secure a release from prison, and it was obvious to Lowenberg that he was doing it again. Sam Faraci, the first to confess and sign a confession, was all too willing to rat on anyone, even an old friend, to save himself.

In a last effort to feign innocence and ignorance, Faraci, in his best Chico Marx impersonation, claimed that he was unfamiliar with the term *rat* by casually remarking, "rats, could be rats, could be mouse, or big rats or anything." Lowenberg wasn't amused.

"You don't consider yourself as low as a mouse that crawls do you? You never crawled on your belly in your whole life, did you? You are not crawling on your belly now are you? In any event, you are not ratting now at all? You are not doing that now to save yourself from the electric chair? Mrs. Antonio did not hire you to kill her husband did she?"

Faraci stubbornly resisted. "I never saw her."[21]

Lowenberg was finished with Sam Faraci, but John Delaney wasn't. The district attorney wasn't about to have Faraci walk away from the witness stand without first clearing the air on his claims of starvation and brutality at the hands of one of his favorites, Jimmy Hynes. For the third time, first it was Duncan and then Lowenberg, Faraci told the court of his experiences at the Third Precinct. The stories just grew more horrific each time he told them. He claimed that he was tortured each day, save one, by a sadistic Jimmy Hynes. Faraci swore that Hynes slapped him ("hit me in the puss") repeatedly while uttering every Italian slur imaginable. He signed a confession, he said, only after being continually beaten on the shins with a bat.

"And of course," said Delaney, "that was a heavy club, wasn't it?"

"Big bat."

"A bat?" sighed Delany in disbelief.

"Some kind of bat, I don't know."

"You don't know it and you saw it?"

"It was long," said Faraci using his hands to illustrate, "like this. I don't know."[22]

He should have. A club or baseball bat end was the weapon of choice fifteen years earlier when he was implicated in the assault and robbery of John Michaelson in his hometown of Geneva. To Delaney, it really didn't matter if it was a bat or a club. Even the size of it was not important. The only thing that mattered was that he once more told an unbelievable tale.

The last thing Delaney wanted to do was to differentiate between the character of "Sam the family man" and "Sam the pimp for Gertrude King." Had he been with Gertrude King at the Fair View Inn, near Dresden on Seneca Lake, a year or two before he arrived in Albany?

The talkative Faraci suddenly fell silent. Startled at the shift in questions from police beatings to the roadhouse inn he once managed, Faraci nodded. It was in the summer of 1930, and, yes, he had been with Gertrude King. Having set the bait, Delaney rattled off a half-dozen cities in the state he had traveled to with King, ending in Newburgh, where she was nabbed in a prostitution sting.

A stunned Faraci knew that all of this information, every city he had been to, could have come only from one person—Gertrude King. In the end, his "lady friend" was no friend at all and was just as big a rat as he was.

17

PERJURY AND ATTORNEY CONSPIRACY

It didn't help Sam Faraci's case that his attorney didn't produce one character witness on his behalf. Faraci hadn't been in Albany long enough to forge any true friendships, and because he really didn't have a job, he had no workplace friends either. The situation wasn't much better in Geneva, where he had more enemies than friends and his relations with his immediate family were strained. Lowenberg fared pretty much the same as his client. He, too, was hard-pressed to find character witnesses who could or would speak well of Vincent Saetta. Not only was his reputation in Albany less than exemplary due to a dismissed weapons charge a few years earlier, but at no time during the trial was what he did for employment ever firmly established. In desperation, Lowenberg sought out the Saetta family, many of whom were more than willing to step forward and help out a member of the family. The presence of his mother and three sisters in the courtroom rallying to his side gave the impression that Vincent Saetta was part of a loving and caring family, a sharp contrast with the estranged nature of Faraci's family and the troubled marriage of Anna Antonio.

The three Saetta sisters were not children but adults living in their parents' house at 63-14, Thirty-Ninth Avenue in Woodside, Queens.

There was thirty-year-old Clara, twenty-eight-year-old Emma, and twenty-three-year-old Esther. All three women were asked the same question and essentially gave the same answer with only a slight variation. The most critical factor in Lowenberg's defense of his client was establishing the time Saetta arrived at his parents' house in Queens. Clara and Esther vividly recalled how excited they were on that Easter Sunday morning when their brother Vincent paid them a surprise visit. "As soon as my brother came into the room and woke me up," recalled Clara, "I looked at the clock and it was exactly ten minutes to eight."[1] Esther concurred, "It was almost eight o'clock."[2] Each swore that it didn't matter if it was Easter Sunday or any other day; both of them worked in factories and had, out of habit, always looked at the alarm clock when they awoke. The Saetta girls were pleasant, sincere, and, above all, liars.

When the three attorneys met for the one and only time at Dan Prior's law office on State Street in March 1933 to discuss the trial, Lowenberg was adamant on one subject. "I'm not here to suborn perjury," he said, "I want that clearly understood." Apparently, the New York City attorney had a discerning mind when it came to this subject, especially when it involved witnesses who could help his client.[3] In an attempt to establish an airtight alibi, Lowenberg asserted that it would have been virtually impossible for Saetta and Faraci to murder Sam Antonio, get to Albany, get cleaned up, collect Gertrude King, and speed off to Queens, arriving there at 8:00 in the morning. From Faraci's apartment at 21 Hamilton Street to the front door of Saetta's parents' house in Queens was approximately 160 miles. This trip—which included stops for gas and oil and New York City traffic delays—would have made it impossible for Faraci to push his Oldsmobile coupe to make the trip in less than three hours. Delaney's own men had taken the exact route to the Saettas' Woodside residence and couldn't duplicate this feat.

Delaney let Lowenberg savor the moment. He knew the Saetta sisters were lying in a vain attempt to save their brother from the electric chair. With only one or two witnesses to testify, what good would it do at this point in the trial to charge them with perjury? Besides, Delaney was more interested in hearing what Lowenberg's next witness had to say.

Throughout the latter part of the trial, the press had made note of the increase in the amount of bickering between defense attorneys

Lowenberg and Prior. Delaney was convinced that this was contrived, an agreed-upon strategy between the two barristers to mislead and confuse the jury. This was hardly the case.

Dan Prior learned a valuable lesson in his defense of Legs Diamond. The "unsolved" suspicious murder of his most famous client was a clear indication that the powers to be in Albany did not want a New York City criminal element establishing a base of operations in their city. Now it was Prior's turn to exact the same style of punishment by attempting to persuade the jury that Vincent Saetta was part of a criminal gang trying to establish roots in Albany. After all, it did look a bit suspicious when his family employed a high-profile criminal lawyer from the city to defend him. Vincent Saetta was an outsider and so was his attorney.

Lowenberg was aware of this animosity and used it in his defense of his client. As an Albany outsider, he was convinced that Dan Prior and Charles Duncan had joined together in an effort to save their respective clients at the expense of his client. What better way to prove this than to call either Prior or Duncan to the witness stand? Since Duncan had been reserved and displayed a calm demeanor throughout the trial, Lowenberg reasoned that this would be the safe move. Far better to deal with him on the witness stand than the argumentative and combative Dan Prior.

Duncan made no secret of the fact that he had met with Prior on four occasions, reminding Lowenberg that he was present at one of those conferences before the trial. The meetings, he assured Lowenberg, were of a general nature and did not delve into specifics regarding the defense strategies they planned to use when defending their respective clients. Lowenberg thought differently.

"You and Prior did not get together on the merits of the defense with the view of putting everything on Vincent Saetta, did you?"

"We did not," affirmed Duncan.[4]

This time Lowenberg had gone too far. Throughout the trial, Duncan hadn't crossed swords with Lowenberg. However, this remark was a blatant attack on his professionalism and ethics. It was true, he said, that he and Prior had lunch together almost every day of the trial. However, he assured the court that they never talked about what had transpired in court because it wasn't necessary. If he needed any information regarding Anna Antonio, Duncan said, all he had to do was ask his own client, which he did when he was on the witness stand. Furthermore, nothing Sam Faraci testified to regarding Anna Antonio surprised Duncan. "I never put a witness on the stand in my life," he said, "that I did not know what they were going to say."[5] As for Anna Antonio's presence on the witness stand, Duncan said it was only natural that he didn't know what she would say, but he was nonetheless moved and impressed. "I presumed she would tell the truth," he said of her testimony, "which I believe she did."[6]

Lowenberg fumed at his candor. If Duncan believed in Anna Antonio's innocence, it was just the same as having believed in Vincent Saetta's guilt. Surely, Lowenberg argued, what better proof did one need to illustrate that a conspiracy of sorts existed between Prior and Duncan? The innuendo-like allegation did not go unnoticed. Dan Prior leapt from his chair and objected to it immediately and in a furious rage called Lowenberg to the witness stand. The exchange between the two was sharp and bitter. Delaney and Casey sat by dumbfounded as the two attorneys assailed each other in a crescendo of allegations and insults. Finally, a visibly angry Judge Gallup had had enough. He slammed his gavel on his desk to restore order.

"We are not trying a lawsuit," he declared. "We are trying the case of the People of New York against three defendants. Whether counsel for each and all of the defendants conferred together and what they said to each other in that conference is immaterial and I will exclude it."[7]

The next day, Friday, April 14, brought the last witnesses to testify. They offered little in the form of new information or doubts as to the innocence of any of the defendants. The new motions that followed, introduced by Prior, Lowenberg, and Duncan, were similar to the old motions, and so was the decision handed down by Judge Gallup. Each defense counsel asked again for a separate trial for his client, and each was once again denied. Gallup quickly brushed aside their motions and asked Prior if he was prepared to make his remarks to the jury. Dan Prior attempted to stall, claiming he wasn't quite ready to address the jury. His hope was that the judge would grant a recess until the following Monday, but Gallup wasn't about to comply. "It is twenty minutes after eleven," said Gallup, "you might possibly be through at one o'clock. If you are not through we will stay until you are."[8] It was fairly clear to all that Judge Gallup wanted to continue into Saturday and end the proceedings.

The closing arguments offered by the three defense attorneys were as diverse as the individuals they represented. Their passion, sincerity, and eloquence were a direct reflection of their personalities. Here was their chance to have the last word.

When Shakespeare penned "All the world's a stage," Dan Prior looked upon the court as his stage where he performed. Those who observed the court proceedings were his audience while the judge and jury were his critics. His trial notes were his script and his glasses, perched upon the end of his nose or twirled in a windmill fashion, his only prop. A gifted orator who didn't need a weekend to prepare a speech, Prior could twist a sentence, interject sarcasm, let loose a pun, or argue the finest detail with relative ease.

The case against Anna Antonio, he told the jury, was challenging yet not entirely impossible to comprehend, given the true facts. The district attorney maintained that Prior had not been forthcoming with vital pieces of information. It was true that Sam Antonio was a brakeman for the New York Central Railroad, but he was also actively dealing narcotics in the Gut district of Albany. Therein, asserted Prior, was the true motive for the murder of Sam Antonio. "It was a racketeer falling out between two people," said Prior, "over money ... somebody was gunning for Antonio. You know that and I know that. It was not this woman."[9]

Now it was time to clear up a few misconceptions or misunderstandings that had arisen during the course of the trial. First on his list was the Steamburg arson. Prior told the jury that the first he heard of the creamery fire was when Lowenberg questioned Anna Antonio about her husband's activities in December 1931. What additional proof did anyone need to illustrate the fact that Sam Antonio was more than a brakeman for the railroad? Next, and perhaps just as important, was Henry Lowenberg's oft-repeated supposition that a prearranged pact had existed between Dan Prior and Charles Duncan in their defense strategies. "He has his client and I have mine," exclaimed Prior. "I am in league with nobody. My responsibility is to this little woman and her three children."[10] The very thought of another attorney remotely suggesting that he was working or plotting to send someone else to the electric chair was ludicrous, said Prior, adding that no self-respecting attorney would stoop so low.

Lowenberg was on his feet in an instant, voicing his objection to anything Prior said or implied with regard to him and his client. If it was his intention to irritate Lowenberg, Prior succeeded. In the short span of fifteen minutes, Lowenberg had objected to or voiced his disapproval at least eight times.

Having sufficiently ruffled Lowenberg's feathers, Prior continued by asserting that someone—and he didn't name anyone—had to be responsible for the murder of Sam Antonio. "It was as cold blooded a murder and as deliberate a killing as I ever heard . . . Antonio never had a chance. Antonio was slaughtered like a butcher would slaughter an ox, there is no question about that."[11] Waving his hand and pointing to individual jurors, Prior said he really didn't care what "nefarious rackets" Sam Antonio was associated with because "a human life is a human life and he is entitled to his just as I am entitled to mine and you are entitled to yours. No one has the right to take the life of another human being in cold blood and with a murderous heart."[12]

Sam Antonio wasn't on trial, but his wife was. Pausing for a moment, Prior drew a deep breath, sighed, and said, "Good character is like money in the bank, you can call on it when you need it."[13] As far as his client was concerned, her character was not in question. Several women had testified from different walks of life and nationalities as to the good character of Anna Antonio. "I could have brought twenty-six or more," boasted Prior. Each one of them would have said that her character was above reproach and that she was an exemplary mother to her children.[14] Her character was true; it was her husband's character that was uneven. Sam Antonio, alleged Prior, was a good husband until he turned his attention and efforts to illicit activities. It was at this point that he abandoned his responsibilities as a husband and as a father to his children.

As to the "dirty, filthy dope money" Lowenberg accused Anna Antonio of accepting to maintain their existence in their Teunis Street apartment, Prior asked if anyone could blame her. Sam Antonio was a provider, but not much else. "Yes, he brought them food and all that," said Prior, "whenever he got the money . . . but providing does not make a good father any more than four walls make a home . . . if he had been a decent man to his wife and children he would be here today . . . he would have not started out at half past one in the morning . . . to some house of prostitution run by Nigger Rose in Hudson."[15]

Highly critical of Flubacher for his ability to recite "detail after detail, and conversation after conversation, and act after act," in his testimony about Anna Antonio without the benefit of notes or an official report, Prior was equally critical of Jimmy Hynes for refreshing his memory by reading her confession a week before he was called to the witness stand.[16] The rebuke was mild compared to the drubbing he had in store for his courtroom nemesis.

"I want to show you the type of case that has been conducted here. The meanest, vilest, cheapest and lowest thing that was ever said in a court room where a woman was on trial for her life was when Saetta's council said here the other day, and whether he said is for you men or the newspapers, or for whom I don't know, but he said, 'I am going to show that this woman hired two men to kill her husband other than these two defendants here.' Do you remember that?"[17]

"Am I on trial here or the defendant?" shouted Lowenberg.

"Maybe my judgment as to what is right and wrong differs a bit," countered Prior, "but I would not say that about any man or woman in the world unless I actually intended to prove it and unless I could prove it."[18] Prior was correct. During the trial Lowenberg seemed more preoccupied with destroying the characters of Anna Antonio and Sam Faraci than trying to prove that others were responsible for the murder of Sam Antonio.

"Let me say something to you about insurance," said Prior. Ever since the details of the crime were reported in the newspapers, the public became captivated by yet another "murder for insurance" crime. Prior believed that the only insurance policy in the Antonio household was the ten-year-old Brotherhood policy. He reminded the jury that Metropolitan Life Insurance agent Samuel Weidman had testified that Sam Antonio had intended to drop the expensive Brotherhood policy once the Metropolitan Policy took effect on April 1, 1932. To illustrate his point, Prior walked to the evidence table and, with his glasses perched on the end of his nose, proceeded to read the first page of the life insurance policy to the jury. It didn't matter that the first premium was paid or not; the policy did not take effect until that date. "Nobody," he said, "can collect a nickel on that Metropolitan policy." To accuse Anna Antonio of orchestrating her husband's death for the purpose of collecting this money was totally unfounded. On this point, Prior was wrong. The Metropolitan policy took effect the same day Sam Antonio affixed his signature to the policy.[19]

Lastly, Prior had more than a few things to say about another piece of evidence directed at his client—the Penta letter. The purpose of this piece of evidence and the questions posed by the assistant district attorney, Casey, had but a single purpose and that was to cast moral suspicion on Anna Antonio. The sensationalist nature of this surprise piece of evidence introduced by Casey reminded Prior of the satisfaction a child received from, as he said, "a boy that had found a prize in a grab bag."[20]

Prior didn't have to go to the evidence table to retrieve the letter as he had a copy of it in his vest pocket. Like a high school English teacher, Prior proceeded to read the letter aloud to the jury. Dissecting the letter sentence by sentence, line by line, Prior told the jury that at no point in the letter was there the least bit of suggestion that Anna was actively plotting to get rid of her husband. The only thing she wished for was a divorce. "I don't blame her for getting tired of married life with Antonio," concluded Prior.[21] Of the tumultuous last few months with her husband, Anna wrote of her time with Tony Penta, "I think a lot of him and I know he does me. We have stuck together through a lot of fights and he didn't like to see me hurt." Prior paused for a moment and asked the jury to weigh this statement. "Anything wrong with that? Any motive there? On an innocent statement like that a woman is to be convicted of murder? This is America. We are free men, and fair men and honest men, things like that are not done here."[22] Using every symbol of imagery he could muster, Prior condemned the motives of the prosecution for introducing the letter into evidence. The sole purpose of the letter was to destroy the character of Anna Antonio and "send her to the electric chair, to burn her life in the chair."[23]

With two seemingly heartless thugs, Saetta and Faraci, as defendants, Prior, as always, softened the image of Anna Antonio. He continually referred to her as "that little woman" or quite often "the mother of three children." At the same time, he endeavored to keep the specter of the electric chair in the forefront of the mind of each man on the jury. In his two-hour recitation, which was interrupted sixteen times by Henry Lowenberg, Prior alluded to the electric chair a half-dozen times. Impressing upon the jurors the seriousness of the task before them, Prior made one thing absolutely clear. Three people were on trial, and although they were tried together in the same court, they were entitled to three separate verdicts. "I ask for a fair and square deal," he said. "If there is any reasonable doubt about this woman's guilt at all, you must give it to her."[24]

18

"WHO IS VINCENT SAETTA?"

Charles Duncan never looked on following Daniel H. Prior's speech to the jury as a tough act to follow. He may have lacked the drama and power of Prior's oratorical skills, but he could be, nonetheless, just as persuasive. After dispensing with the niceties of addressing the jury, Duncan got right to the point. "As far as Sam Faraci is concerned, the evidence in the case is not so much."[1] The only real evidence against his client was not one but two signed confessions obtained under dubious circumstances while being detained by the police. "I know just as well as I am standing here," said Duncan, "that Sam Faraci was beaten to get that statement."[2]

Whereas a near hysterical Faraci, while on the witness stand, recalled the numerous beatings he had received at the hands of the police, Duncan recalled a singular statement made by Albany chief of police David Smurl. When Faraci was brought in to be fingerprinted after he had signed his confession, Chief Smurl said to his police officers, "Boys, I don't want you to touch Sam anymore."[3] What further proof did anyone need that Sam Faraci was mistreated? The statement reportedly made by Smurl would have carried a lot more weight in the defense of Faraci had Smurl been sworn in as a witness during the trial. He wasn't and therefore his statement fell flat.

As to who wielded the knife in the murder of Sam Antonio, Duncan said that this was a matter of speculation. If Faraci did the stabbing, as Delaney and Casey charged, were his bloody fingerprints on the knife? Duncan reminded the jury that when fingerprint expert Thomas Straney testified, it was never firmly established that any fingerprints were found. Duncan assured the jury that had Straney discovered any fingerprints on the knife, he would have certainly said so on the witness stand.[4]

So much for the evidence. Now what about motive? Duncan told the jury that there was absolutely no reason and no proof in the world for Sam Faraci to want to kill Sam Antonio. Faraci was not mixed up in the dope racket or participated in the Steamburg arson like Saetta. He didn't have a falling-out with Sam Antonio over money and didn't have a sidewalk brawl with him like Saetta had done. Simply put, there was no bad blood between the two Sams. The most ridiculous thing Duncan had ever heard of was the paltry forty-dollar payment after the murder. Duncan shook his head in disbelief and asked the jury when was the last time they heard of a hit man taking a job *before* he got paid? You get paid before the job, and you usually get a lot more than forty dollars.

Not only did Sam Faraci harbor no grudge against Sam Antonio, he didn't really know Mrs. Antonio. One meal at her house can hardly can be looked upon as a connection between them in this case. And as long as they were on the subject of Anna Antonio, Duncan reiterated what Prior had said earlier. There was no prearranged deal made before the trial in defense of their respective clients.

"Sam Faraci was not a model citizen," concluded Duncan. "Sam Faraci had the misfortune to have been convicted of a crime. Sam Faraci consorted with a prostitute; there is no doubt about that. He admits that and he admitted it to you on the stand. Sam Faraci is being tried for his life for the crime of murder and nothing else, and having been convicted of a crime before and his being in the company of a prostitute is not murder, and it is no more of an indication that he committed murder than your peaceable and pleasant life is that you committed murder; not a bit."

He continued, "I am going to leave it to you gentlemen as I close with my opening statement: For God's sake make no mistake."[5]

As he returned to his seat, Judge Gallup received a nod from the court stenographer. He needed a rest. It was almost 5 P.M. and Henry Lowenberg was expected to deliver a speech to rival that of Dan Prior. After a brief recess, Lowenberg approached the jury box. Given his previous comments during the trial, Lowenberg could be counted on to deliver stinging rebukes, nasty innuendos, and his style of big-city sarcasm. He didn't disappoint.

Standing in front of the jury, Lowenberg gestured toward Dan Prior. "I did not know whether he was trying the case of the People against Henry Lowenberg or whether he was trying the case People against Anna Antonio."[6]

Unlike his predecessors, Lowenberg opted not to have his client take the witness stand. "I did not put him on because I do not have to disprove what the People failed to prove. That is the point I want to make. If you want to believe these two fairy tales that jibe so perfectly you can believe them—but I don't think you will."[7] Since Anna Antonio and Sam Faraci had testified to their dealings with Vincent Saetta, now was the time for Lowenberg to defend his client. Everyone in the court had heard of Anna Antonio's troubled marriage and Sam Faraci's life of painting and pimping. Now it was time to hear all about Vincent Saetta.

"Who is Vincent Saetta?" asked Lowenberg. "Who is this great killer that Mr. Prior would have you believe he is? He is the man who would endanger the life of this poor woman and he is the man who would endanger the lives of small children. Why it is unbelievable. As I sat there and listened to that argument, baseless as it is, it made me smart because it made me feel that Pancho Villa the ex-Mexican bandit, the destroyer of human life and property was just a baby in comparison to what they would want to paint that poor Italian boy."[8]

Lowenberg reminded everyone that gangsters and racketeers of this era were for the most part high-profile criminals who found their way into the newspapers. So, had anyone on the jury, he asked, ever heard of this "poor Italian boy" being bantered about the press side by side with other racketeers? The only problem with this rationale was that this "little Italian boy" he spoke of was not a boy but a twenty-nine-year-old man. The only reason no one had ever heard of him in Albany was that except for an incident a year earlier in which the charges against him were dismissed, Saetta had a clean record. So, who was Vincent Saetta? Lowenberg really didn't say. He never divulged any pertinent details about Saetta. There was no work history, no war record, and little family information to elicit sympathy for his client. Instead of defending Vincent Saetta, Lowenberg chose to point the finger of guilt at the other defendants.

Prior, in his closing statement to the jury, had used the expression "If the truth hurts" when defending Anna Antonio's testimony about her relationship with Vincent Saetta. Now it was time for Lowenberg to do the same. "If I hurt anybody I can't help it," he informed the jury, "if I hurt anybody to get to the truth I am going to hurt that person. That is all there is to it."[9] The first person he intended to hurt was Anna Antonio.

He began first by mocking her previous testimony as a "loving wife," one who "revered and respected" her husband. Her sincerity on the witness stand in describing her home life with Sam Antonio was an act. "It was almost drama," said Lowenberg sarcastically, "but it would be a comedy afterwards."[10] All one had to do was read the letter Anna had written to her husband's niece. Although Prior had contended that the letter was innocent in nature and should be taken at face value, Lowenberg vehemently disagreed. The city attorney looked upon the letter as the most damning piece of evidence in the trial. When Anna wrote that she and Tony Penta were "pals," Lowenberg interpreted that as "lovers." After that letter was read in court, Lowenberg told the jury that it cleared up any misconception one may have had about her future plans if she could not obtain a divorce from her husband. When the divorce was not forthcoming, Anna, he claimed, made other plans to unite with Tony Penta.

"I'll wager now that within the day after she leaves this court if she is acquitted, she will run to the arms of Tony Penta, three children or no three children."

Anna Antonio vaulted from her seat and screamed, "You lie!"[11]

The sudden outburst stunned the crowded courtroom as all eyes turned to Anna Antonio. There was no need for Judge Gallup to reprimand the visibly distraught woman as Dan Prior gently tugged at her arm to return her to her seat. Prior may have been surprised by her outburst but was smart enough to know that her denial was in concert with his earlier statement to the jury regarding her relationship with Tony Penta. For her to sit idly by and let this statement pass without any reaction could possibly be interpreted by the jury that a relationship between the two actually existed, something Lowenberg had said all along.

"Well, now we come to Sam Faraci." Lowenberg didn't deny that a "bosom" friendship had developed between Sam Antonio and Sam Faraci.[12] What's more is that he said a different friendship of sorts had arisen between Sam Faraci and Anna Antonio. After his cross-examination of Faraci, Lowenberg steadfastly maintained that their claims of not knowing each other was a contrived lie. It was Faraci, not Saetta, who was desperate for money. "She hired Sam Faraci to kill her husband," said Lowenberg, "her motive being Tony Penta. That is the curse of this case."[13] It was only natural, claimed Lowenberg, that Faraci, behind on car payments and living off the earnings of his prostitute girlfriend, would agree to a murder scheme in order to reap the profits of an insurance settlement. And as long as he broached the subject of money, Lowenberg offered a different slant to the Steamburg arson.

Like Charles Duncan's arguing the merits as to who actually used the knife in the murder, Lowenberg took the same path by denying his client's involvement in the arson. He claimed it was a ruse. "It never occurred. . . . Just a fantastic tale. Just something conjured in the mind" of Anna Antonio.[14] No one argued that the milk plant was destroyed as a result of arson; it was in all the newspapers, but no one but Anna Antonio made the claim that her husband and Vincent Saetta torched the building. This was a clever scheme on her part to plant the seeds that would eventually grow into a falling-out between the two. "She constantly saw money," claimed Lowenberg, "thousands of dollars, she saw hundreds of dollars, she saw money all the time, it never ended, lots of money."[15] The dispute over the payoff from the Steamburg arson was contrived on the part of Anna Antonio, as Lowenberg said, "to slip another nail in the casket of Vincent Saetta."[16]

Not only was Vincent Saetta not an arsonist, Sam Antonio was not a racketeer. Lowenberg tried to convince the jury that Sam Antonio wasn't the menacing fellow he was made out to be by his wife or Dan Prior. Lowenberg said that he just didn't fit the racketeer mold. For one thing, he had a job, albeit a hazardous one, as a brakeman on the railroad. Most of the racketeers Lowenberg had encountered in the city never wanted to get their hands dirty, let alone put in a full day's work. If Sam Antonio was the racketeer Dan Prior made him out to be, there was the question of money. Where was all the money he made burning buildings and selling narcotics in the Gut? There was no such money, claimed Lowenberg, and contrary to what federal narcotics agent Richard Kelly observed, Sam Antonio was not involved in any illicit activities.

Like Prior before him, Lowenberg was highly critical of the witnesses called to testify against his client. He was highly critical of Flubacher, the lead investigator who didn't keep any of his notes, Jimmy Hynes "the ice cream boy" who assisted the other detectives in forcibly extracting a confession from Saetta, but reserved his most venomous attack for railroad detective Joseph Genova. He was nothing more than "A Doctor Jekyll and Mr. Hyde" to Lowenberg. It was the Italian-speaking detective who weaseled his way into the good graces of Mrs. Saetta in an effort to extract information about her son.[17] Still, his contempt for Sam Faraci remained firm.

In his final attempt to sully the reputation and blatantly accuse Sam Faraci as the true murderer of Sam Antonio, Lowenberg reminded the jury that the Genevan was beset with money problems since the day he arrived in their city. Lowenberg scoffed at the number of homes Faraci claimed to have painted in 1931. "The town must have changed its color because he labored there," said Lowenberg.[18] How could anyone supposedly make all that money in 1931 and then the following year up and abandon his family in order to run off with a prostitute? Lowenberg said that not only was it impossible for him to support his family and take up with Gertrude King, but it was a flat lie. Sam Faraci lived off the earnings of Gertrude King. Earlier in the trial, Lowenberg asked Sam Faraci if Gertrude King was a "kept woman." She wasn't really a "kept woman" as much as he was a "kept man."

"She kept him," said Lowenberg, "That's the point. She kept him and there isn't anything lower on this earth than a pimp and that is what he is, nothing else. There isn't any lower animal known to man that crawls on its belly than a man that will live off the wages earned by a woman selling her body, and that is Sam Faraci, and that is the man who would want Vincent Saetta to go to the electric chair so that he could walk out of this court room."[19] Faraci had no scruples. He could take money from a prostitute as well as take money from Anna Antonio.

Lowenberg concluded his summation to the jury by chiding the way in which his antagonist, Dan Prior, attempted to evoke compassion for

Anna Antonio and her three children. "Don't be swept away by these emotional pleas of mercy," advised Lowenberg, "anybody that makes a merciful plea has a weak case."[20] However, tugging at the heartstrings was an entirely different matter when it came to his client. "I am making an emotional plea," he said on behalf of Saetta, "he has an old mother who is not well ... he should not be turned out because he did not commit the crime ... I have no weak case." Not one to beg for God's mercy the way Duncan and Prior had done, the nonpracticing Jewish lawyer asked the jury to perform its duty by declaring Vincent Saetta not guilty so that he might be able to "live on with his sisters and his mother and his father."[21]

19

"DO EQUAL JUSTICE"

When Dan Prior asked the court that the testimony of John Campion, the Poughkeepsie patrolman who had apprehended Saetta and Faraci, not be allowed in the Anna Antonio case, he established a precedent. From that moment on, a certain degree of confusion arose when the testimony of one witness was accepted for one defendant and excluded for another. The confusion this created was inevitable and quite often led to arguments between the three defense attorneys that could not be ignored. "The bickering among the defense counsel during the trial was characterized by having only one objective," observed a reporter for the *Albany Evening News*, "creating confusion in the jury's mind and make one defendant seem to be less guilty than another."[1]

On Saturday, April 15, John T. Delaney rose from his desk in the courtroom and slowly walked to the jury box. It was a little after 10 A.M., and, like the previous day, the courtroom was filled to capacity. The day before, the last day of the trial, the jury had put in a long day. The jurors listened to four witnesses and the latest motions for a new trial and heard Prior, Delaney, and Lowenberg before retiring at 6:15 P.M. Today, Delaney was rested and so was the jury.

Delaney began by telling the members of the jury that this case wasn't as confusing as the other attorneys might want them to believe.

What he lacked in hard physical evidence (there was no gun and a knife with no fingerprints) he made up for by calling over thirty individuals to the witness stand. He had a solid case and he knew it. Whether contrived or not, Delaney sought to minimize the confusion by presenting a simple fact-based case to the jury with only one end in sight. "Each and every one of these defendants," said Delaney to the jury, "is just as responsible as the other for the death of this man on last Easter morning; each and every one took his or her part in bringing about that death. The woman is just as much a conspirator in that crime as the man who actually fired the shots into his body, or put the knife into the fourteen places that you heard testified here."[2] As far as John T. Delaney was concerned, they were all guilty.

The previous day, Dan Prior expostulated on the virtues of good character, referring to it as "money in the bank" to be called upon when necessary. Delaney disagreed, at least in the instance of Anna Antonio, whom he considered morally bankrupt. He told the jury not to be fooled by the demure and seemingly innocent little housewife. "I say she is no credit to motherhood," said Delaney. "We expect a wife who is an ideal mother. We do not expect a woman who will not shed a tear for her dead husband, who will plot with two other men to kill her husband. She is not a credit to motherhood. A woman who will not resort to the courts for a divorce but plots her husband's destruction, is not entitled to sympathy. She is entitled to condemnation."[3] Never in his career, Delaney told the jury, had he encountered a more coldhearted woman than Anna Antonio. She was as manipulative as Ruth Snyder and just as ruthless. Once Anna Antonio set her mind to doing away with her husband, there was no stopping her.

Could it possibly be that the frail woman with a fifth-grade education sitting in court was capable of all the plot twists and alibis to plan a perfect crime? Apparently, Delaney believed that this was well within the realm of possibility and warned the jury not to underestimate the cunning mind of Anna Antonio. He refreshed the minds of the jurors by telling them how Anna had given them false leads in the initial stages of the investigation. Flubacher discovered that the mysterious letter from the grocer Pacelli was as innocent as the man himself. There was the question of the missing wad of bills her husband purportedly had on his person the night of the murder, and there was the mystery of the Steamburg arson.

Her cunning mind was well at work, said Delaney, when it came time to draw in Saetta. The story of the Steamburg arson was part of her plan to present the image of her husband having underworld connections and at the same time introduce Vincent Saetta. The arson remained an unsolved crime in the western part of the state. Who was to say that Sam Antonio and his gang of burlap-bagged men with kerosene cans were involved? It was a story she told that no one corroborated.[4]

Delaney continued to assail Anna Antonio by insisting that, with the promise of an $800 payoff to Vincent Saetta, she could do away with her husband and take up with her lover. Unlike Dan Prior, who interpreted the letter as an innocent correspondence, Delaney took Lowenberg's approach. The letter Anna Antonio wrote explaining her "just pals" relationship with Tony was much more than that. "This vicious woman who plotted the murder of her husband when she besought him to divorce her so that she might go with Tony Penta." With that, Anna buried her head in her hands and, for the first time, openly wept in court.[5]

While Anna blotted away her tears, Delaney directed his verbal assault on the remaining defendants. Although not quite as harsh as he was with Anna Antonio, the district attorney wasn't going to let them escaped unscathed. Since Vincent Saetta didn't take the witness stand in his own defense, Delancy had no other recourse but to attack his character witnesses. The chorus of claims by the Saetta sisters of having been awakened at or about 8 A.M. Easter Sunday morning by their brother were "pretty well rehearsed" to Delaney.[6] Clearly, they were lying. As for Sam Faraci, Delaney went after him in a roundabout way.

Delaney made no secret about the fact that this wasn't the circumstantial evidence case the defense team had alleged. The most important piece of evidence he had was three signed confessions. Just how he obtained these confessions was the subject of debate and conjecture. Now was the time to clear up any misconceptions on how they were received into evidence.

"When you were selected as jurors," said Delaney, "there was a great howl about third degree methods and brutality."[7] That being said, he went on to remind them that he had paraded a bevy of detectives before them. In each instance they denied that Saetta and Faraci were tortured. There were no beatings or bread-and-water diets. If they were abused, as they had claimed, why didn't they tell Dr. Brenenstuhl?

When Dr. Brenenstuhl testified, he said that he was called to the precinct by the detectives to examine Saetta for "gas in the stomach" and Faraci for "ulcers," which turned out to be indigestion. Why, then, didn't he mention any bruises or marks on either of the two defendants? What Lowenberg alluded to about the beatings inflicted on his client were unproved. And Faraci's performance on the witness stand was simply unbelievable when referring to the beatings he received at the hands of Flubacher and Hynes. "What a mess he made of that," said Delaney.[8]

Not only did third-degree methods not take place, they weren't necessary once Gertrude King was brought in to see Faraci. After that, both men talked and getting signed confessions was relatively easy. It was King who gave Delaney the first break in the case. Faraci turned on Saetta, and Saetta implicated Anna Antonio. "If they are willing to rat on one another," said Delaney, "all well and good."[9]

From the moment Judge Gallup had ruled in his chambers that one trial was sufficient for the three defendants, Delaney was driven by pride, ego, and a sense of duty to present a case to the jury that had only one end in sight and that was to achieve a triple conviction. "Favor none," he said in his parting words to the jury, "sacrifice none, do equal justice, whether it be a man or a woman, if that evidence is there that condemns, do your part under your oaths."[10]

An eerie stillness fell over the court as Delaney walked back to his chair. Judge Gallup broke the silence with a gentle rap of his gavel and declared a recess. Delaney's address to the jury had been the fourth rendition of the same crime the jury had to consider. Each address, with the exception of Duncan's, had been long, passionate, and to some degree tiresome. Now, with the seventeen-day trial nearing completion, Judge Gallup saw no need to rush the jury along.

An hour and a half later, Judge Gallup called the court to order. After thanking the jurors for performing their "patriotic duty" and sacrificing their own personal time to take part in the judicial process, the judge told them that in his estimation, serving on a jury for a capital murder case was the most tremendous responsibility anyone could undertake. He reminded the jury that all three defendants were charged with murder in the first degree, emphasizing the severity of the crime by quoting directly from the law book upon his desk. "The killing of a human being, unless it is excusable or justifiable, is murder in the first degree, when committed from a deliberate act and premeditated design to effect the death of the person killed."[11] In the mind of Judge Gallup, the terms *premeditated* and *conspiracy* were one and the same. He used both terms interchangeably no less than twenty times in his hour-long dissertation to the jury. In essence, he reminded them that it was not necessary for Anna Antonio to be physically present at the scene of the crime to be charged with murder. After a careful review of the evidence, the jury should, if they deem so, find her just as guilty as the person who fired the fatal shot or the one who wielded the knife.

Setting the text aside, Judge Gallup reviewed the facts surrounding the murder of Sam Antonio in a "this happened first" and "this happened next" manner, ending with the eventual apprehension of Saetta and Faraci, which in turn led to the implication of Anna Antonio. Judge Gallup instructed the jurors to determine the guilt or innocence of all three defendants based solely upon the evidence and credibility of witnesses presented at the trial. He readily admitted that of the twenty-five documents and material entered into the court record, the signed confessions of the three defendants were the most important and at the same time most controversial pieces of evidence. He cautioned them to weigh the merit of each confession carefully. "No confession," warned the judge, "is by itself sufficient to warrant a conviction without additional proof that the crime has been committed."[12] If they believed that any of the confessions were obtained in a questionable "involuntarily" manner, they were to disregard it. However, if they believed otherwise, he told them to give the confessions their highest consideration.[13] As two of the defendants had testified on their own behalf, Judge Gallup conveyed his own thoughts to the jury.

The piece of evidence that caused quite a stir was undoubtedly the letter written by Anna Antonio in which she recalled her friendship with Tony Penta. Prior dismissed it, Lowenberg and Delaney embraced it, and Judge Gallup never mentioned it. The judge ignored this controversial piece of evidence while at the same time failing to mention the

Steamburg arson or Sam Antonio's drug trafficking in the Gut. Instead, after reviewing at length Anna Antonio's several clandestine meetings with Vincent Saetta, Judge Gallup broached the subject of her attorney's use of character witnesses. He was unimpressed with any character witnesses and said so. "It is true," said Gallup, "that evidence of good character may of itself create a reasonable doubt of guilt where, without it, no doubt would exist. On the other hand, good character has been repeatedly said not to be a defense for a guilty man."[14] Or in this case, a guilty woman. A reliable witness who could come forward and offer an alibi carried more weight than one who could vouch for good character.

As far as the character witnesses for Vincent Saetta were concerned, Judge Gallup came short of calling the Saetta sisters liars. He instructed the jury to pay close attention to what they claimed. "From Albany to Woodside Long Island, by automobile, it would have been impossible for him [Vincent Saetta] to have been at the scene of the murder at the time it is claimed by Faraci that the crime was committed."[15] This was not in the realm of possibility and neither were the claims of both men that they were persistently beaten by their captors. Each and every witness who had come in contact with both suspects said, the judge testified, "that there were no threats made against or abusive and cruel treatment accorded to either of the defendants at any time."[16]

All the time stressing the importance of the evidence and the credibility of the witnesses, Gallup eased back in his chair and said that the fate of all three defendants was now in their hands. "The responsibility, gentlemen, is with you."[17] With that, the bailiff led the jury out of the court. Six hours later, at 10:23 P.M. on Saturday night, the jury returned with its verdict.

"Gentlemen of the jury," asked the court clerk, "have you agreed on a verdict?"

"We have," replied the foreman.

"What is it?"

"If your honor pleases," said the foreman, "we find the defendants, Anna Antonio, Sam Faraci and Vincent Saetta, guilty as charged."[18]

In what must have seemed an eternity, Judge Gallup postponed the sentencing for four days. On Wednesday, April 19, a small crowd was on hand as the sheriff's motorcade approached the rear entrance of the courthouse. Anna Antonio entered the courtroom first, followed by Saetta and Faraci. She wore a plain black coat and dress, with a felt hat. As she made her way to her seat next to Dan Prior, she caught a glimpse of her brother Patsy in the crowd that had gathered in the courtroom. Patsy and his wife had brought her children, and although eight-year-old Phyllis beamed with joy and waved frantically, her mother did not return even a smile to the child. Seated a few rows behind them, Anna Antonio caught sight of her husband's sister, Mary DeSisto. Only recently had Anna been made aware that her sister-in-law was making designs to adopt all three of her children if she was not exonerated.

After denying motions of all three defense attorneys to set aside the verdict, and at the insistence of the district attorney, Judge Gallup proceeded.

"Vincent Saetta, rise please."

"Saetta," said Gallup in a somber tone, "the duty incumbent upon me is not a pleasant one. . . . It is my duty to sentence you and pronounce the judgment of the Court upon you . . . you will be taken by the Sheriff of Albany county to Sing Sing Prison at Ossining, N. Y. . . . and kept in solitary confinement until the week beginning May 29th, 1933 and upon some day within the week so appointed . . . the Warden is commanded to do execution upon you, Vincent Saetta, in the mode and manner prescribed by the Laws of the State of New York. You may sit down."[19]

Vincent Saetta looked straight ahead in a trancelike stare. He didn't flinch, bat an eye, or betray any emotion whatsoever. He appeared unmoved by the death sentence imposed upon him. He slowly sat down and turned about to acknowledge several of his family members seated a few rows behind him. "The stoic calm," noted one Albany reporter, "Saetta maintained throughout the trial was unbroken."[20]

"Sam Faraci," announced Judge Gallup, "will you stand up? Defendant Faraci, have you anything to say why sentence of the court should not now be pronounced upon you?"

"If your Honor please," replied Duncan, "we have nothing further to say at this time."

"Sam Faraci," said the judge, "what I said with regard to Vincent Saetta applies to your case. Under the contention of the People, the only crime of which you could be found guilty was that of murder in the first degree. You were so found guilty and it is now my duty to sentence you and pronounce the judgment of the court upon you."[21]

Sam Faraci was visibly shaken when Judge Gallup sentenced him to die in the electric chair at Sing Sing prison. Nervously, the ashen-gray Faraci turned and slowly waved his hand toward the only member of his family present, sixteen-year-old Josephine. He then sat down in denial and disbelief. He didn't expect a slap on the wrist, but he didn't expect to receive the ultimate punishment either.

"Defendant Antonio," announced Gallup, "have you anything to say why the sentence of the Court should not now be pronounced upon you?"

Standing next to Dan Prior, her eyes had already begun to swell with tears. Grasping her small purse with white-knuckle fear, Anna twisted her fingers nervously in anticipation of her fate. With Saetta and Faraci both sentenced to die, she naturally feared the worst.

"As I said to the other defendants," said Gallup with a deep sigh, "the duty incumbent upon me is not a pleasant one. As the jury have found the facts under the law, you stand convicted as guilty of murder in the first degree.... the Warden of Sing Sing Prison of the State of New York at Ossining, New York is commanded to do execution upon you, Anna Antonio."[22]

Sobbing hysterically, Anna darted from the side of her attorney and warmly embraced her three children. She hugged, cried, and kissed them. It was a tender scene that ended only when the jail matron gently tugged at Anna's arm. It was time to say good-bye to her children and prepare to move to the Death House at Sing Sing prison. After leaving her children, she said good-bye to her attorney. Prior told Anna, who was still crying, that all was not lost and to keep up her courage. He was taking her case to the Court of Appeals and, if need be, to the governor.

As the remainder of the spectators and family members filed out of the courtroom, Dan Prior paused for a moment, shuffling papers into his leather satchel. He wasn't in any real hurry to leave the courtroom. Outside in the hall, throngs of hungry reporters waited anxiously to get a newsworthy quote from the man who had saved the notorious Legs Diamond but was unable to save a frail little woman. As he turned to leave, he was stopped by Henry Lowenberg, the last person he wanted

to speak to. Dan Prior didn't have any statement for the press and certainly didn't have one for the man who, save the prosecution team, had
worked so diligently to convict his client.

Lowenberg jogged Prior's memory and asked if he recalled their
only meeting at his law office on State Street with Charles Duncan. At
that meeting he asked Prior if he recalled how he, Lowenberg, had insisted that the defense counsels should coordinate their strategies in
defending their respective clients. If they didn't cooperate, Lowenberg
maintained, all three would in all likelihood go to the electric chair.
"Dan, I don't want to rub it in," said Lowenberg, "but I told you so."[23]

Part III

SING SING PRISON

20

THE BIG HOUSE

In 1921, Rev. Edward J. Flanagan embarked upon a totally unique social experiment when he founded Boys Town in Douglas County, Nebraska. Troubled youths, orphans, and those boys who had an occasional brush with the law found a safe haven where Father Flanagan believed they might find their way in an adult world that had forsaken them. "There are no bad boys," he insisted. "There is only bad environment, bad training, bad example, bad thinking."[1] Several years later, on the banks of the Hudson River, Lewis E. Lawes embarked upon a social experiment of his own when he became warden of Sing Sing Correctional Facility.

At first, the Elmira, New York, native had no desire to follow in his father's footsteps and join the ranks of the penal system. As Lawes was to recall later, he tried his hand at a variety of jobs and quickly discovered that some, especially desk work, were not to his liking. It was only after a brief stint in the Coast Guard Artillery that he made the decision to return home and join his father as a prison guard at Elmira Prison.

In the years that followed his apprenticeship at Elmira, Lawes climbed the ladder of several New York prisons. His postings to Dannemora, Auburn, and Hart Island in New York City eventually led to his appointment as warden at the Massachusetts State Prison. Soon his efforts in penal reform came to the attention of others. On January 1, 1919, New York State governor Al Smith offered Lawes the helm of the most troubled ship in the state penal fleet—Sing Sing prison.

The reputation of Sing Sing had been firmly cemented in the mind of the public long before Lewis Lawes passed through the main gates of the prison. This was "The Big House," and since the vast majority of the prison population hailed from the boroughs of New York City, the courts sent them "up the river." Here, too, was where the condemned walked their "last mile" to the electric chair.

At thirty-seven years old, Lawes was the youngest warden in the history of Sing Sing. Although conditions at Sing Sing were harsh when he arrived, the reform-minded warden was determined and driven to make great changes to an already antiquated system. Cramped cells, poor food, dilapidated buildings, and questionable finances ($30,000 was missing from the account ledgers) were just a few of the problems Lawes inherited when he accepted the position of warden. His chief concern was the use of prison labor and physical punishment inflicted upon the inmates. The former he resolved by having inmates rewarded financially for their work. The latter was more difficult. It wasn't all that long ago when prisons were synonymous with revenge. Here, behind the stone walls of the prison, society exacted its revenge, its pound of flesh from that incorrigible element of society. When Lawes arrived, he beheld a burgeoning prison population that seemed as hard as the stone walls of the prison. "If you treat a man like a dog," he was fond of saying, "he'll act like a dog."[2] Beatings and floggings came to an end under his watch.

In quick succession he oversaw the construction of a new administration building, chapel, library, hospital, and mess hall. Inmates tended to gardens, sports were introduced, concerts were held, and educational courses were offered. All of these reforms dovetailed nicely into his vision of modern prison reform, save one. In February 1922, Lawes saw to the completion of the Death House.

The brick building with its signature bars was a self-contained prison within a prison. It boasted thirty-nine single cells, of which three were set aside for women. It contained its own kitchen, hospital, dental office, chaplain's office, reception room, and a tiny outdoor exercise yard. The centerpiece of this macabre structure was the death chamber, which contained the visitors' gallery and the electric chair. The half-dozen cells nearest to the execution chamber served as a staging area to which the condemned were brought before they walked their "last mile." Inmates and guards alike sardonically referred to this area of the Death House as "the dance hall."[3]

An ardent and outspoken opponent of capital punishment, Lewis Lawes used his position as one of the leading penologists of his day to express his views in a bully-pulpit fashion. The death penalty didn't stop crime, he argued, and many who walked that last mile were not career criminals. Furthermore, it was not equal justice. "Did you ever see a rich man go the whole route to the Death House? I don't know of any. Have you ever seen the sons of the rich on Condemned Row, no matter what they do?" he asked, "I don't know any."[4] Statistics bore him out. Of the 139 "legal" executions he had witnessed in the fourteen or so years he had been warden, many were black, almost all were poor, and only one of them had been a woman. Then, on April 19, 1933, Lawes received word that three prisoners from the Albany County Jail were being transferred to his facility to await execution. He recalled the day as "one of turmoil" due to the fact that one of them was a woman.[5]

Murder trials may take weeks, but sentencing is swift. The same day, April 9, 1933, that Judge Gallup sentenced Anna Antonio, Vincent Saetta, and Sam Faraci to death, the trio arrived at the gates of Sing Sing prison. Lawes recalled that a small crowd had gathered by the front entrance in hopes of catching a glimpse of the condemned. It didn't matter if they were reporters or spectators. Lawes looked upon them as one and the same. They were nothing more than morbid curiosity seekers, as he said, "Trying to give the public last minute word pictures of the reactions of the three who were beginning their last journey."[6] He reasoned that all of the reporters present would have gladly passed by Saetta and Faraci in the hope of seeing Anna Antonio, the first woman to face the electric chair since Ruth Snyder.

The unusually chaotic day described by Warden Lawes was nothing more than business as usual for twenty-three-year-old records clerk Michael D'Ambrosio. When a prison guard announced himself in his doorway, D'Ambrosio motioned him and the woman he was escorting to come forward. As the frightened little woman sat down in a chair beside his desk, the guard handed over a packet of papers from the Albany court. After glancing at a few of the documents, D'Ambrosio set the envelope aside. On his desk was the Receiving Blotter, an admittance ledger book with sequentially numbered pages. After number 87513, he entered the name Anna Antonio.

At first, D'Ambrosio didn't ask Anna any questions. The court documents that had accompanied her to Sing Sing contained all the pertinent information about the location of the crime, the court, and the sentence. He made only one alteration. Taking his pen, he drew a line across "Term" and beside it wrote "Execution Week of May 29, 1933."[7]

The bottom half of the form was made up of questions concerning family history, personal habits, work history, and so forth. Here, Anna answered each question with complete honesty. She neither smoked nor drank and had always been a housewife. Her religion was Catholic, but she added that since she had been in the Albany County Jail for over a year, she hadn't been to church.

When the form was filled out, D'Ambrosio motioned to the guard. The paperwork was completed, and now he could bring Anna to the Death House. Turning the page of the Receiving Blotter, he motioned to another guard to bring the next prisoner forward.

A master at twisting and turning the truth to suit his own needs, Sam Faraci told D'Ambrosio that his habits were moderate. He never used drugs, but he said he used tobacco. This was interesting because at his trial he said that he refused all offers of cigarettes from the detectives because he didn't smoke. His employment history as a house painter in Geneva was about as plausible as his claim of having supported his family of nine children. The one thing he couldn't lie about was his criminal past. Sing Sing authorities had already contacted Auburn State Prison. In his final attempt to portray himself as an honorable, somewhat decent person, Faraci never mentioned the Hamilton Street bungalow he shared with his prostitute girlfriend, Gertrude King. Instead, he lied and gave his residence address at the time of his arrest as "69½ Wadsworth Street, Geneva," and his nearest relative as his wife, "Mary Faraci." The wife he had abandoned still went by her married name of Ferugia.

During this time, photographs and fingerprints were not required as part of the admission process at Sing Sing. A signature at the bottom of the page attesting to the factual content of the admission form was all that was required. Despite the fact that Sam Faraci had said on numerous occasions while being detained by the police that he could neither read nor write, he managed to pen a legible signature on his admission form.

When it came time for Vincent Saetta to sign his name at the bottom of the Receiving Blotter page, he casually remarked that he really didn't expect to be executed. Naturally, a remark like this caught the attention of D'Ambrosio. Saetta exhibited a certain air of indifference. It was as if his presence at Sing Sing was a temporary or minor inconvenience. He didn't have the careworn look of Anna Antonio or display the restless, agitated demeanor of Sam Faraci. When D'Ambrosio asked him why he felt this way, a confident Saetta said that he wouldn't be going to the electric chair because a woman was involved. He then went on to say that if his appeal was not successful, he was prepared to make a last-minute statement. D'Ambrosio and another clerk in the same room, Jesse Collyer, were somewhat taken aback. They didn't really know what to make of Saetta's remarks. He certainly didn't appear to be taking his situation as serious as the others.

If the gravity of his situation did not become immediately apparent to Vincent Saetta when the door slammed shut on his Death House cell, it most likely did the next day when Bruno Polowicz and Alex Kasprzcak were electrocuted.

In a case that eerily mirrored his own predicament and that of his partner Sam Faraci, the two Niagara Falls natives were accused of orchestrating a murder in an attempt to collect a $6,000 life insurance policy. After weeks of cajoling, thirty-nine-year-old Alex Kasprzcak had convinced his sixty-nine-year-old uncle to purchase a life insurance policy. The uncle eventually acquiesced and named his nephew, Alex, as the beneficiary. This being done, Alex then enlisted the aid of his friend, Bruno Polowicz.[8]

As with Faraci, Bruno "The Bear" Polowicz, had done time in Auburn State Prison, and, like Saetta, he was a heartless killer. Payment in advance was not necessary. "Never mind the cash," Polowicz brazenly told his coconspirator, "I will do the murder on credit."[9]

In the early evening hours of July 5, 1932, Polowicz and Kasprzcak, having secured the services of a getaway driver, made their way to the farmhouse of Alex Kasprzcak. While the driver waited, the duo crept slowly toward the front porch of the unlit house. Their knock on the door was soon acknowledged by the elderly Kasprzcak. The door opened, and before the old man could utter a word, he received five slugs from the gun of Bruno Polowicz. As the old man slumped to the porch in a pool of blood, the duo fled the scene in the awaiting auto.

Like the Antonio murder, the crime took place at night, the victim knew his assailant, the murder weapon was never recovered, and the duo was quickly apprehended. Kasprzcak and Polowicz signed confessions, later disavowed these confessions, and were tried jointly for first-degree murder. Found guilty and sentenced to the electric chair at Sing Sing prison, they were executed on April 20, 1933, after the Court of Appeals upheld their original conviction.

In the women's wing of the Death House, Anna Antonio also had cause for concern. At the time of her arrival at Sing Sing, she was the only woman in the wing, but that changed four months later when the matrons escorted Mrs. Addie Exum, a black woman, down the corridor to her cell. The forty-year-old housewife from Staten Island had been convicted of presenting $400 to former Fisk University football star, Lovell Landers, a black man, to do away with her husband in order for her to collect a $1,800 life insurance policy. Exum and Landers were tried jointly in a case that was fraught with confusion, circumstantial evidence, and conflicting testimony.[10]

For Anna Antonio, the case of Mrs. Exum offered a glimmer of hope. After ten months in the Death House, Mrs. Exum was released. The Court of Appeals ruled in her favor regarding the circumstantial evidence presented at her trial. Landers escaped the chair as well and was given a life sentence.[11]

While the fate of each of the latest arrivals at the Death House hinged upon the decision of the Court of Appeals, the trio acclimated themselves to their present existence. "As a rule," observed Lawes, "prisoners in the condemned cells give us little trouble." Totally isolated from the rest of the prison population, life behind bars in the Death House with its few privileges was something akin to state-sponsored boredom. It was, as Lawes was fond of saying, "a drab affair."[12]

As intended when constructed, cells in the Death House were designed in such a way so that prisoners had absolutely no interaction with other inmates. For the most part, prisoners were confined to their locked cells with only a few exceptions. They could only be let out to receive a visitor, bathe, or, in the case of men since razors were not allowed, visit the Sing Sing barber. The only time they could leave the Death House proper to catch a breath of fresh air was when a guard escorted them outside to the tiny exercise yard. Here, they were permitted to wear shoes instead of their prison-issued felt slippers.

There were no dining or mess halls in the Death House. Inmates had their meals passed to them by guards through an opening in their cell door. Smoking was allowed in the cells, but matches were forbidden. Guards carefully lit the cigarette or cigar for them a slight distance from their cell bars. To while away the hours, the prison library provided books, magazines, and newspapers. The only form of entertainment was radio, and the only time it was silenced was on the day of an execution. The moment of silence was a gentle reminder to the entire prison population of Sing Sing just how serious things were in the Death House section of the prison.

Almost everyone who was familiar with the prison agreed that the only thing that successfully interrupted this boring daily routine, while awaiting the ruling of the Court of Appeals, was the arrival of a visitor. During their yearlong stay at the Albany County Jail, access to Anna Antonio, Vincent Saetta, and Sam Faraci was relatively easy. All one had to do was drive out or take the Quarter Cab to Shaker Road during visitation hours and sign the visitor logbook. This fairly simple process changed dramatically when all three were transferred to Sing Sing. Visiting someone who was part of the regular prison population differed greatly from visiting someone in the Death House. Any potential visitor, and this included attorneys as well as family and friends, had to make an application of sorts in a letter to a local judge. If the request was approved, the judge sent a letter to the prison in the form of a court order allowing that person to visit the condemned. The only ones exempt from this regulation were immediate family members—spouses and children. For Anna Antonio, the last person to say good-bye to her at the Albany County Jail was the first person to visit her at Sing Sing. Her name was Elizabeth Fox, and Anna was overjoyed to see her.

Fifty-eight-year-old Elizabeth Fox had been a matron at the Albany jail since 1928. A widow supporting her daughter and son-in-law on wages of less than twenty dollars per week, it was all she could do to make the trip to Sing Sing, and she did it twice. She had looked after Anna for over a year at the county jail, often accompanying her to the courthouse. She respected and guarded Anna's privacy by never speaking to the press before, during, or after the trial. A month later, another Albany County Jail matron, Alice LaCooke, paid Anna a visit.

When Catherine Gianetti, Anna's sister, applied for permission to visit, she evidently made such a strong impression on Schenectady judge John Alexander that she never had to ask again. "This woman," ruled Judge Alexander, "is to visit inmate ONCE A WEEK FROM DATE OF COURT ORDER TO DATE OF EXECUTION." The other family member who frequently made the trip to Sing Sing was her brother Patsy. Sometimes in the company of his wife Concetta, Patsy was especially welcomed because the conversations they had invariably centered on Anna's children. Frankie, the youngest, had been in Patsy's care since the day Anna had been arrested and sent to the Albany County Jail. Phyllis and Marie were a different matter. Patsy assured his sister that as soon as he was able to pick up more hours at his job with General Electric, he would be able to take the girls out of St. Vincent Female Orphan Asylum and reunite them with their little brother Frankie. This was welcome news for Anna, who, after the trial, feared that her sister-in-law Mary DeSisto might attempt to take custody of all three of her children.[13]

The handful of visitors Anna received from the time she was brought to Sing Sing ended abruptly with the onset of cold weather. During the winter months, no one ventured to the great prison to see her. However, this did not necessarily mean that she was alone. Her constant companions at this time were the jail matrons assigned to look after her by Warden Lawes. Dr. Amos Squire recalled that there was no shortage of applicants to be a matron in the Death House when Anna Antonio arrived. "Numerous applications were received by the Warden from substantial housewives in Ossining who wanted one of the three positions as matron," said Dr. Squires. "Although somewhat distressing, to say the least, the work is not tedious, and the pay is unusually good."[14] Two of the matrons chosen were ones who had served him in the past. Lucy Many, a forty-six-year-old mother of two, lived not too far from the prison on Spring Street in Ossining. The last woman she looked after was Ruth Snyder. The other matron was Carrie Stephens. Married with no children, the sixty-two-year-old Stephens was a tall, broad-shouldered black woman who in her time had watched over seven women in the Death House.[15] As had been her experience in the Albany County Jail, Anna forged a great friendship with both of these matrons.

There was only one other person to visit Anna Antonio unannounced from time to time who didn't require permission from any judge or even the warden. Her appearance at the door of the Death House was all that was needed for the guards to grant her entry. She was the warden's wife, Catherine Lawes.

When Catherine Lawes announced that she intended to accompany her husband to Sing Sing prison in 1919, her friends were a bit dismayed. These same friends were then horrified when they discovered that Mrs. Lawes intended to take up residence within the prison. The confidence her husband had in prison reform was shared by her as well. "My family and I," she reassured her doubters and critics, "feel safer living among thousands of convicts than we would if we lived in New York [city]. Life is much more tranquil. Our neighbors are more considerate and polite—nice in every way."[16]

Although not as famous as her reform-minded husband, Catherine Lawes created a legacy within the prison walls on her own terms. She visited inmates, listened to their concerns, wrote letters for them, sat among them in the spectator stands during basketball and football games, and helped distribute fruit and tobacco at Christmas. She was especially kind to those who were in the Death House. On a few occasions, her name was the last word on the lips of the condemned as they were strapped into the electric chair. "Tell Mrs. Lawes," said Francis "Two Gun" Crowley, "I appreciate all she did for me."[17]

When Ruth Snyder was brought to the Death House, newspapers across the country were quick to point out that the stylish flapper's wardrobe would be radically altered as soon as she entered the great prison. One paper, the *Rome Daily Sentinel,* informed its readers that Mrs. Snyder "must relinquish the pleasures of silk underwear, and other niceties of feminine apparel, including silk stockings." The "modest widows weeds" she wore at her trial would soon be exchanged for the "coarse garments made by the felons in the prison factory."[18] The paper noted that Mrs. Lawes had taken it upon herself to purchase appropriate underclothing for Mrs. Snyder.

Mrs. Lawes saw to Anna Antonio's needs in a different way. Naturally overwhelmed at being in the Death House, Anna Antonio never complained about the creature comforts of life in her small, narrow cell. She accepted the drab prison clothing, but when she expressed the desire to make clothing for her children, not herself, Mrs. Lawes was quick to oblige. She made arrangements for a sewing machine and fabric to be sent to the women's wing of the Death House.

Vincent Saetta and Sam Faraci forged no such friendships at the Albany jail or at Sing Sing. In his first few months in prison, Saetta had been visited by a cousin, George Intelisano, and friends from the city, Mr. and Mrs. Lawrence Pellerino. His immediate family, living in Queens, had the shortest distance to travel and visited him from time to time. It was a much different situation for Sam Faraci. For the first time in his life, he was totally abandoned. The distance between Geneva and Sing Sing apparently didn't make the heart grow fonder for the family he never supported. The illiterate house painter from Geneva languished in his cell for an entire year before receiving a single visitor.

21

THE COURT OF LAST RESORT

The swiftness with which Anna Antonio, Vincent Saetta, and Sam Faraci were whisked to Sing Sing was matched only by the speed in which the trio was forgotten by the Albany press. Once the three were safely tucked away inside the prison, the press simply had no news to report to its readers until the finding of the Court of Appeals was announced. While Anna and the others passed their days on death row during this cruel waiting game in anticipation of the court's decision, the press looked elsewhere for stories.

There was no shortage of newsworthy events in the summer of 1933. Abroad, Nazi Germany dominated the foreign news while here at home, Americans waited in hopeful anticipation that Franklin D. Roosevelt's New Deal programs would lift the country out of the depths of the Great Depression. In the Midwest, outlaw bandits Bonnie and Clyde were still making headlines, and many people were beginning to wonder if the kidnapping and murder of the twenty-month-old son of famed aviator Charles A. Lindberg at his Hopewell, New Jersey, estate would go unsolved. Closer to home in Albany, authorities were investigating their own kidnapping.

In the early morning hours of July 7, 1933, four kidnappers positioned themselves behind trees and shrubbery near the driveway at

11 Putnam Street in Albany. Their intended victim was twenty-three-year-old John J. O'Connell Jr., scion of the politically powerful O'Connell family. When young O'Connell arrived home and stepped out of his automobile, he was immediately accosted. One kidnapper placed a gun to his head while the others hustled him toward their getaway car. Blindfolded, gagged, and bound, O'Connell was tossed into the trunk of the car. Hours later, the kidnappers placed a call to John's uncle, Edward O'Connell, and demanded a ransom of $250,000.[1] Days later, Manny Strewl, a onetime Prohibition beer runner and recently released convict, stepped forward and offered his services to mediate between the kidnappers and the O'Connell clan. Twenty-three days later the family delivered $40,000, apparently enough to satisfy the kidnappers. Eventually, Strewl, who in fact orchestrated the entire affair, was arrested with his entire gang. On February 26, 1934, Strewl was brought to trial at the Albany Courthouse.[2]

The public followed the two-and-a-half-week Strewl trial with the same fascination as they did the Antonio trial. It was a courtroom drama with essentially the same cast. Judge Earl Gallup presided over the trial, with John T. Delaney and Joseph Casey on one side and Daniel Prior representing Strewl on the other. The trial made headlines, and there was no shortage of courtroom antics or barbs traded by the opposing attorneys. Still, Manny Strewl didn't stand a chance. He was doomed the moment Judge Gallup dropped his gavel and called the court to order.[3]

There was no public sympathy for Manny Strewl. He was looked upon as a small-time racketeer who didn't threaten the O'Connell political machine as much as he threatened the O'Connell family. For the guilty Strewl, his next stop was Dannemora Prison, while Dan Prior's was next door at the Court of Appeals to argue the case of a client whom he believed was innocent—Anna Antonio.

The Strewl trial did have an effect on the Antonio appeal. Due to Delaney, Casey, and Prior's participation in the Strewl trial, the Antonio appeal was moved back on the court calendar. On April 23, 1934, a year and four days since Anna Antonio was brought to Sing Sing, briefcase-toting Dan Prior, in the company of his secretary, arrived at the Court of Appeals on the corner of Eagle and Pine Streets. Located on the same side of the street as the county courthouse, the Appeals building, with its half-dozen grandiose granite columns, was just as imposing. Topped by a magnificent dome, the building evoked the finest qualities of Greek and Classical architecture. Inside, the court chambers took on the semblance of a great English country estate where oil portraits of past judges, instead of nobility, graced the paneled walls in their gilded plaster frames. The architecture and beauty of the surroundings were quickly set aside when six robed figures were announced, entered the room, and sat at a large oak tribunal-like table.

Having failed to sway a jury of twelve men in the cause of their respective clients, each attorney now had to convince a jury of a half-dozen judges that justice had been denied his client. A year had passed since each of them had filed the necessary papers, ample time for them to prepare their individual arguments for a new trial. This time there would be no verbal sparring, interruptions, insults, or long, drawn-out soliloquies. Their arguments to the judges would be brief and precise.

In the year that had passed since the trio of attorneys had been in Gallup's court, Prior and Duncan had seen each other countless times due to the proximity of their law offices on State Street. Neither of them had communicated with Henry Lowenberg. A year's respite, however, hadn't softened the animosity between Prior and Lowenberg.

For Duncan, standing before the appellate judges, there was only one argument he could present on behalf of his client. Since Sam Faraci's own words condemned him in the mind of the jury, Duncan insisted that these words, his signed confession obtained by the Albany police, were extracted "involuntarily and by forceful coercion."[4] In a rare moment of solidarity, Duncan echoed the sentiments of Henry Lowenberg in that his client's civil rights had been grossly violated. Duncan spared few details as he recited, mostly from the court transcripts, a litany of abuses inflicted upon his client. Not only was Faraci slapped and punched repeatedly, he was denied food and water, claimed Duncan. His ears were stretched and he was beaten unconscious when he refused to cooperate with the police.

When his turn came, Lowenberg based the thrust of his argument for a new trial on the absence of rights guaranteed to his client outlined in the Constitution. Saetta, and this included Faraci, had been held incommunicado for more than two weeks by the police before being arraigned. It was only after the duo had signed their confessions, which Lowenberg claimed had been obtained by questionable methods, were they formally charged and allowed to seek legal representation. A confession obtained by these methods without the benefit of counsel, he argued, should have never been used as an exhibit in the trial.

For the most part, Duncan, and the same could be said for Lowenberg, offered conjecture in their arguments before the judges. The accusations of police brutality could be interpreted simply as a case of "he said, they said." Saetta and Faraci claimed they were beaten, but the police said it never happened. What weakened the argument for the two attorneys was an inherent lack of facts. Where was the proof in terms of eyewitnesses and doctor statements?

Dan Prior had the facts that his fellow colleagues lacked. When Dan Prior arrived at the Court of Appeals, he was accompanied by his secretary. Present each day at the trial of Anna Antonio, she sat by with her steno pad, making notations each time Prior nodded to her. Now these notes proved to be the crux of his argument to the judges before him. Pointing toward the five volumes of court transcripts on the desk before the judges, Prior claimed that justice had been unequivocally denied his client. He cited 239 instances where Judge Gallup had specifically instructed the jury to disregard the testimony against one defendant or another who was on trial. "This was so confusing," said Prior, "that the court was unable to recall 23 instances against which of the defendants certain of the testimony had been allowed."[5] He argued that the confusion this presented to the jury could have been avoided if his client had been tried alone.

A month later, on May 22, the Court of Appeals unanimously announced their decision. "As to each defendant judgment of conviction affirmed; no opinion."[6]

Two days later at Sing Sing, Lewis Lawes received word of the failed appeal and had his records clerk make the proper notation in the files of Antonio, Saetta, and Faraci. He then went to the Death House to meet with each of them individually. A very somber Lawes told them that the week of June 25 had been set aside by the courts for their date of execution.[7] As the three on death row tried to come to terms with having four weeks to live, they learned that they had one last chance. If the Court of Appeals was "the court of last resort," the last stop on the judicial road, the state governor's intervention was their last hope on earth. Following on the heels of the court's decision, the three attorneys requested an interview with Gov. Herbert Lehman. On June 21, they met at the governor's office to plead for the lives of their clients.

Lowenberg spoke first and struck hard. "Before I open my argument, I want to file this petition, signed by the jurors, asking that you commute the sentence of death against Saetta to life in prison." The governor casually glanced at the paper and set it aside on his desk without comment. Nearby, Prior and Duncan seethed with anger. Granted, the petition was an important step in avoiding execution, but it was totally self-serving. As they were all tried together, the petition may have carried more weight with the governor if it included the names of their clients as well.

"Now," said Lowenberg, "if your Excellency please, before I proceed with a discussion of the case itself, I want to give you a background of the life of Vincent Saetta." For a quarter of an hour, Lowenberg painted the picture of the typical Italian immigrant, fresh off the boat at Ellis Island, who had endured all the hardships and deprivations imaginable. He was poor, lived with his aging mother and father, quit school to go to work, and then along came the Great War. In an effort to impress Lehman, who had served as a colonel in the war, Lowenberg said that Saetta displayed a deep love and loyalty to his adopted country by immediately enlisting in the army. In what sounded like a wartime propaganda speech, Lowenberg said his client was doing his patriotic duty in defending American ideals. "American institutions were in danger," said Lowenberg, "and required the backbone of America to lend their aid to the preservations of American institutions."

Carefully omitting that Saetta had never served overseas during his brief stint in the army, Lowenberg revealed to the governor a postwar troubled youth. Although his client had a brush with the law on one occasion, the charges were dismissed. The only crime Vincent Saetta committed was the one for which he stood to forfeit his life. "I know," said Lowenberg, glancing at Prior, "following me in the line of argument will be the counsel for Anna Antonio; and I say to you in all seriousness that if your Excellency for one moment considers the commutation of the death sentence in the case of Anna Antonio, I say to your Excellency, with all due respect and humility that can command, that the commutation to life imprisonment should follow as far as the other two cases are concerned to be consistent." On this note, Charles Duncan was in agreement. He would have gladly traded the electric chair for life behind bars for Sam Faraci.

The constancy Lowenberg asked Lehman to consider was an impossible request to consider. Lowenberg was vehemently opposed to executive clemency for Anna Antonio while Vincent Saetta sat on death row. The entire affair, he insisted, was of her doing. She was the mastermind who plotted and duped his client, an innocent man, to do her bidding. "We have only to refer to the pages of history," said Lowenberg, "that wherever there has been connivance, where there ever has been a woman that has plotted and wherever there has been an unscrupulous woman, there has also been a man to atone for her wrong doing. Civilizations and empires have been cast into oblivion because of the enterprises of women. I say as far as this particular type of woman is concerned." When it was apparent that his chauvinistic rant had drawn a sharp look from the governor and his staff, Lowenberg quickly added, "not all women."

Once more Lowenberg echoed his belief that not only had a conspiracy existed to murder Sam Antonio, another conspiracy was played out at the trial. "Mrs. Antonio took the stand and joined hands in her defense with Sam Faraci trying to place on the lap of Vincent Saetta the full responsibility of the murder. She gave Faraci a lift wherever possible, and Faraci in turn put a boost in her case by giving her consideration." The collusion between the two was obvious. How could the two of them swear under oath that they didn't know each other and at the same time swear that they had dealings with Vincent Saetta?

Finally, Lowenberg brought to the attention of the governor that this entire affair was totally unnecessary. "At the beginning of the trial I called into Mr. Delaney's office and told him that I stood by ready to plead Vincent Saetta guilty to murder in the second degree, and I will now ask Mr. Delaney, before your Excellency whether that was so or not." All eyes in the governor's office turned toward the Albany district attorney. Delaney nodded his head and quietly said, "Yes, he did." If Delaney had accepted the plea, said Lowenberg, the county would have saved the expense of a lengthy trial, the Court of Appeals hearing, and he would not be in the governor's office pleading the case of his client. But this did not happen, and in the end, said Lowenberg, Anna Antonio and Sam Faraci did their best in the trial to "leave Vincent Saetta holding the bag."

In an attempt to soften his stinging rhetoric, Lowenberg brought an outsider with him to offer a few words to the governor on behalf of Saetta. Lowenberg didn't dare bring the perjuring Saetta sisters to plead for their brother's life, so instead, he opted to invite a Catholic priest to bolster the "good boy gone wrong" image of his client. Rev. Nicholas Paglia had perhaps a more difficult time pleading for mercy on behalf of Saetta than did Lowenberg. The parish priest may have "known the boy for many years," but the boy was no longer a youth—he was thirty-two years old. What the parish priest could possibly say, or did say, to Lehman about a former parishioner who had committed cold-blooded murder on Easter Sunday will never be known.[8]

Prior preferred a gentler approach when pleading his case before Lehman. Sweeping aside the sarcasm and bitterness of his predecessor, he spoke directly from the heart. Here was a woman, a largely misunderstood woman, the mother of three small children, driven to despair, trapped in a loveless marriage. Her life was hanging in the balance and the fate of her children was unknown. In an effort to elicit as much sympathy as possible from the governor, Prior had arranged for the children to be present during the clemency hearing. Sitting behind Prior and wearing the dresses that their mother had sewn in prison were Phyllis and Marie. Beside them was their uncle Patsy, doing his best to keep three-year-old Frankie entertained.

Since this was the first time Governor Lehman had the opportunity to consider clemency for a woman, Prior stressed the importance of not making comparisons. In the Snyder case, the evidence richly supported the supposition that Ruth Snyder acted in concert with her paramour, Judd Gray, in the bludgeoning death of Albert Snyder. The same could not be said for the case against Anna Antonio. The prosecution's attempt to portray Anna Antonio as an unfaithful spouse, akin to Ruth Snyder, was baseless. "Mrs. Antonio," asserted Prior, "had no desire to dispose of her husband to take another mate."[9] The "other mate" Prior referred to was the mysterious Tony Penta. The letter introduced at Anna's trial by the prosecution and assailed by Lowenberg was not so much evidence as it was innuendo.

The time had come for Dan Prior to play his ace card by leveling a serious accusation. "Her husband beat her and abused her," he declared, "the wonder is, she didn't kill him herself."[10] The remark sent shock waves throughout the room. During the trial, Prior carefully skirted the issue of domestic abuse in the Antonio household. The wary attorney knew that any reference to actual physical abuse would most likely be used against his client as a motive for murder. On more than one occasion, Anna Antonio testified that she feared her husband, but she carefully avoided giving specific details about what may have justified that fear. She gave the impression that her marriage was troubled, due in part to her husband's dope dealing, philandering, and long mysterious absences from home. His accusation of an abusive husband reverberated in the press. In an instant, the public's image of Anna Antonio changed from that of a cold-blooded killer to a desperate housewife.

John T. Delaney dismissed this latest allegation. Sam Antonio wasn't the unsavory character Dan Prior made him out to be. The real villain, he told Governor Lehman, was Anna Antonio. "The murder was planned coldly and cruelly," he said, adding, "she intended to throw suspicion on some other person. Our suspicions were first aroused when state police noticed she showed no emotion when informed of Antonio's death."[11]

Making the claim that Sam Antonio wasn't a bad person depended upon one's point of view. Since Antonio didn't have a police record, he was an innocent victim in the eyes of John Delaney. Federal narcotics agent Richard Kelly might disagree. Just because you hadn't been caught selling dope in the Gut didn't necessarily mean that you were a model citizen.

Governor Lehman listened to everyone without comment or question. A mere nod of his head in the direction of his secretary, James J. Mahoney, and the solicitor general, Henry Epstein, signaled the end of the two-and-a-half-hour hearing. The governor's decision, they were told, would be forthcoming. As it turned out, the session was all for naught. Lehman had no intention of commuting the sentences or granting clemency to any of the accused. It had always been his policy not to interfere with any judgment made by the Court of Appeals in which their decision had been unanimous.[12]

22

AN UNFORGIVING PRESS

Throughout the trial, reporters from in and around the capital district of Albany presented to their readers a fairly accurate presentation of the events that transpired within the courthouse. Quotes that were attributed to attorneys and witnesses matched those that were recorded in the transcripts. When arguments between the attorneys were lengthy, and there were quite a few, the press paraphrased them in such a way as to give their readers a real sense of what had taken place. Few papers outside the Albany region devoted any ink to the Antonio trial, the lone exception being the *Poughkeepsie Eagle News*, due no doubt to the testimony of patrolman John Campion. Press coverage virtually ceased when Anna Antonio, Vincent Saetta, and Sam Faraci were transferred to Sing Sing prison. For almost a year, the time it took for their case to be heard in the Court of Appeals, they were ignored by the press. There was simply nothing new to report. The failed appeal, together with the governor's refusal to intervene on their behalf, changed everything. With the execution date more firmly established, the press wasted little time in creating stories about the last days and hours of the murderous trio from Albany.

Local reporters who had covered the trial for the Albany papers found themselves pushed aside in favor of large wire services that, up to this time, had never heard of the Antonio case. Some of their stories were credible, a few weren't, and there were some that were incredible. Underneath it all, they agreed that there would be little interest to the general public if three men were to be executed. Anna Antonio made this a front-page story.

Of all the news agencies, the International News Service (INS), owned by communications mogul William Randolph Hearst, was the greatest offender when it came to reporting the final days of Anna Antonio. The INS freely mixed partial truths, misquotes, and just enough facts in its efforts to stimulate the public's imagination about Anna Antonio. On May 26, 1934, the INS, which up to this time had never published any stories about her, released an incredible story purported to be the reaction of several inmates of the all-male prison as Anna walked across the prison grounds to the Death House. "Not bad looking" was the reaction of a few when sizing up the "dark, slim looking woman of 29." The description of her most likely came from a newspaper photograph. Isolated in the women's wing of the Death House, Anna Antonio had absolutely no contact with any male prisoners at Sing Sing.

In an exclusive interview with Anna Antonio, the INS quoted her as saying, "Wasn't he a bad man? A dope peddler? Didn't he beat me and often let my children go hungry while he spent his money on other women? My husband forgave me, I saw him smile at me in the coffin. . . . So why must I die now?"[1] With the exception of the "smiling in the coffin" passage, Anna Antonio never said anything like this at her trial. She never spoke ill of her husband, suspected his drug dealing, or claimed that her husband had in any way mistreated the children. Stories like this sold papers, and the INS was just getting started.

The INS insisted that after Sam refused to entertain the idea of a divorce, tempers flared at the 3 Teunis Street apartment.

"I hope," screamed Anna in a fit of rage, "you die soon."

"Me?—I will never die. I will live a long time and I will have many sons."[2]

In this volatile exchange, the INS went so far as to tell its readers that this shouting match was overheard by a neighbor and could be read in the trial transcripts. The only reason they didn't identify the neighbor who overheard this exchange was because they couldn't. It never happened. If it had, John Delaney would have surely subpoenaed this person as further proof that Anna wanted to do away with her husband.

The only neighbor to testify at the trial was Margaret Zimmerman. She lived in the upstairs apartment for ten months and spoke very highly of Anna Antonio.

As for the actual planning of the murder, the INS did its best to portray Anna Antonio as a hard-as-nails female Mafioso contract killer. "How much to kill Salvatore?" she was to have said to both Saetta and Faraci. "They haggled," reported the INS, "as a housewife might haggle over the price of a fish." They claimed that Anna had at first offered Saetta $75 up front and promised to pay the balance of $100 when the job was completed. When her husband wasn't killed in a timely manner, the INS reported that Anna flew into a fit of rage. "You are yellow, you lost your nerve—do it Sunday night or give me back my $75. . . . Why do you let him live? Cowards! I have a mind to take my money back and do it myself."[3] Once more, the INS erroneously reported that this, too, was taken from the trial transcripts. How they arrived at $75 was anyone's guess. When Prior addressed the jury in his closing remarks, he said that no money had been exchanged before the murder of Sam Antonio. The only time this exact sum of money was mentioned during the trial was when Prior called former addict William Dempsey to the witness stand. Dempsey claimed that he had paid that sum of money to Sam Antonio for morphine.

At the same time, the chief rival of the INS was the Associated Press (AP). The reporter assigned to the Antonio story was Dale Harrison. The veteran news reporter did his utmost to garner as much sympathy for Anna Antonio as he possibly could. Often his stories bordered on the melodramatic. Such was the case when he reported a day before the execution the supposed mental state of Anna Antonio. "In the Death House," he wrote, "she weeps for her children, she weeps too, for her 80 year old father. Most of all she weeps for Anna Antonio."[4]

Harrison reported the news and occasionally created the news. Such was the case when he suggested that there was a slight chance Anna Antonio could escape the electric chair if it could be proven that she was mentally unbalanced at the time of the murder. "If it could be shown she were insane," suggested Harrison, "or if new evidence could be produced, the regular channels of law might stay her death."[5] Immediately after Harrison planted this seed, his competition, the INS, quickly announced "Sanity Plea Fails" and then proceeded to inform its readers that a "sanity commission cut off escape on plea of an un-balanced brain."[6] There was no sanity commission. The mental state of Anna Antonio before, during, and after the trial was not an issue until the press made it an issue. In the same press release, Harrison claimed that Warden Lawes, apparently moved by the plight of Anna Antonio, had made a special trip to Albany to confer with Governor Lehman. "The visit was a closely guarded secret," wrote Harrison, "and neither Governor Lehman nor the warden would discuss it."[7] The reason they wouldn't discuss the meeting is because it never took place.

On the local scene, H. Eric Liljeholm, of the *Albany Times Union,* was capable of doing the same when it came to embossing a few details. Since reporters were forbidden to enter the Death House to obtain "exclu-sive" interviews, Liljeholm took a different path and sought out Anna's brother. In his exposé on the Antonio household, Liljeholm asserted that, according to Patsy, Anna lived under the heel of her husband in total fear. "He [Patsy] tells of sordid racketeers coming to her house all times of the night, and Antonio waking his wife and making his wife pre-pare meals for his 'friends.'"[8] If Liljeholm had consulted the trial tran-scripts, he would have discovered that Anna had been roused from her bed to prepare just one meal and that was for Sam Faraci. As to the "sor-did racketeers" who frequented 3 Teunis Street, Liljeholm was mistaken. The only instance of "racketeers," if one would call them that, coming to the apartment was when Sam Antonio was preparing for the Steamburg arson job. If Anna had made the claim that racketeers were regular vis-itors to the apartment, Dan Prior would have not hesitated to use this testimony to further cement Sam Antonio's reputation as a gangster.

At best, Liljeholm's interview with Patsy Cappello appeared sus-picious. "I often pleaded with Salvatore," said Patsy, "to get out of the rackets and work an honest job, and get along like I do, poor, but happy and safe. He sneered at me."[9] It is difficult to imagine that this interview took place. First, Patsy and Sam Antonio never had the close relation-ship that this passage suggests. If they had been close, Dan Prior would have called on Patsy to offer testimony about these racketeers. Finally, he was never called Salvatore. To all who knew him, he was referred to by his birth name, Sam. The only ones who called him Salvatore were the police and the press. The former because they didn't want to confuse him with Sam Faraci, and the latter because Salvatore sounded Italian, more gangster-like.

The *New York Times* didn't cover the trial, but afterwards they let their readers know that on Mother's Day 1934, a special religious service was held at the Sing Sing chapel and later the prison staff presented a bouquet of flowers to the only mother in the prison. Following the failed appeal, which was announced on her son's birthday, the *Amsterdam Evening Record* informed its readers that Anna Antonio's thoughts and energies remained with her children. When not sleeping or in the exercise yard, Anna was continually cutting out patterns and sewing outfits for her children.[10] She estimated that she had completed enough outfits for her children to last an entire year.[11] Grateful for the fabric and sewing machine provided to her by Mrs. Lawes, Anna saved the scraps of fabric to make clothes for Marie's favorite doll.[12]

As far as the press was concerned, Anna Antonio was the real story. "No one," said Dale Harrison of the Associated Press, "pays much attention to Faraci or Saetta."[13] While a portion of the public gradually embraced the worn woman with the sad eyes who expressed deep love for her children, they had no compassion for the two killers. Vincent Saetta remained cold and mysterious. Reporters found it impossible to craft a story around a man they could not quote. Denied access to the Death House for an interview, reporters discovered that the trial transcripts were of little help as Saetta never testified. The man they could and did quote was his attorney. The irascible Henry Lowenberg was still exploring avenues to prevent the execution of his client.[14]

Nearby in another cell, Sam Faraci was fully aware that his attorney didn't have a last-minute appeal for him. Charles Duncan was a court-appointed attorney who had done his job during the trial and at the appeal. Time was running out, and he couldn't see any legal loophole or obstacle that stood in the way of his client walking directly to the electric chair. He knew this, so did Faraci, and so did the reporters. The large newspapers ignored the plight of Sam Faraci, but the local press in his hometown of Geneva didn't.

It didn't really matter to Mary Ferugia that her errant husband had used the name Faraci. The name change meant little since everyone in Geneva knew of her husband's troubled past and what was in store for him at Sing Sing. The *Geneva Daily Times* kept its readers abreast of the trial but respected her privacy. They never interviewed her or members of her immediate family or printed stories from her friends. This changed on June 16, 1934, when Mary Ferugia discovered that not only did she have a husband in prison but now had a son in the local jail. On that day, twenty-one-year-old Raymond Ferugia and twenty-two-year-old Joseph Cook were arrested by the local police and charged with statutory rape, stemming from an incident involving two young women from the nearby village of Newkirk in Wayne County. Unable to post bail of $10,000 apiece, the pair was remanded to the Canandaigua jail to await trial.[15]

Nine days after her son's arrest, the *Geneva Daily Times* reported that Mary Ferugia had traveled to Sing Sing to visit her husband. The paper noted that the trip was made possible by the generosity of the convicts' Mutual Welfare League. Joining her on this trip was her father, Joseph Calabrase, and her four-year-old son Charles. In the fourteen months Sam Faraci had been in the Death House, these were the first and, as it turned out, only visitors he received.

What she and her husband had to say to each other will never be known. The *Geneva Daily Times*, however, was able to learn what had transpired between Mary Ferugia and Warden Lawes. Having been the warden of "The Big House" for a number of years, Lewis Lawes had heard his fair share of stories from the family members of those who sat on death row. What Mary Ferugia had to say to him came as no surprise. She first thanked the warden for the funds sent to her by the Mutual Welfare League, which enabled her to purchase train tickets to Ossining. With nine children, one of which was currently in jail, she told Lawes that after the birth of Charles, her husband took off with Gertrude King. Since that time, she was so poor she was never able to obtain a divorce. Grateful for train tickets, a somewhat embarrassed Mary Ferugia asked a favor. Would it be possible for her husband's body to be returned to Geneva for burial? Lawes quietly assured her that the Mutual Welfare League would provide funds to make this possible.[16]

Still, Anna Antonio was the real news, and the press had to rely on jailhouse gossip to tell the story of her final days. Unfortunately for the members of the fourth estate, the man who could tell the story wasn't granting any interviews. Lewis Lawes zealously guarded the privacy of anyone in the Death House no matter who they were or what they had done. Executions, Lawes maintained, were not entertainment. Besides, when it came time, he'd rather tell the story himself.

23

THE STATE ELECTRICIAN

Once, when a condemned inmate was led through the green door of the death chamber and beheld the electric chair for the first and soon to be the last time, he nervously turned to the guard and asked, "What kind of guy is this Elliott? Does he know his job?" The guard solemnly nodded and directed the inmate's attention to the tall, gaunt figure with the silver-gray hair tending to the leather straps of the chair. The inmate, apparently satisfied with what he saw, sat down and was strapped into the chair. The man who was about to end his life was Robert G. Elliott, and he knew his job all too well.

Unlike Lewis Lawes, Elliott had no family ties to the penal system. In fact, there was nothing in his early life to remotely suggest that he might be drawn to this peculiar calling. The fifth of six children born on a farm in Wayne County, New York, his deeply religious parents had named him after the local Methodist minister. He recalled how in his youth his mother encouraged him to pursue the ministry and admitted that he was considering such a path in life had it not been for a chance encounter with one of the local farmers who at one time had been a telegraph operator. The inquisitive sixteen-year-old was fascinated by tales of this power that could send messages and light up rooms.[1] Eager to absorb this new technology, Elliott enrolled in a nearby teaching col-

lege, Brockport Normal, to study physics and electricity. After he graduated, Elliott secured a position with the Brockport Electric Company
and two years later accepted a position as an assistant engineer at the
electrical plant at Dannemora Prison. It was here that he witnessed his
first execution.

Elliott was the greatest enigma to be associated with the penal system. The man who once said, "That is a job I would like to have" after
reading about an electrocution, was a staunch opponent of capital punishment. Not nearly as vocal as Lewis Lawes, Elliott viewed the practice
as a form of societal revenge. By the 1930s, his services were in demand
in six states, including New York, where his official title was "The State
Electrician." He never considered the $150 he received for each execu-
tion as "blood money," never had nightmares, and never lost sleep after
adjusting a dial and turning a switch that killed 383 men and 6 women.
In his mind, Elliott believed that he hadn't killed anyone. The judicial
system was responsible, and he was merely an instrument in the hands
of that system.

Whenever a prison was in need of his services, a letter was sent to
Elliott at his home at Richmond Hill, Long Island. The short, businesslike communiqué lacked any formalities. An execution was scheduled
for this date, for this prisoner, and "we shall expect you to be present
at the regular time."[2] In the last week of June, Elliott received just such
a note in the mail from Warden Lawes. He was to report to Sing Sing
prison on Thursday, June 28, to perform the executions of Anna Antonio, Vincent Saetta, and Sam Faraci.

A Thursday execution came as no surprise to Elliott as all Sing
Sing executions took place on that particular day of the week. Elliott
believed that Lawes purposely scheduled executions on this day in the
off chance that if there was a last-minute reprieve, lawyers and judges
couldn't possibly resolve the situation by the next day, Friday. This,
together with the weekend, would guarantee three more days of life.
Another thing that didn't catch Elliott off guard was a triple execution. Several had taken place at Sing Sing, and the press wasted little
ink in telling the story. When John McKinney, John Tinsley, and Henry
Edmonds were put to death on September 1, 1933, the press virtually
ignored the three black men. The same could be said for John Jordan,

George Swan, and Stephen Witherill. When they went to the chair, the press seemed more interested in their last meal than in the crime they had committed. The *New York Sun* and the *Ossining Citizen Register* reported that the trio consumed the largest meal that any condemned prisoner ever ordered.

In the early evening hours of June 28, Elliott arrived at the front gate of Sing Sing and was quietly ushered to the Death House. Meticulous, he routinely arrived four hours early. "It is a project," he euphemistically declared, "that must be taken and carried through without mistake, with the slighting of no detail. The least slip may make it more brutal even than need be. My responsibility is to make impossible that slip."[3] Arriving at the death chamber, that "windowless, bright most cheerless room in the world," Elliott spoke briefly with a few of the guards and then got right to work inspecting each nut, bolt, and screw of the electric chair. Eight leather straps with their buckles bound the chest, waist, arms, and legs where they needed to restrain a body that would receive a thunderbolt of two thousand volts of current. Riveted to the floor, the oak chair was, in the words of Elliott, "a fearsome looking piece of furniture."[4]

Elliott was completing his inspection of the electric chair when the first group of witnesses to the execution entered the room. He never quite understood why anyone would want to witness an execution. A few, he reasoned, were morbid curiosity seekers and then there were reporters, a group that was a class unto themselves. "To him it's a show," said Elliott, "he must get a thrill or he wouldn't return for a second, third, fourth or tenth time, as he often does."[5] Equally perplexed was Lewis Lawes. "It does not seem fitting to me that such a solemn and gruesome matter should be regarded in the light of a sideshow for the entertainment of morbid minded and abnormal people."[6] Despite his beliefs, the law in the state of New York required Lawes to send out invitations to the judge who had sentenced the condemned and the district attorney who had prosecuted the case. In all the years he served as warden of Sing Sing, Lawes noted that not one judge or district attorney accepted the invitation.

What worried Lawes was not so much the countless others who wanted to attend an execution but were denied, but the few he considered were much more than morbid curiosity seekers. Lawes was particularly wary of the reporters and steadfast in his determination not to have a repeat of the Ruth Snyder execution.

On January 12, 1928, Tom Howard, a reporter for the *Chicago Tribune,* managed to smuggle a miniature camera past the guards when he entered the death chamber. Seating himself in the front row, with the camera affixed to his ankle, Howard waited for the precise moment and carefully lifted his pant leg to snap a photograph of Ruth Snyder receiving her life-ending burst of electricity. The blurry image, which appeared in the *New York Daily News* the next day, became one of the most sensational images of the 1920s. While Howard received one hundred dollars for the picture from the *Daily News,* Lawes felt betrayed by the press. Following this breach of trust, Lawes required all reporters to lift their pant legs to ensure that this incident would never be repeated.

On the other side of the green door, preparations of another sort had been taking place for the triple execution. When her brother Patsy and his wife Concetta left Sing Sing with her children, Anna was brought back to her cell and composed a short will. She had no estate. All the worldly goods she had from her Teunis Street apartment had been placed in storage after she had been arrested. Presumably these things had been disposed of by her brother when it became difficult to pay the monthly storage fee. All she had was her children. "I want my brother Patsy to bring up the three children," she said, "he has been very good to them and me. It's them, more than myself that I am thinking of."[7] Setting the will to one side, she stared intently at the picture of the children she had in her cell and reread Phyllis's last letter.

> I received your doll and was glad to have it. Please do not worry, because I got home safely Sunday night. We had a flat tire but Harry had another tire with him. Uncle Patsy is going to come and see you this week. Next week he is going to bring me, because he came to see me and told me so.
>
> I am praying and praying for you day and night. Uncle Patsy said that he is going to give me a doll he has home for me. I forgot to give Sister Germaine the doll. I will give it to her when Sister Antonio fixes it. It will look nicer then. I am going to see how long I can keep it. The doll that Uncle Patsy is going to bring me I will let Sister Antonio mend it for me. You would think that she is my mother the way she treats me so.[8]

Brushing away her tears, Anna set the letter aside and silently prayed before the two lit candles that flanked the crucifix in her cell. When one of the matrons presented her with the menu to choose the customary last meal, she graciously declined. "I want nothing," she said and continued to pray. In the last twenty-four hours, she had sipped on a small cup of coffee.

No one knows where or how the custom of the last meal originated for those on death row. Some scholars look to the Bible in Isaiah 22:13: "Let us eat and drink, you say / for tomorrow we die." Others say the tradition dates back to the ancient Greeks or Romans. Whatever the origins, it was a time-honored tradition at Sing Sing with no racial discrimination whatsoever. Black, white, Chinese, or immigrant, no one was ever denied a last meal before he or she walked the last mile.

On the morning of June 28, Saetta and Faraci were taken from their cells and moved to a staging area closer to the death chamber, referred to by all as the "dance hall," where they ordered their last meal. Saetta and Faraci feasted on chicken, veal cutlets, and a variety of desserts. "I only wish I had their appetite," quipped one guard.[9] With only a few hours remaining, the two smoked one cigar after another.

Saetta, puffing on his cigar and blowing copious amounts of smoke into the hallway, appeared relaxed. "I don't expect anything," he replied when a guard asked him if there was the possibility of a last-minute reprieve. "I expect to pay the price." Nearby in another cell, Faraci still harbored a resentment toward the legal system. "I told the truth," he said bitterly, summing up his belief that Delaney had reneged on a promise of a lighter sentence in exchange for testimony that would convict Saetta.[10]

It was close to 10 P.M. when the Sing Sing barber made his way to the dance hall. In order for the brine-soaked electrode to make contact, the barber shaved a neat four-inch square on the back of their heads. Having completed this, he made his way to the women's wing of the Death House to do the same for Anna Antonio. Wearing a pink gown with a white lace collar, up to this time Anna was doing well. As the barber clipped the first truss of hair from her head, she broke down and sobbed hysterically. Father John P. McCaffrey, the prison chaplain, did his utmost to console her by encouraging her to pray with him. In between prayers, she fought back tears and said, "I have nothing on my conscience. I never killed anybody."[11] She continued her prayers with Father McCaffrey until she looked up to see Lucy Many and Carrie Stephens standing in front of her cell door. In a soft whisper, one of the matrons told her that it was almost time. She prayed and waited. Soon 10:50 passed to 10:55, and then to 11:00. Still, she prayed and waited.

24

SAETTA SPEAKS

How Vincent Saetta spent his final hours in the Death House is as mysterious as how he spent the last thirteen months in a seven-foot by three-foot cell. What he did to occupy his time was anyone's guess. He had access to the prison library, but no one knows if he read any books or the newspapers. Like anyone else, he was allowed a radio in his cell and was permitted to use the exercise yard, where for a brief moment he could stretch his legs and catch a breath of fresh air. Although his family and friends from Long Island were closer to Sing Sing than those of Sam Faraci and Anna Antonio, he still didn't have many visitors. If anything, Vincent Saetta had time to think. He had a lot of time to consider what had happened on that Easter Sunday morning and what should have happened.

Saetta was a poor planner and an equally poor assassin. His choice of Castleton Road to commit a murder wasn't thought out. True, the road had no streetlights, but it was a well-traveled road even in the early morning hours. If he wanted to make the murder appear as if it were a gangland affair, he should have taken a wrong turn onto a lonely country road. The only flawless part of his plan was the seating arrangement in the car on that fateful morning. Positioning Sam Faraci in the middle was a good idea. When Faraci announced that he had to answer the call of nature, Sam Antonio was forced to exit the car.

By all accounts, it was a sloppy murder. Saetta's expertise with a pistol at a range of a dozen or so feet was wanting. By aiming at the silhouette of Sam Antonio against a car headlight, he managed to hit his mark four out of five times. Only when his victim fell to the ground after being struck in the palm of the hand and both thighs was Saetta able to deliver the fatal shot to the hip. When he told Faraci to "finish the job," he erred again. Of the dozen or so stab wounds inflicted upon Sam Antonio, the coroner reported that not one of them hit a major artery or vital organ.

A dead body discovered in a roadside ditch by a passing motorist the next day would have placed a lot of distance between them and the authorities. Here, he erred once more. Saetta sped away and never made sure that his victim was dead. Instead of having a dead man with no wallet or papers, he had a live body who identified himself as Sam Antonio.

In hindsight, Saetta probably realized that his escape plan was about as flawed as his partnership with Sam Faraci. The only reason Saetta included Sam Faraci in the murder plot was his need for an automobile. It didn't take two people to lure Sam Antonio to Hudson and then to Castleton Road. He should have borrowed the car, done the job himself, and left town. It was bad enough not to have an escape plan when he planned the murder, but after the murder he involved Gertrude King. When Faraci said he wanted to go to Oswego with Gertrude King, he should have let him go. It would have been relatively easy for Saetta, as a former employee of the New York Central Railroad, to pack a suitcase and purchase a one-way ticket to Grand Central Station. With sisters and cousins scattered about Long Island, it would have been easy for him to stay hidden for a week or two.

Finally, Saetta's lack of patience proved to be his undoing. It's not too often that a murder on a country road in upstate New York finds its way onto the pages of a New York City newspaper. Saetta should have skipped the call to his landlady and placed a call to some of his friends in the Gut. "I haven't heard from Sam" or "Can you give Sam a message, I can't seem to find him" phone conversations would have been a discreet way of finding out if the police suspected him and Faraci. Saetta never did this and instead headed back to Albany into the waiting arms of the Poughkeepsie police.

Now, with less than an hour remaining before his own execution, Saetta put his final plan into motion. The man who did not speak at his own trial was about to make the biggest speech of his life. "She's innocent," he screamed, "I tell ya, she didn't do it I . . . I gotta save her . . . she didn't do it!"

On the other side of the green door, in the death chamber, Lawes had positioned himself near the electric chair. Elliott was making a last-minute inspection of the electrodes in the hooded headset while a gallery of witnesses stared intently at the green door, waiting for Anna Antonio to appear. Minute after minute passed and nothing happened. Another minute went by and suddenly the door was flung open with such force as to startle everyone in the death chamber. A guard appeared and went directly to Lewis Lawes and whispered in his ear. The somber expression on the face of Lewis Lawes changed to that of deep concern. Lawes made his way quickly through the green door that led to those cells near the dance hall and came face-to-face with Saetta. "She didn't do it," shouted Saetta, "I've gotta save her."[1] The appearance of the warden had a calming effect on Saetta. Now a less excited Saetta told Lawes he was prepared to make a statement. Lawes listened intently as Saetta gave his version of the events that eventually led him to the electric chair. Most of the names and places were the same, but with one startling omission. Saetta didn't mention Anna Antonio. Lawes was intrigued. This wasn't what he had expected. These were not the hysterical cries of a condemned man. Lawes noted the time—it was 10:45 P.M.—and told the guard nearest him to bring stenographer Clement Ferling to the Death House.

Ferling arrived, steno pad in hand, and recorded Saetta's statement. "It was long and rambling," said Lawes of the three-page deposition. "I could have helped him out, but I thought it was fairer to let him tell the story in his own words."[2] When Saetta finished, Ferling made his way across the prison grounds to his office in the administration building, typed out several copies of the confession, and returned to the Death House. He gave Saetta a copy of his confession and asked him to read it and, if necessary, make any alterations or additions before signing it.

I, Vincent Saetta, being duly sworn, state that the following statement is being made by without promise or duress and in the interest of justice.

I knew Sam Antonio when I worked with him on the railroad. After a long time, perhaps four or five years, I came in contact with him again, that is, I saw him often.

We had dealings of our own, and we had some trouble in our dealings. These problems were straightened out okay.

I left Albany after this. I went to New York City and I was there about two weeks and Sam came up to me, or rather he got me on the telephone, and I met him at 99th Street and Second Avenue.

I was with my nephew, Antony Saetta. Sam said to me, "Vincent, I need some money." I said, "How much do you need?" He said, "How much you got?"

I told him I had $75, as I had my bonus check cashed, and I gave it to him. I told him that I had some oil bills to pay.

There were about 11 cases of oil, and I got a note to meet later. I told him. He told me that he would return it in about a week or so. When a few weeks went by and I didn't get the money, I went to Albany.

I finally got in touch with Sam and asked him when he was going to pay me. He said he used the money in the house and that he would take care of it soon on pay day.

He stringed me right along and then a couple of weeks went by. One morning I met him on Green Street in Albany, and asked him for the money. He said come on down to the river and we will settle it.

I said, "So you don't want to pay me, eh?" He said, "I have always made a living out of people like you," I turned around and swung at him.

This, what I am saying right now, is on the record. So we had a fight and when we got to the corner of Green Street a couple of friends of ours, came along and broke up the fight.

He was going to make me pay for this all right. Well, about two or three weeks later I am still in Albany in a pool room on Madison Avenue. Somebody came in and said that Blackie wanted to see me.

He (Blackie) met a fellow who has a restaurant at 66 Green Street. At the same time Sam Faraci was with me and I asked him if he wanted to take a walk.

He said, "Yes." As I walked in the place the proprietor, Blackie, came and told me that Sam Antonio was in there and please do not make any trouble because he wanted to make up.

And I said, "Okay." I got in and the man is sitting there. He laughed at me, and I laughed at him. He gets up and shakes my hand, and we both said we were sorry.

After leaving the kitchen of 66 Green Street, Antonio said to me as he pulled out a knife, "You were lucky that I didn't have this with me that day."

I told him to "Forget about it, we are friends again." Two or three weeks went by and I used to see Sam Faraci once in a while, and Faraci told me that Sam Antonio was going to take me for a ride.

I asked Sam, "Do you think that is right after all the doings we had?" He said, "No." He also said Antonio should be killed and that he would help me kill him.

He said, "That is the only way to do because the fellow was going to take me for a ride," He said, "Don't say anything," I said, "Okay."

After a while I met Sam and said, "I will be back right away." So I went to my room where I had a bottle of whiskey and I drank about half of it. Not all at once. I poured some in a glass.

Then I got the gun out of the drawer and put it on my hip. I walked out then and it took me about a half an hour to get to Green Street, and it was about a half hours time to get back. We had all arranged to go for a ride.

We all intended to go to Hudson. Finally we reached Hudson and got to a restaurant and I said it was too late to go any place as it was about 3 o'clock.

Sam was telling me to stop the car along the road but I wouldn't stop, so after we were a little below Castleton, going from Hudson to Albany, and Sam Faraci stopped on the side of the road.

I was on the other side of the road and Sam Antonio was on the same side with me. Sam Antonio was holding the door for me.

All of a sudden it came to my mind and I fired at him. He went down and Faraci rushed over and wanted to know what happened.

I said, "I don't know." He reached over in the pocket of the car and got a knife. Whatever he did with it I don't know because it was dark.

Mrs. Antonio is absolutely innocent of this crime. I got $40 from her before the crime, but that didn't have anything to do with it.

> Afterwards I wanted to get away as I was desperate and asked her for
> $40 more. She was frightened and gave it to me.
>   VINCENT SAETTA[3]

The instant Saetta affixed his signature to the statement, Ferling notarized it and presented it to Lawes. With the signed confession in hand,
Lawes went to the nearest telephone and called Governor Lehman. After
giving a brief rendition of what had transpired, Lawes proceeded to read
Saetta's statement. Lehman listened intently but with a certain degree of
caution. He agreed with Lawes that what had just occurred was totally
unprecedented, but given his position as governor, he also believed that
if he acted too quickly and commuted the sentence of one or all three,
it would lead to a dangerous precedent. To make a hasty decision might
make eleventh-hour confessions on death row an accepted practice.
Lehman needed time to consult with his advisers and discuss the merits
of Saetta's statement. At this moment, Lawes needed direction. Around
1 A.M., Lehman authorized him to make the following statement on his
behalf. The governor dictated it over the phone to Lawes, who in turn
immediately released it to the press.

"I have directed the warden of Sing Sing to postpone the electrocution
of Vincent Saetta, Sam Faraci and Anna Antonio until Friday night, June
29, in order that I may have time to study and consider the long statement made by Saetta just before 11 o'clock tonight, the general substance
of which has been repeated to me by telephone by Warden Lawes."[4]

By now, mystery and confusion replaced the steady routine of the
Death House. In a cell nearby, Sam Faraci had no idea what had just
taken place. The unusual traffic in the hall convinced him that something was amiss. Saetta's screams and shouts were now followed by an
eerie silence. On the other side, in the women's wing, Anna Antonio had
been sitting in her cell for two hours. Her matrons were still waiting for
the signal to escort her to the electric chair.

Equally confused were the reporters and witnesses seated in the gallery of the death chamber. After Lawes left his post near the electric
chair, no one in authority had come forward to offer any explanation
as to why the execution had not taken place. One reporter who had been
patiently waiting for an explanation as to this delay was Robin "Curly"

Harris of the *New York Daily News*. When the green door opened, Warden Lawes calmly approached the gallery of witnesses. Because of the nature of Vincent Saetta's last-minute statement, Lawes told them that he had consulted with Governor Lehman. The execution would be postponed for twenty-four hours. Harris scribbled in his notepad as quickly as he could. Execution or no execution, this was news and he had to contact his newspaper. What Harris found disturbing, though, was the reaction of a small group from Oswego who had, no doubt from some sort of political influence, received invitations to the execution. "They acted as if they were at a football game and it just got called off," said Harris. When he turned to confront one of the disgruntled spectators, one of their number angrily snapped, "How do you like this? I may never get another chance like this again."[5]

The small contingent of Oswego witnesses may have been disappointed, but the man standing behind the electrical panel wasn't. An eleventh-hour postponement had never happened before, and Elliott took this as a good sign. He turned off all the switches, gathered up his electrodes, and went home, confident in his belief that Mrs. Antonio would receive a commutation of her sentence.[6] Lewis Lawes didn't share that confidence. Although grateful for the governor's action, he was nonetheless disappointed with a twenty-four-hour postponement. One day wasn't much of a reprieve. This meant that the macabre ritual had to be reenacted. He could not comprehend why the governor would not extend the reprieve past the weekend. Still, it was one more day of life.

Saetta and Faraci received the news of the one-day reprieve with little or no emotion. Each simply nodded and made no comment. It was a far different scene in the women's wing. "It was hellish hot in her cell," said Lawes, "she had been under terrific strain. By the time word came from the governor that he would grant a 24-hour stay, she fainted. When she came to, she looked about in great surprise. In a weak voice she asked the matron to say something. I am sure she thought she was dead, and needed reassurance of a human voice to convince her that she was still on earth."[7] After she regained her composure, the matrons told her what Saetta had told the warden. A mentally frayed and physically weak Anna Antonio exclaimed, "I appreciate that statement a million times."[8]

While the governor and his advisers studied Saetta's statement in Albany, Warden Lawes braced himself for yet another Saetta surprise.

The following day he learned that two of his record clerks had known all along that Vincent Saetta would make a last-minute statement. His chief clerk, Donald L. Parsons, in an interdepartmental memo, stated that Saetta, when being interviewed by clerk Michael D'Ambrosio, said in effect that he would make such a statement. D'Ambrosio told Parsons that Saetta, while being processed for admittance into the prison, seemed to appear quite confident that he would receive a commutation of the sentence due to the fact that the crime involved a woman. Jesse Collyer, another clerk who was in the same room as D'Ambrosio, not only corroborated the story but added one piece of vital information. "Saetta stated that Mrs. Antonio was innocent of the crime for which she, Saetta and Faraci were convicted and at the proper time he would make a statement and he also stated that he was positive that she would never go to the electric chair."[9]

That morning, word of Saetta's last-minute manifesto reverberated about the state as front-page news. Perhaps no one newspaper was more excited to receive a transcript of this confession than the *Albany Times Union*. The reporters who had followed the trial from beginning to end wasted little time in their attempts to either validate or dismiss Saetta's statement. Of particular interest to them was restaurant proprietor Blackie of 66 Green Street. *Times Union* reporters discovered that at the time of the Antonio murder, Tony Black had owned a restaurant at that address. Now, two years later, neighbors in the vicinity of Green Street hadn't seen him in over a year. Some speculated that he had moved to Utica, New York. Authorities in Utica were contacted, and they, in turn, questioned leaders of the Italian community. No one matching his name or description had been in Utica.[10]

Dan Prior was as surprised as everyone else when he learned of Saetta's statement. When he received his copy of Saetta's confession, he immediately made arrangements to meet with Governor Lehman. In light of this new evidence, Prior told the governor that he needed time to file a motion for a new trial. Lehman was hesitant. He wasn't about to make any decisions without at least conferring with the district attorney.

When district attorney John T. Delaney arrived at the governor's office, he expressed his reservations regarding the statement. It wasn't so much evidence as it was "an absolute fabrication of lies." The story that Vincent Saetta wanted everyone to believe, said Delaney, didn't come close to "anything that was brought out by our investigation of the murder or that was testified to at the trial."[11] As public sentiment now shifted in favor of Mrs. Antonio, Delaney reminded everyone in the governor's office of another confession. "The general public seems to forget," said Delaney, "that Mrs. Antonio confessed this crime orally and then to a stenographer."[12] Nevertheless, Delaney believed that Prior should have an opportunity to have his say in court. With both counsels in agreement, it was much easier for Lehman to make his decision: "I am granting a reprieve, until the week of July 9, in the case of all three."[13]

If Dan Prior breathed a sigh of relief at this news, it was no greater than the relief felt by the woman he was defending. That evening, the matrons were once again preparing to escort Anna Antonio to the electric chair when a guard arrived and announced that the governor had granted yet another reprieve. Her eyes swelled with tears as she slowly eased herself onto her prison bed. "Oh, thank God," she cried.[14]

On the other side of the Death House, the painter from Geneva merely nodded when told of this second reprieve. Nearby, his partner Saetta seemed equally unmoved by the announcement, but inwardly he may have harbored a certain degree of smug satisfaction as to what he had accomplished. The man who couldn't commit the perfect murder had succeeded in halting his own execution.

25

"THE PORTALS OF MERCY"

As far as Dan Prior was concerned, Saetta's confession literally breathed new life into the case of Anna Antonio. Could this be the piece of evidence he needed to obtain a new trial for his client and hopefully save her from the electric chair? Despite its ramblings, the street-language soliloquy of Saetta reinforced two salient points Prior had made in defense of his client. Not only was this not a murder for insurance money, but no conspiracy had ever existed between his client and Vincent Saetta. On July 2, four days after Saetta made his midnight confession, Dan Prior filed a forty-five-page brief in the Albany Courthouse requesting a reargument of the case on the grounds that this critical piece of evidence had been overlooked. On the face of the signed confession, Prior hoped that the court would look upon what Saetta had to say as the missing chapter in this murder case. Now was the time to put Vincent Saetta on the witness stand and get his version of what had happened. In a slightly vengeful tone, Prior reminded the court that when his client was on the witness stand, she was cross-examined by Delaney and Casey, but was also at the mercy of Saetta's attorney, Henry Lowenberg. Prior never forgot nor forgave Lowenberg for his ruthless attacks upon Anna Antonio's credibility and character while she was on the witness stand. "His counsel," said Prior in reference to Lowenberg, "was a bitter prosecutor of the appellant and his attitude and enmity toward the appellant Anna Antonio continued even to the hearing before the Governor on the application of executive clemency."[1] So incensed was Prior by Lowenberg's remarks at that meeting that Prior included a typed transcript in his brief to the court and had a copy forwarded to John Delaney.

In a trial that had no shortage of attorneys, Prior reminded the court that there was a real shortage of evidence. The key piece of evidence used against Saetta in the trial was his signed confession, a confession that Prior now believed was obtained in much the same manner that Faraci claimed his was obtained, "under circumstances which are to say the least bit suspicious from a legal viewpoint."[2] This new confession changed everything. Saetta never alluded to any insurance money. The only money he speaks of is a seventy-five-dollar loan to Sam Antonio and the forty dollars he received from his wife as a partial payment of this loan. The additional forty dollars he received from Anna was obtained, said Saetta, without her knowing that he had just killed her husband. There was no promise of a big-money payout from an insurance settlement, and therefore there was no conspiracy. The bad blood that existed between Saetta and Antonio escalated into murder on Castleton Road.

"He does not deny his guilt," said Prior, "but he does now say that the statement that he made [in police custody] involving this woman were false. . . . Saetta would have nothing to gain from such testimony, there would be no hope of reward for him. He must go to the electric chair."[3]

Having granted a reprieve until July 10, a relieved Governor Lehman saw that his role in the entire affair had become moot. With Dan Prior filing papers with the Albany court for a new trial based on Saetta's confession and John T. Delaney investigating the credibility of the confession, Lehman stepped aside. Now the decision of what to do—retrial or completion of the death sentence—was in the hands of the court and not him.

In addition to causing quite a stir outside the prison walls at Sing Sing, Prior discovered that Saetta's confession had inspired others to take up the cause of Anna Antonio. One such group was the Men's League of Mercy. Founded by playwright Ernst W. Cortis, the organization, which had its headquarters at his office at 309 Fifth Avenue in New York City, was ostensibly an anti–capital punishment for women organization. Moved by the plight of Ruth Snyder, Cortis announced plans, seven months after her conviction, to present a multitude of signatures to then Gov. Alfred E. Smith in hopes of convincing him to commute her death sentence. The *Philadelphia Inquirer* noted that the League was not seeking clemency for her paramour, convicted murderer Judd Gray.[4]

Cortis had been relatively quiet throughout Anna's stay in Sing Sing and hadn't taken up her cause until twelve days after Saetta's confession hit the newsstands. It was only then that he announced that the Men's League of Mercy had completed its own five-week investigation into the murder of Sam Antonio. Not surprisingly, Cortis claimed that Anna Antonio was totally innocent and deserved another day in court. A confident Cortis announced that he had forwarded his findings to some of the most famous trial lawyers in the country. Clarence Darrow, of Leopold and Loeb fame as well as the Scopes Trial, reportedly received a copy, as did Arthur Garfield Hays of the Sacco and Vanzetti case.[5] The *New York Times* claimed that the report was also sent to Cardinal Hayes, who in turn forwarded it to Pope Pius XI.[6] Later that month, Cortis announced that the Men's League of Mercy would form two splinter groups, the United States Alliance of Jews and Christians and the Allied Italian Societies of New York, to aid in the cause of Anna Antonio. The publicity that Cortis generated was admirable, but his claims remained suspect. Dan Prior never received a copy of this report, nor did John T. Delaney, and it didn't find its way to the desk of judge Earl Gallup. Cardinal Hayes never received it, and it is not among the papers of Clarence Darrow. The investigative report may never have existed, but the mere mention of it in the *New York Times* kept alive in the mind of the public the possibility that a miscarriage of justice had occurred in the case of Anna Antonio.[7]

Saetta's confession, together with the postponement of the execution, turned public sympathy in some quarters of New York toward Anna Antonio. One contributor to the *Brooklyn Daily Eagle* questioned the moral duty of the governor after it had been reported that Mrs. Antonio had fainted when told of the canceled execution. "Must [she] ever go through that again? Surely through your paper you will help save Mrs. Anna Antonio. I am sure that anyone with a soul will feel as I do. She has suffered twice. I am sure our Governor will never let it happen."[8] People may have expressed sympathy for Anna Antonio, but they were suspicious of Vincent Saetta. Newspapers across the state were divided over the issue. Was this confession simply a "crudely phrased, ungrammatical statement blabbered out by a man who thought he had only a quarter hour to live," leveled the *Albany Times Union,* or should it be accepted, in the words of the *Saratogian,* as "a gallant gesture to save a woman's life . . . the solemn truth spoken by a man about to die"?[9]

Either "a gallant gesture" or a desperate act to delay the execution, the man whose responsibility it was to determine what Saetta had in mind was the Albany district attorney. As it turned out, Henry Lowenberg was just as much a thorn in the side to John T. Delaney as he was to Dan Prior. Whereas Prior had clashed with Lowenberg throughout the trial, Delaney had to contend with the antics of the derisive attorney afterwards. A week after the failed clemency hearing at the governor's office, Lowenberg contacted Delaney with new information concerning Vincent Saetta. Lowenberg told Delaney that he had recently learned from a member of the Saetta family that Vincent Saetta had received a severe head injury while in the employ of the New York Central Railroad. This injury necessitated the insertion of a metal plate in Saetta's head by a medical team at Bellevue Hospital. Family members told Lowenberg that after this operation, Vincent was subject to violent mood swings. Information of this magnitude, maintained Lowenberg, justified a stay of execution so a team of psychiatrists could review the medical records.

Delaney disagreed. He told Lowenberg that as far as his office was concerned, the time for introducing Saetta's medical history had long passed. If it was as important as he said it was, family members should have come forward earlier and introduced this evidence during the trial—not on the eve of his execution. Besides, if Saetta did experience head trauma, he didn't display any signs of neurosis or violent behavior when he was arrested and none during the year he was in the Albany County Jail.

Receiving no satisfaction or support from Delaney's office, Lowenberg appealed directly to Governor Lehman and was summarily refused. Lehman told him that it was impossible for him to consider because a separate commission had already performed psychiatric evaluations on all three and declared each of them sane. Rebuffed by the governor, Lowenberg once more turned to Delaney. At 6:30 P.M. on the evening of the execution, Lowenberg telephoned Delaney and pleaded with him. Would he join forces with him and ask the governor for a stay of execution?

Any patience Delaney had with Lowenberg suddenly disappeared. He refused to join in and told Lowenberg that "no such delay would be tolerated."[10] An angry Lowenberg shot back. If a delay was not immediately forthcoming within the hour, his client was prepared to make a last-minute statement that would damage Delaney's reputation as a district attorney and eventually lead to his disbarment. Saetta would announce that he was the victim of a double-cross. Delaney had heard this before and couldn't believe that he was hearing it again. During the trial, Lowenberg had insinuated that Delaney had made a deal with Saetta. In return for a signed confession implicating Anna Antonio in the murder, Delaney was to ask for a reduced sentence for Saetta. Now, with the execution only a few hours away, Lowenberg offered a different version of an old story. On his way to the electric chair, Saetta would announce that Delaney had double-crossed his parents. Saetta would swear that Delaney had promised his parents that at the clemency hearing he would ask the governor for a reduced sentence. As an extra precaution, Lowenberg told Delaney that the Saetta family was willing to swear that this was promised them.

Delaney ignored the veiled threat of blackmail. Last-minute confessions and last words were as old as capital punishment. Saetta had every right to speak, just as Delaney had the right to ignore the troublesome attorney. It didn't take long for Delaney to discover that Lowenberg wasn't bluffing. Saetta made his speech right on cue, but with a dramatic twist. He didn't cry "double-cross" as Lowenberg had threatened but instead accepted full responsibility for the murder and at the same time declared the innocence of Anna Antonio. A little after midnight, Delaney received a phone call from the governor explaining what had transpired at Sing Sing and informing him of his decision to postpone the execution. Delaney assured the governor that he and his assistant, Joseph Casey, would go to Sing Sing the next day to interview Saetta. Lehman agreed, adding that his own counsel, Charles Poletti, would join them.

When the three arrived at Sing Sing and descended upon the warden's office, Delaney was immediately presented with a notarized copy of Saetta's confession together with a signed statement from Michael D'Ambrosio. Glancing casually at both affidavits, Delaney set them aside and asked to see Saetta. He wasn't interested in the confession. He had read it several times before he arrived at the warden's office. What he wanted now was to hear a more detailed account of the murder from the man who was never a witness at his own trial. Lawes, realizing the seriousness of this situation, instructed Clement Ferling to bring along his steno pad and join them in the consultation room in the Death House.

Escorted by the guards and later joined by the prison chaplain, Rev. John McCaffrey, Saetta half smiled at Delaney and Casey. The last time he had seen these two men was at his trial. Delaney was anxious to hear what Saetta had to say, and he wasn't disappointed. Answering a series of rapid-fire questions, Saetta flatly denied meeting with Anna Antonio at the Leland Theater to discuss the demise of her husband. Since he didn't meet with her, he had absolutely no knowledge of insurance money. When Delaney gently reminded him that Anna Antonio had mentioned the meeting in her own confession, Saetta said she was lying. Not only did he not meet with her, Saetta denied the multiple phone conversations that had taken place between the two of them. This was not a complicated affair, alleged Saetta. A grudge had existed between him and Sam Antonio over a long-standing debt of seventy-five dollars. He didn't deny killing him, but he now asserted that Sam Faraci had encouraged him.

For almost an hour, Charles Poletti had listened to the back-and-forth question-and-answer banter between the district attorney and Saetta. When his turn came, Poletti asked Saetta two questions. When, and at what particular moment, did he decide to speak out on behalf of Anna Antonio? What's more, Poletti wanted to know if Saetta had discussed his plans to make this dramatic statement with anyone during the year he had been incarcerated at Sing Sing. Saetta turned to Poletti and told him that he had always planned to say something to help Mrs. Antonio before the scheduled execution. He also told him that he was fairly certain that no one in the prison, save D'Ambrosio, knew of his plans. However, outside of the prison, he was absolutely positive that he had told his attorney of Anna Antonio's noncomplicity in the crime. Lowenberg was aware of this? Now it was Delaney's turn to smile. Lowenberg hadn't asked to be a part of this interview. He was in another part of the Death House interviewing Sam Faraci, trying, no doubt, to obtain a sworn statement from him.

A week later on July 5, Dan Prior arrived at the Albany Courthouse to argue for a new trial for his client, while John T. Delaney stood by determined not to let it happen. Prior, as passionate as ever in his defense of Anna Antonio, implored the judge to consider Saetta's latest statement as a justification for a new trial. Saetta's confession changed the entire texture of the last trial. Not only had Saetta admitted that he had killed Sam Antonio, he unequivocally stated that Anna Antonio was innocent of the crime. A new trial was needed so that his client would not once more be denied, as he said, the "full opportunity of justice."[11]

Delaney agreed with Prior on Saetta's guilt, but he didn't believe a new trial should be granted based solely on this latest confession. Saetta's denial of so many known facts surrounding the case made this a ludicrous request. As far as Prior's assertion that his case was hampered by Saetta's inability to testify at the trial in the case against his client, Delaney sharply disagreed. As all three defendants were being tried in the same court, Saetta had the right to testify against Anna Antonio and Sam Faraci. Exercising his Fifth Amendment right, Saetta did not have to testify on his own behalf and did not on the advice of his attorney. In hindsight, said Delaney, it would have been a great gamble on the part of Dan Prior to have Saetta testify. Prior, he said, "Did not know whether he would tell the truth or would tell a story tending to vindicate the defendant. Would his story on the stand be favorable or unfavorable to defendant Antonio? As long as that questioned remained unanswered they did not dare call him as a witness. Now, as a last resort to prolong his worthless life he has agreed to tell a new story exonerating her."[12]

The decision to order a new trial lay in the hands of the judge who had presided over the existing case, and he wasn't about to change a thing. Judge Gallup viewed the first confession signed by Saetta as a critical piece of evidence in the case. "This confession," said Gallup, "was very voluminous, went into great detail to tell all the plans and preparations of the crime, as well as the manner in which it was committed."[13] Saetta's first confession contained information that was substantiated during the investigation and later at the trial. This second confession was not new evidence as it simply lacked substance. If a new trial was to be granted, ruled Judge Gallup, credible evidence was needed. Echoing the sentiments of John Delaney, Gallup said that the most important piece of evidence at the trial were the signed confessions. "The fact that the defendant Antonio herself confessed to her part in the crime and that her confession was accepted by a jury as voluntary and representing the truth, the Court is satisfied that if the case were retried the same verdict would probably be rendered," concluded Gallup. "The motion for a new trial must, therefore, be denied."[14]

Prior expected nothing less from Gallup and made plans to appeal his ruling. On July 16, Dan Prior, in the company of Charles J. Duncan, appeared before the Court of Appeals. Since Saetta's confession vaguely implicated Sam Faraci, Duncan was in favor of a new trial for Anna Antonio. If she was granted a new trial, Sam Faraci would most likely receive one. Prior and Duncan spoke for approximately a half hour each on behalf of their respective clients. The court, however, reached a unanimous decision in less time. The motion to reargue the case for the purpose of having a new trial was denied. A disappointed Dan Prior left the courtroom and was immediately beset by reporters eager to quote him on this latest setback in his defense of Anna Antonio. "It would appear," said Prior, "to be a denial of justice to refuse a review of the order denying her a new trial."[15]

Still, Prior wasn't about to give up on his client. With only three weeks remaining before the scheduled execution, Prior made plans to introduce another motion for a new trial. Obviously, the failure of the last motion—that of Saetta's impromptu confession—was based in part on Delaney's postconfession interview with Saetta. If Prior hoped to secure a new trial for his client, he would need a respected reliable witness. Since Saetta was looked at as a sinner, Prior looked elsewhere and found a saint. On July 30, Prior announced that he was once again filing a motion for a new trial based upon the sworn affidavit of Father William A. Brown, assistant pastor at St. Joseph's Roman Catholic Church in Albany.

Father Brown claimed that by sheer coincidence, he had, on July 19, a chance meeting with Dan Prior in New York City. In the course of their conversation, the priest mentioned that it was he who had administered the last rights of the Roman Catholic Church to Sam Antonio at Memorial Hospital. He then went on to say that after leaving the hospital and upon his return to the rectory, he called Anna Antonio. "I asked if she was Mrs.

Antonio and she answered that she was. I then told her that her husband had been in an accident and was at Memorial Hospital. She screamed when I told her this. I then advised her to get in touch with the hospital and hung up." Father Brown told Prior that although he was aware of the murder trial, he didn't follow it closely in the newspapers. He didn't feel that the conversation he had with Mrs. Antonio was important. Prior assured him that it was and asked if he would swear to this in court. Brown assured him that he would "testify at any trial or proceeding."[16]

On August 2, Dan Prior raced to Elizabethtown in Essex County and went directly to the home of Supreme Court Justice O. Byron Brewster. After Prior introduced himself, he explained the purpose of his unannounced visit and then presented the jurist with Father Brown's affidavit, together with motion papers for a new trial. The case Prior described was not unknown to the forty-eight-year-old judge. He had read all about the Antonio trial in the newspapers and was aware of the appellate court ruling denying her a new trial.

Prior said that the sworn statement of Father Brown changed everything. On the witness stand, Anna testified that she did not suddenly appear at Memorial Hospital as Flubacher had insinuated. She testified that in the early morning hours of Easter Sunday, she had received a phone call from someone who informed her that her husband had been seriously injured. When she was unable to identify the person who made the call, Delaney had his doubts that such a call actually existed. In addition to this, Father Brown's statement changed another trial misunderstanding regarding Anna Antonio. He said she screamed on the telephone when told of her husband's injuries. Delaney said that one of the most disturbing things about Anna Antonio was her utter lack of emotion when informed of her husband's death at Memorial Hospital in the presence of Flubacher and none at the precinct station when told that Saetta and Faraci were the men who killed her husband. Anna's scream on the telephone was a clear demonstration of emotion that Delaney claimed was suspiciously lacking.

Justice Brewster was intrigued. He knew Dan Prior by reputation only, but he may have admired his tenacity. How many attorneys would, with only days before the scheduled execution, make a one-hundred-mile dash to his doorstep to personally deliver the affidavit and motion papers for a new trial? Brewster nodded to Prior and told him that a

Show Cause Order would be sent to the Albany district attorney's office. Delaney would now have to appear and explain why, in light of his new evidence, a new trial should be denied to Anna Antonio.

Delaney's reaction to the Show Cause Order was sharp and swift. Believing that he had heard the last of the Antonio motions and delays, he looked upon Prior's latest move as "a last minute effort to make something out of nothing. Of course she is not entitled to a new trial and we will oppose it."[17] Delaney didn't deny or suspect the sincerity of Father Brown, but clearly his statement did not absolve Mrs. Antonio of any wrongdoing. "It may well be that Father Brown was the person who called Mrs. Antonio," said Delaney, "but how is that material to the question of her guilt?" This latest installment of "new evidence," said Delaney, was as meaningless as the Saetta confession and should not be considered by the court. It was, as he said, another effort by Dan Prior "to evade justice and to make a mockery of the administration of the criminal law in this state."[18]

Delaney's main concern regarding Father Brown's sworn statement was the time frame of the phone calls Anna Antonio received on that Easter morning. At her trial, Anna Antonio testified that she had received a telephone call somewhere between 4:00 and 4:30 A.M. from Vincent Saetta. After speaking with him, she took a taxi from her Teunis Street apartment and met Saetta at the corner of Broadway and Columbia Streets. Saetta told her what had happened and was either presented with or demanded forty dollars. In his affidavit, Father Brown clearly states that after administering the last rights to Sam Antonio at Memorial Hospital, he returned to the rectory and called her at 5:00 A.M. She may have screamed when Father Brown called, but she was most certainly already aware of what had happened to her husband.

On August 8, townspeople as well as summer tourists descended upon the courthouse in Elizabethtown to hear firsthand the decision of Justice O. Byron Brewster. A reporter for the *Albany Times Union,* upon viewing the red brick courthouse for the first time with its lush green lawn, thought it "looked more like a country club," noting that many present had set aside their golf clubs and tennis rackets to attend the day's proceedings. Elizabethtown was a small community, and the locals took note of strangers in their midst. Heads turned and people whispered when

John T. Delaney walked to the front of the courtroom. A while later, at 10:20 A.M., the bailiff announced the arrival of Justice Brewster.[19]

After reading aloud Father Brown's affidavit, along with Prior's statement asking for a new trial and Delaney's opposition to a new trial, Justice Brewster announced his decision. "The jury," said Brewster, "probably would have found her guilty even if this evidence had been introduced at the trial." Basing his decision on the chronological sequence of the telephone calls, Judge Brewster was in agreement with Delaney. "She knew her plan to have her husband killed had been executed before she received the call from Rev. Brown. . . . I am perfectly aware of the gravity of my decision. I find, however, that the difficulty of its rendition is due to considerations that have no proper place in the stern administration of justice, eloquent and potent as they may be, at the portals of mercy. I am placed and limited by our procedure and statutory rules. Motion denied."[20]

In a matter of minutes, it was all over. The sharp bang of his gavel broke the silence of the courtroom. Townspeople filed out of the court and went about their day while reporters raced to the nearest telephones to call their editors. One reporter from the *Albany Times Union* called Dan Prior to get his reaction to yet another setback in the defense of Anna Antonio. "I honestly don't know what I am going to do right now," said Prior. "I just learned of the decision, but I have not seen the opinion. I must read over the opinion before deciding anything."[21] Sadly, Dan Prior knew that there was nothing more he could do to help Anna Antonio. The *Yonkers Herald* translated Brewster's eloquent decision in plain words: "His decision closed every legal avenue of escape from the chair for Mrs. Antonio."[22] Only the governor's direct intervention could save her, and Prior knew that this would never happen. Previously, Lehman had agreed with the courts, and Prior didn't see any reason why he wouldn't do the same again.

Meanwhile, at the district attorney's office in Albany, there were no self-congratulatory plaudits or shouts of victory. Immediately after Justice Brewster had rendered his decision, Delaney called his office and directed one of his assistants to release a statement to the press. As his assistant, Joseph Casey, had been an outspoken critic of Prior's latest effort at Elizabethtown, characterizing it as "merely an attempt to make a mockery of administration of the criminal law of this state," Delaney chose another member of his staff to make an official statement to the press.[23]

"We feel," said the assistant district attorney, Henry Kahn, in a prepared statement to the *Albany Times Union,* "that the decision was in accordance with the law. While the district attorney's office is not elated over the decision, we feel that we have done our duty."[24]

In the Death House at Sing Sing, Anna Antonio had been exercising in the corridor with one of the matrons and seemed cautiously hopeful. Earlier that day she said, "I am so anxious to learn what is to become of me. I've been through so much torment I wonder if my troubles will ever be over. I haven't lost faith for the future yet." Now, that faith and optimism were dashed. When told that the motion for a new trial had been denied, the matron observed that Anna was "momentarily stunned, too dumbfounded and thunderstruck" to speak. Her eyes slowly filled with tears. She slowly walked into her cell, laid on her cot, and wept bitterly. The next day, August 9, she would go to the electric chair. It was Marie's seventh birthday.[25]

26

AUGUST 9, 1934

When news of the Elizabethtown decision reached the Death House, the three who had waited so anxiously for the outcome reacted in ways that reflected their personalities. The toughest of the three, Vincent Saetta, seemed indifferent. He knew all along that he would eventually walk the last mile. His last-minute confession simply stalled the inevitable. The bluff, the lie, the charade, the game, whatever one might want to call it, was over. On Saetta's last day, Warden Lawes arrived at his cell and informed him that several people were there to see him. Escorted to the visitors room, he was met by his mother, four sisters, a brother-in-law, a nephew, and an old girlfriend, Marie Pellerina.[1] Noticeably absent was his father. On this last day, Antonio Saetta saw no need to reconcile with the son who had been so troublesome in the past and now had brought shame upon his family. Vincent Saetta kissed his mother and sisters good-bye and was returned to his cell near the green door to await execution. As was the case six weeks earlier, the thought of death didn't diminish his appetite. Saetta sat in his little cell and gorged himself on a last meal that consisted of a roast chicken, Italian sausage, salad cucumbers, ice cream, pineapple pie, and orangeade.[2]

Nearby in a cell sat a despondent Sam Faraci. For the most part, his fate had been inextricably tied to that of Anna Antonio. A new trial for her would naturally result in a new trial for him. Slightly encouraged that his attorney, Charles Duncan, assisted Prior with several of the appeals, Faraci knew that the decision at Elizabethtown was the end of him. As he waited his turn to have the prison barber shave the necessary square on the back of his head, his thoughts may have wandered. Perhaps he was thinking about the dozen or so men he witnessed walk that last mile toward the dreaded green door to the death chamber. Because the cells were arranged in such a way that inmates could not see each other, they had to be content with conversation. It was in this way that Sam Faraci became acquainted with Frank Canora.

A gas station and restaurant owner from Lodi, New Jersey, the fifty-one-year-old Canora was waiting his turn in the Death House after being convicted of the torch murder of his wife. Following an intense argument with his wife on the subject of divorce and dividing property, Frank Canora momentarily feigned reconciliation and lured his unsuspecting wife into his vehicle. On a pretext of a ride in the country, the silver-haired Canora drove a few miles across the New Jersey border to Spring Valley, New York. After viciously slashing his wife's throat, Canora attempted to conceal her body by dragging it behind a large boulder. He then doused the unconscious woman with a five-gallon can of gasoline and set her ablaze. Canora surrendered to the authorities in New Jersey, waived extradition, and went to trial in Rockland County. An unsympathetic jury declared him guilty, and an equally unsympathetic judge sentenced the father of two boys to the electric chair.[3]

In Canora, Faraci had found his only friend in the Death House. Both were immigrants from Italy and had estranged marriages and children who had for the most part been abandoned by them. Save for the presence of the prison chaplain, Canora had not seen one visitor in the year he had been sitting on death row. His only company was Faraci. From cell to cell the two spoke each day. The only time their conversation was interrupted was when an inmate was escorted past them to the dance hall cells nearest the green door. When this happened, Canora wept hysterically and prayed aloud each time a man—and there were twenty-one of them in the time he had been in the Death House—passed by his cell. When his turn came on July 12, Canora bade farewell to each of the eleven men in the Death House. His last words to Sam Faraci were to be brave when his time came. Now, it was Faraci's turn to weep.[4]

When the prison barber had finished shaving the back of his head for the placement of the electrodes, Sam Faraci was given the prison menu. As with his partner, the thought of death didn't interfere with his appetite this time either. He ordered a steak, fried potatoes, strawberry shortcake, apple pie, and ice cream.[5]

On the opposite side of the Death House, in the women's wing, Anna Antonio struggled with her emotions. Direct intervention on the part of Governor Lehman was her last hope. As the minutes passed to hours, she grew more restless. "The Governor knows everything," she said in despair, "why doesn't he say something?" As more hours slipped by, she realized that the governor's silence meant that he wasn't about to interfere. Turning to one of the matrons, she said, "It looks as if they've all turned me down." With a great sigh, she gazed about the small cell that had been her living space for the last sixteen months. Pictures of her children adorned the drab walls. Staring at the crucifix of her faith and with tears streaming down her cheeks, she shook her head. "God alone can help me now." Dazed from lack of sleep and weak from refusing to eat, her confused mind began to drift. For a moment she rambled incoherently about her children and then quietly asked one of the matrons, "When I go, who will get the canary?"[6]

That evening, the mild sedative prescribed by Dr. Amos Squire was only mildly effective in helping her sleep. For most of the evening and into the morning hours, she slipped in and out of consciousness. She would suddenly awake, stare at the cell door in a trancelike way, and then sob hysterically. "I've been through enough to kill a million people," she said in her delirium, "I am almost dead now. I feel at times as though I am not breathing."[7] The next morning, she rose from her prison cot and set to work immediately at the sewing machine, completing a dress for her daughter. It was Marie's birthday, and although just a few days earlier she had held out hope for a cheerful reunion, she worked feverishly to complete the dress. "Just because I must die," she confided to a matron, "is no reason that little Marie should suffer on her birthday." The dress and a box of chocolates was all she could do. Then, in a rare moment of self-pity, she added, "Maybe it would have been better if I had died the night she was born. The children would have been spared the disgrace."[8]

As with the previous day and some of the ones before that, Anna refused any suggestion of food. She passed up the customary last meal and instead sipped a cup of coffee while she sewed. The mental strain and anguish she had suffered for the last few months had clearly taken their toll on her health. "I don't think I'll be able to stand up at the end," she confided to one of the matrons. "They'll have to carry me." One man on the prison staff who was inclined to agree with her was Dr. Amos Squire. "During her fifteen months of confinement," noted the Sing Sing physician, "her weight had dropped off twenty pounds, until she weighed scarcely eighty pounds."[9] She was simply flesh on bones and in such a weakened emaciated state that Dr. Squire felt certain she would literally have to be carried to the electric chair.

Whereas Saetta received many visitors on his last day, Anna Antonio had just two, her brother and her son. Three-year-old Frankie entertained himself by running down the corridor of the women's wing, chasing a red ball, too young and innocent to comprehend what was taking place. Warden Lawes, who was present, remembered the poignant moment: "It's not often that the sound of a child's laughter can be heard in the Death House at Sing Sing, but it was that evening."[10]

The conversation between Anna and Patsy inevitably centered on the children. "She asked about her babies," he recalled. "She wanted to be sure they would be taken care of." Patsy assured his sister that he would raise Frankie as if he were his own child. In time, he told her that he would do his utmost to remove Phyllis and Marie from St. Vincent Female Orphan Asylum and reunite them with their little brother. "I told her that I would look after them just as if they were my own."[11]

When it came time to say her final good-byes, Anna, fighting back tears, called to little Frankie. He had been bouncing a ball in the corridor when his mother presented him with a bright red apple. "Here, Frankie," she said, "here's another ball for you. It won't bounce but it's a nice ball, just the same." The little boy laughed. "You can't fool me, it's no ball, Mama. It's an apple!" Anna held him in her arms one last time and whispered, "I hope you grow up to be a good man, Frankie."[12]

With tears in her eyes, she embraced the brother who had stood by her side throughout this long terrible nightmare. They held each other in their arms one last time in a warm embrace. The emotional strain Patsy had endured the last few weeks had broken him. As he sobbed aloud, his sister comforted him with little Frankie's thoughts of a tomorrow. "Patsy," she whispered, "let's make believe it isn't going to happen. Let's pretend I will still be here tomorrow, and the next day and the next. Let's look forward to your visit with me the next time. No end at all. I shall be here the next time you call." As Patsy turned and walked down the corridor with Frankie, Anna, still sobbing, cried out one last time. "Promise me, that you will look after the children."[13]

At the orphanage in Albany, there were more tears. Marie was sitting next to one of the nuns, eating a piece of birthday cake, when her sister Phyllis, with tears in her eyes, sat beside her. Unaware of what was about to take place in Sing Sing, Marie asked, "Why are you crying? Aren't you happy because it's my birthday?" Phyllis broke down and sobbed with no one to comfort her but her little sister. Marie soon learned the truth and for the rest of her life never celebrated her birthday again.[14]

Alone in her cell, Anna sank to her cot, buried her face in the pillow, and bitterly wept. The matrons, who were never far from her, did their best to console her but to no avail. It was only through the intervention of Father McCaffrey that she was able to regain her composure. As the hours slipped by, she still held out hope that a phone call from the governor would save her as it had done on two previous occasions. "Surely the Governor won't let them do this to me," she lamented.[15] Unbeknownst to Anna, Dan Prior and her brother Patsy had telephoned Governor Lehman in hopes of obtaining another postponement, and with the execution only hours away, a delegation of Brooklyn officials descended upon the executive chambers to make a final plea for Anna's life. Brownsville party boss Hyman Schorenstein, King County commissioner of records, who had been instrumental in securing the nomination of Lehman to the governorship, was joined by Walter R. Hart. Lehman accepted the petitions presented to him by his old friend and benefactor but offered no comment. When Hart, who spoke on behalf of the large Italian American community of Brooklyn, ended his speech, Lehman once more politely listened and offered no comment.[16]

When the prison barber appeared at her cell to shave the back of her head for the placement of the electrodes, she knew her situation was hopeless. She gently sobbed as locks of her thick black hair tumbled to the cell floor. Shortly after that, Warden Lawes appeared. As was his habit, he always visited anyone who was about to walk the last mile. He offered his heartfelt apologies for what was to take place and also apologized for his wife, who was unable to be there. "I'm not afraid to die," she said, "I did not tell those men to kill my husband for insurance money of $5,000. I could have killed him a dozen times, the house was always full of dope and guns. One of these men came to see me and said they were going to kill my husband and I said 'I do not care what happens to my husband. I care only for my children.'"[17]

At 11:00 P.M., the somber procession began. Prison chaplain Father McCaffrey, attired in a black cassock with a purple stole, carried a small wooden crucifix and walked beside Anna down the hall and through the green door, reciting the "Litany of the Dead." Her voice trembled as she repeated, "Lord have mercy, Christ have mercy." In the death chamber, witnesses in the first row could hear Anna continue with her prayers. "O God the Father, creator of world, have mercy on the souls of the faithful departed." For many of the witnesses, including reporter Robin Harris, this was the first time they had ever seen Anna Antonio. Up to this time she had been only a grainy image in a newspaper. "She was the smallest thing you ever saw," he recalled.

To the surprise of many, Anna walked unfaltering to the electric chair. She sat herself down, and while Elliott adjusted the leather straps about her, Harris noted that Anna's "big brown eyes were fixed in an unseeing stare." He, too, stared at the little woman in the soft blue gown and thought how, in an instant, electricity would spoil what remained "of her Latin prettiness." From his vantage point, Harris watched as Elliott made his final adjustment. "Her black hair," noted Harris, "dank from being moistened so that the electrode would not singe it hung drearily over her thin face."[18]

Elliott stepped back, and with a nod, Father McCaffrey leaned forward toward Anna. After she had kissed the crucifix, Elliott placed the hood over her head. As he walked to his electrical panel, Lucy Many and Carrie Stephens stepped forward and positioned themselves directly in front of Anna, thus obscuring the view of most of the witnesses. They were determined, and Lawes was in total agreement, that the first woman to be electrocuted since Ruth Snyder would not face the same ignominy of having her picture appear in the newspapers.

At his electrical panel, Elliott paused. He, too, felt a tinge of remorse. "A wave of pity for this frail little mother swept over me."[19] He then turned a switch and released two thousand volts into her body and did it again. "Her skinny frame stiffened against the straps as electricity shot from head to foot," observed Harris. As a small puff of smoke drifted out from beneath the hood, he distinctly heard the crackle of electricity. "A small shower of sparks when a drop of water from her wet hair fell on the metal electrode attached to her leg," wrote Harris, causing one of the witnesses to faint. Dr. Charles Sweet stepped forward and placed his stethoscope to Anna's heart and in a solemn voice said, "This woman is dead." It was all over in two minutes.[20]

If it had been a tradition or unwritten rule of the prison during multiple executions to send the weakest to their death first, it didn't hold true that evening. "In life woman may be the weaker sex," said Lewis Lawes, "but on the road to death, no one has walked with stronger and swifter feet than Anna Antonio. . . . Mrs. Antonio was as brave as any man who ever walked the last mile."[21]

Minutes after the lifeless body of Anna Antonio had been placed on a gurney and wheeled into the autopsy room, the green door was opened again. Sam Faraci seemed oblivious to the prayers that Father McCaffrey was reciting. Staring at the crowd that was about to watch him die, he calmly sat down in the electric chair. "There was a stupid bewilderment smile upon his face," noted one journalist, while another panned his attire. Faraci wore a "violent salmon colored shirt" open at the neck with rolled-up sleeves and gray trousers. The Catholic scapula about his neck seemed out of place as he was all but ignoring the prayers of Father McCaffrey.

When the leather straps were tightened about his body and the electrodes soaked in brine were placed on his leg and skull, Faraci looked out at the twenty-five witnesses and offered some final words. "I want to thank you gentlemen," he said in a loud voice, "I'm going to the chair, but I'm innocent. That's all I can say. I thank you gentlemen and I wish you all good luck, every one of you, for the rest of your lives. I want to thank you all." When Elliott placed the hood over Faraci's head, one reporter, unmoved by the sentimental last words of a man who had knifed Sam Antonio a dozen times or so, commented, "I think it's a case of—'thanks for nothing.'"[22]

With Elliott in position, Lawes nodded, and the process began again, the only difference being that the witnesses didn't have an obstructed view. As a whirring sound and the crackle of electricity filled the air,

Faraci lurched violently forward as Elliott sent a five-second blast of electricity into his body. Gazing at his watch, Elliott reduced the voltage to one thousand volts and thirty seconds later sent another two thousand volts into Faraci. Dr. Sweet came forward, applied his stethoscope to Faraci, and motioned to Elliott that he detected a pulse. The doctor stepped to one side and Elliott administered an additional surge of electricity. Once more, Sweet applied his stethoscope to Faraci. "I declare this man dead."

Now, it was time for Vincent Saetta. As the green door opened, Saetta walked into the death chamber and, like Faraci before him, ignored the prayers recited by Father McCaffrey. With the ease as if he was walking up to a bar in the south end of Albany, he cheerfully exclaimed, "Hello, Doc." Dr. Charles Sweet, taken aback by his gallows humor, simply nodded. Of the three, Saetta was viewed with perhaps the most skepticism by the press due to his "confession" of June 28 a scant fifteen minutes before Anna Antonio was to be executed. Was he, as one reporter surmised, a Sydney Carton–type of character from A Tale of Two Cities, who would selflessly go to his death to save another? Many reporters, however, found it difficult to accept the idea that this last-minute statement was indeed a "gallant gesture" to save Anna Antonio. To many journalists, Saetta was "the jailhouse gallant," nothing more than "the speaker of the beautiful lie."[23]

Oddly, the man who had plenty to say on one occasion offered no last words as he was being strapped into the electric chair. He grinned broadly at the crowd as Elliott drew the hood over his head. Within minutes, he, too, was sent to eternity. While the witnesses filed out of the death chamber, Lewis Lawes went to his office and placed a phone call to the governor. "It's all over," he said.[24]

The next day at 10:00 A.M., Michael DeMarco arrived at Sing Sing prison to collect the body of Anna Antonio. The Schenectady undertaker was greeted by Warden Lawes, who politely asked if he would be interested in touring the Death House and seeing the electric chair. DeMarco graciously declined. Understandingly, Lawes led him to the morgue, where the shroud-covered bodies lay. Gently drawing the shroud of the corpse of Anna Antonio, DeMarco stared for a moment at the lifeless body of the woman Patsy Cappello had entrusted to him.

Lawes broke the silence by calmly remarking that the blue dress Anna was wearing was a gift from his wife. Mrs. Lawes, he said, was extremely fond of Mrs. Antonio. DeMarco nodded and went about preparing the body for the long ride home.

On the drive north to Schenectady, DeMarco had plenty of time to think about the funeral arrangements. His main concern was crowd control. A sizable crowd had gathered outside the main gate at the prison the night she was executed. DeMarco thought her funeral would attract an even bigger crowd. Since the *Schenectady Gazette* had already announced that the funeral would take place at the Cappello home at 1027 Barrett Street, DeMarco had to convince Patsy Cappello that given the size of his second-floor apartment, it would be impractical, if not impossible, to conduct the service there. Later, Patsy agreed with DeMarco, and the service was moved to the DeMarco Funeral Home at 548 Strong Street.

The abrupt change proved to be a wise move. DeMarco, like many funeral directors, was more concerned about the living than the dead. After more than a dozen years, he knew what to expect when family and friends entered his establishment. What he had no control over were the throngs of morbid curiosity seekers. Buoyed by the latest headline in the *Albany Times Union*, "Curious Banned from Antonio Funeral," DeMarco could only hope that the public would respect the family's privacy.[25] They didn't. The line of mourners, sincere and otherwise, stretched a good five blocks from the front door of the funeral home and down Summit Avenue near Jane's Card Shop near Albany Street.[26]

The scene wasn't that much different the next day at the church service at St. Antony's. Before the hearse arrived at the church, the *Schenectady Gazette* estimated that well over two hundred people had gathered on the sidewalks, prompting Father Michael Bianco to address the crowd. Speaking in Italian from the front steps of the church, he implored the crowd to show some decency and respect for the family. The paper noted that his appeal had little effect. The crowd seemed to swell as the DeMarco hearse pulled up in front of the church. While some drew as near as they could to catch a glimpse of the casket, others filed into the church.[27]

The family was already seated in the front pews when the pallbearers entered the candlelit church carrying a small white casket. Patsy was there with his wife Concetta, as was Ferdinando, his aged father. Anna's sisters, Concetta Audi and Marie Gianetti, sat with their husbands. Marie's sons, Michael and Victor, served as pallbearers. The only ones missing were the children. Patsy thought it best to leave little Frankie with a babysitter and not to remove Phyllis and Marie from the orphanage.

Although the press made the claim that Anna's dying wish was to be buried next to her husband, it was never considered. Mary DeSisto, Sam's sister, would have never allowed this to happen, nor would Patsy, who had made the funeral arrangements. Anna was buried in the Cappello family plot at St. Anthony's Cemetery in Glenville. The graveside service was small and simple. The immediate family was present along with two special friends. At the last minute, Mrs. Lawes announced that she would be unable to attend the service, but not before making arrangements to have her husband's car made available to the matrons. Lucy Many and Carrie Stephens wept at the graveside of the woman they had cared for and loved for the last fifteen and a half months. The warden's wife never forgot Anna Antonio and held her in the highest regard. Later, when a reporter asked the warden's wife of her opinions on other women who had gone to the electric chair, Mrs. Lawes said, "Mrs. Antonio was a saint."[28]

In Geneva and Queens, it was a much different story. For Sam Faraci and Vincent Saetta, there were no crowds or flowers. The Sing Sing Mutual Welfare League had provided funds to have Faraci's body returned to Geneva, where it was received with little fanfare. His wife Mary arranged for a small funeral service for her estranged husband and had the body buried at St. Patrick's Cemetery.[29] Saetta's funeral was held at his parents' house at 63-14 Thirty-Ninth Avenue in Woodside, Queens. It, too, was a small affair attended by family and a few friends. Vincent Saetta was buried at Calvary Cemetery in Queens.[30]

Part IV

AFTERWARDS

27

THE CUSTODY WAR

Two days before his sister's funeral, a reporter for the *Albany Times Union* asked Patsy Cappello how he was going to tell the children their mother had died. "I guess," he said with a deep sigh, "I'll tell them that Anna got sick and went to heaven." He also made it a point to tell the reporter that he had made a solemn pledge to his sister to look after all three children. Frankie had been in his care since the day Anna had been arrested and sent to the Albany County Jail, while the girls were in St. Vincent Female Orphan Asylum. "Later, I'll take them," he said, "That's what Anna was worried most about."[1]

What Anna Antonio "was worried most about" wasn't so much *how* the children would be cared for as it was *who* would care for them. On several occasions prior to her June 28 execution date, she communicated with Albany Children's Court judge John J. Brady, imploring him not to award custody of her three children to sister-in-law Mary De-Sisto. The *Albany Times Union* correctly predicted that a custody battle would be the next chapter in this ongoing drama. While Patsy Cappello made arrangements for his sister's funeral, Mary DeSisto moved forward with plans of her own. With the death of Anna Antonio, her three children were officially declared orphans and as such became wards of the state. If no one stepped forward to gain custody or adopt them together or separately, they would be placed in foster homes. From her home in the Bronx, Mary DeSisto moved quickly and secured the services of Albany attorney George Rothlauf. She instructed him to draw up the necessary papers for her to obtain legal guardianship of all three Antonio children.

Rothlauf presented her request to Supreme Court Justice Gilbert V. Schenk. In the papers, Mary DeSisto based her claim to guardianship on the premise that not only was she better suited to care for all three children, but as a sister of their deceased father, she was the nearest living relative. No one, she asserted, had any legal right to the children as neither Sam Antonio nor Anna had a will. Incredibly, Justice Schenk signed the guardianship papers knowing full well that Patsy Cappello could make the same claim as Anna's brother. It was common knowledge in Albany that little Frankie had been in Cappello's care. Heartwarming pictures of the little boy with his uncle had been in all the newspapers. By awarding Mary DeSisto guardianship, Justice Schenk simply put phase one of the custody battle into action.

Mary DeSisto knew that she would have little trouble serving papers to the nuns at St. Vincent to gain the release of Phyllis and Marie. Frankie, however, was a different matter. The hatred she harbored in her heart toward her sister-in-law carried over to Anna's brother. Fearing an unpleasant encounter at the Cappello home, she elected to remain in the car while her attorney and a sheriff's deputy served papers and retrieved Frankie.

It was an astonished Concetta Cappello who answered the door that afternoon. After overcoming the initial shock at seeing a uniformed officer on her doorstep, Concetta had a fair idea of what was about to happen when the gentleman next to him introduced himself as Mrs. DeSisto's attorney. With court documents in hand, and motioning toward the parked car on the street, Rothlauf told her that Frankie was no longer to be in their care. His legal guardian, Mary DeSisto, was waiting for him. Concetta replied that Frankie was outdoors playing with one of the neighborhood children and that her husband was at work. Could she call him? Rothlauf thought for a moment and agreed that as this was a delicate situation, it would perhaps be best for her husband to be present.

Patsy Cappello raced home from work, parked the car in the garage, and dashed into the house, where he immediately broke down and wept hysterically. He was still sobbing when Concetta, who had momentarily left to get Frankie, reentered the house with the boy in tow. With tears streaming down his cheeks, Patsy asked if he might be able to give the boy a bath. "I want to dress him up nice." Rothlauf, seeing how emotionally distraught Cappello was at the prospect of losing the child, agreed. As fifteen minutes slipped by to a half hour, Rothlauf became concerned. How long does it take to give a little boy a bath? After shouts to Patsy and Frankie went unanswered, the sheriff's deputy searched the house, only to discover that the pair had escaped. When Rothlauf and the deputy were in front of the house with Concetta, Patsy and Frankie made their getaway out the back door. Meanwhile, Mary DeSisto correctly deduced that something was wrong when she saw Rothlauf and the deputy leave the Cappello home without Frankie. Apprised of the situation by her lawyer, a furious Mary DeSisto said this was kidnapping and demanded that Cappello be arrested. By the end of the day, police agencies across the state received a teletype message alerting them to be on the lookout for "Pasquale Cappello, residing this city. He is 35 years old, 5 feet, 7 inches, wavy black hair, 145 pounds. Accused of kidnapping on Frank Antonio, three years old, from 1027 Barrett Street, after having been served with a Supreme Court notice signed by Justice Schenk of Albany county, to deliver the child to his guardian."[2]

In the 1930s, kidnappings often involved high-profile individuals who had the ability to obtain ransom money in an expedient manner. The kidnapping of famed aviator Charles Lindbergh's son in 1932 and Canadian beer mogul John Labatt two years later were typical. Closer to home, everyone in Albany recalled the 1933 kidnapping of John O'Connell. In Schenectady, chief of police William Funston remained calm in his belief that the Cappello affair was not your typical kidnapping. This was not as much a kidnapping for ransom as it was a desperate act motivated by love. The *Schenectady Gazette* told its readers that Patsy Cappello should be pitied rather than punished for what he had done. Cappello, they said, was driven "half mad over the prospective loss of a child which he was fond," adding that this wasn't the work of "a professional snatcher."[3] Chief Funston was inclined to believe this, but he was duty-bound to actively search for Cappello. Soon after the teletype was released, his office was inundated with Cappello sightings. A man and a boy were seen on this street or that street, near this store or that park.

Some contacted his office claiming that they had just received a phone call from Cappello. Funston's men investigated as many of these leads as they could. In one instance, he received a report that Cappello had been spotted making a phone call from a service station two miles west of Scotia. When police arrived at the gas station, owner Fred Balder said that a man matching Cappello's description, in the company of a small boy, had been there hours earlier and had asked to use the phone. Not only could Balder not remember what direction they drove off in, he couldn't recall the make and model of the car. Funston soon discovered that the Barrett Street neighbors weren't much help either. In fact, Funston discovered that sympathetic neighbors and friends had assisted Cappello in eluding the authorities. "He left home in a taxi," concluded Funston, "going in the direction of Amsterdam. He dismissed the driver several miles out, went to a house and made a telephone call, and then started walking back to the city. We think an automobile met him."[4] The automobile in question was Cappello's car, driven to him by one of his neighbors. As soon as Funston confirmed the reports that Patsy Cappello was in constant contact with his wife, neighbors, and friends, he relaxed the search. "I am certain now," he said in a statement to the press, "he is perfectly alright. I have discarded any fears I may have had."[5]

With Patsy on the run, Concetta suddenly found herself, for the first time, in the public eye. She turned on the charm and presented to the press an image of a struggling husband trying to maintain a household on the meager wages he earned at General Electric. Entertaining neighbors as well as the press, Concetta now took the opportunity to dispel rumors that had appeared in print regarding Phyllis and Marie. The statement she made regarding three letters she had received from families in New York City interested in adopting the girls was taken out of context. "We'd like to keep Phyllis and Marie," said Concetta, "but Pasquale spent every cent he had in an effort to save Anna. We have paid for the lawyers she had and for her funeral and we are in debt. My husband is working only two or three days a week and we could not provide properly for the girls. Both of them need tonsil operations and other attention and we want them to have every advantage of a good home." And what of Frankie? "Of course," she said emphatically, "we are going to keep the baby. I'm the only mother he ever knew anyway. I've had him since he was ten months old and have cared for him through babyhood. I have no children of my own, except Frankie, and he's just as much mine as though I was his real mother. My husband and I will take steps to adopt Frankie as soon as we can and will give him our name."[6]

Concetta delivered her lines, performing admirably for the press. It would have been a different story if the journalists had interviewed her after Anna was arrested or even when Anna was on trial. When Anna was sent to the Albany County Jail, her three children were in the care of a neighbor until Patsy arrived and brought them to his house. This arrangement turned Concetta's world upside down. She was thirty years old, had no children, and had no responsibilities. She had fine clothes, a wide circle of friends, and despite the economic hardships of the Great Depression, her husband had a good job. A careful look at their finances might indicate that they were not so far in debt as she led everyone to believe. Patsy hadn't spent "every cent" on Anna's lawyers. First, there was only one lawyer, Dan Prior, and he did the job for free. As to the funeral cost, gossip columnist Walter Winchell claimed that Warden Lawes "buried the late Mrs. Antonio paying $225 from his own jeans."[7] Concetta Cappello was riding out hard times in relative comfort until now. She made no secret of the fact that she hated having Phyllis and Marie in her house. Phyllis was a little headstrong and had a rebellious streak, and Marie, well, Marie just could not stop wetting the bed. Concetta loathed the babysitting role she was suddenly thrust into and wanted it to end. These were not her children, and she didn't want them in her house. She therefore gave her husband an ultimatum—either the kids go or she would. Patsy begged her to reconsider. He had promised his sister that he would look after all the children. Concetta agreed on one condition. Little Frankie could stay, but the troublesome girls had to go. Since the trial and Anna's first days in Sing Sing, Concetta gradually warmed to "the boy." She had changed, and so had Frankie. He was no longer the ten-month-old who had taken his first steps in her living room. Now, he was an active three-year-old who greeted her with affection. Frankie was a part of their home, but as far as she was concerned, the girls could remain at St. Vincent Female Orphan Asylum.

When reporters prodded Concetta about her husband's whereabouts, she lied again. She swore that she had not heard from him since his disappearance. As it turned out, Patsy had disappeared in plain sight. As his picture was in all the local papers, he felt sure that the authorities would find him at any given moment. He didn't lie low like your typical kidnapper but instead spent most of his time, as he later said, "cruising around" the outskirts of Schenectady, going so far as to pick up a couple of hitchhikers. Once the pair had settled into the backseat of the car and drove away, Cappello asked if they had any news of the kidnapping. One of the hitchhikers shook his head and said that there was really nothing new at this point and that the police were still searching for the kidnapper. Cappello casually turned his head and told them that they were doing a better job than the police because *he* was the kidnapper. The hitchhikers stared at each other in disbelief. When they noticed a little boy in the front seat, they knew it was the kidnapper and demanded to be let out of the car. Cappello complied with their demand and simply drove away.[8]

That evening, Patsy and Frankie spent the night in a roadside cabin on the outskirts of Schenectady. Evidently the manager took no notice of the man with no suitcase and the small boy clad only in pajamas with one shoe and one sock. Surely, thought Patsy, he must know who we are. Fearing that the police would greet him at sunrise, Cappello woke Frankie at dawn and sped off to the nearest gas station. His encounter with the hitchhikers troubled him as they were clearly frightened. Kidnapping was a serious offense, and Patsy realized that he had to turn himself in for the sake of Frankie. At the same time, he didn't want to lose the little boy whom he had grown so attached to. Scared and confused, Cappello got to the nearest gas station and placed a call to Dan Prior.

Apprised of the situation, Prior sprang into action. He had fond memories of the Antonio children and looked at this as a debt he owed the mother he could not save. Prior immediately obtained a restraining order to nullify the kidnapping charge against Cappello and then filed a Show Cause Order with Justice F. Walter Bliss in response to Mary De-Sisto's claim to full guardianship of all the children. She was wrong, said Prior. Anna did have a will dated June 27, and he had it on file in his office. When Chief Funston was made aware of these latest developments, he announced that his department was suspending its search and invited Patsy and Frankie to return home. When Patsy picked up a copy of the Sunday edition of the *Albany Times Union* and learned that the charges against him had been dropped, he brought Frankie home the next day. Of their great adventure, Cappello told the waiting reporters on his doorstep that little Frankie wasn't at all scared. "Frankie didn't cry once," he said, "he had a good time."[9]

Frankie may not have been scared but Mary DeSisto certainly was when she read in the papers that Dan Prior was involved. The attorney who had fought long and hard for Anna Antonio could be expected to do the same for Anna's children. The custody battle would turn into a custody war.

After postponements and delays that lasted close to a year, the court hearing that would decide the future of Phyllis, Marie, and Frankie got under way the first week of June in 1935. Interviewed by the press before the hearing commenced, Cappello reminded everyone of his promise to his sister to care for all the children. "They must come together and learn how to know each other like good children. I promised their mother, my sister, I would take care of the children. All of them, not one, or two, but Frank, Marie and Phyllis."[10] Mary DeSisto expressed the same sentiment. The children should be allowed to grow up together, under one roof, preferably hers. After both sides presented their arguments, it would be up to Justice Schenk to decide in favor of a maternal uncle or a paternal aunt. The only evidence Dan Prior presented at the hearing was Anna Antonio's signed statement assigning custody of all three children to her brother.

"Know all men by these present, That I, Anna Antonio, a resident of the City of Albany, the mother of Phyllis Antonio, Marie Antonio and Frank Antonio, infant children, whose father, Salvatore Antonio, is now deceased, have appointed, nominated and constitute, as guardian of the persons and estates of said infant children after my death and during their minorities, my brother, Pasquale Cappello, residing in the City of Schenectady, hereby disposing of the custody and tuition of said infant children their respective minorities each of said children to Pasquale Cappello."[11]

Attorney George Rothlauf, speaking for Mary DeSisto, said that this wasn't so much of a will as it appeared to be a deed. Why then, asked Rothlauf of Patsy Cappello, if you had charge of all three children did you find it necessary to place the girls in an orphanage? Now it was Patsy's turn to lie. At the time, he said, his wife was ill and could not properly care for them. At the same time, it was noted, Mary DeSisto went to St. Vincent only once, and that was to remove the girls and take them to her home in the Bronx.

If there was any surprise testimony at the custody hearing, it came from Victoria Penta. The twenty-three-year-old informed the court that she had been living with the DeSistos for almost all her life. She was an infant when her mother, Meaka, suffered a near-fatal accident at their home in Savanna, New York, in 1912. Since that time, she had lived with Peter and Mary DeSisto.[12] Dan Prior didn't need to be introduced to Victoria Penta. He didn't know her personally, but he did know the name. This was Tony Penta's sister. Recalling how the Tony Penta letter had seriously damaged Anna's defense, he wondered if Victoria's testimony would have the same effect on the custody case.

Victoria testified that on two occasions, that previous November and January, she had brought Phyllis and Marie from the DeSisto home in the Bronx to the Cappello home in Schenectady to see their little brother. At the dinner table, Victoria claimed that Cappello had given Frankie a full glass of wine. While this drew a gasp or two at the hearing, Prior didn't seem to notice. He gently asked Miss Penta if wine was something out of the ordinary at the Cappello home. No, said Victoria hesitantly, "wine drinking is common among Italian people." Prior then turned to ask his client if what Miss Penta had said was indeed true. Cappello didn't deny that this had happen, but he said that it wasn't a full glass of wine. He said he gave Frankie "a little wine to taste." As for his drinking habits, Cappello said he drank wine at dinner, adding, "I know when I have had enough." Victoria also said that she wasn't overly impressed with Frankie's appearance or his behavior. "Frankie wasn't dressed so well when I got there," she said, "he was dirty and didn't look so good. Frankie told Phyllis that he was going to sock her and swore at her. I told him that was not nice and he didn't answer." When Prior asked her how Cappello reacted to this incident, Victoria said that he shrugged it off. "I can't help it," he said, "he picks it up."[13]

When the proceedings began, both Mary DeSisto and Patsy Cappello knew that full custody would be awarded to the one who had the best ability to provide for the children. Mary claimed that hers was a working household. She and her husband Peter, as well as Victoria, had full-time jobs at the Commercial Decal Company in Mount Vernon. They were not rich by any means, but they were comfortable. Patsy Cappello had to do better than this, and he did. In a surprise move, the man who had told newspaper reporters a year earlier that he was financially drained due to attorney fees and his sister's funeral was suddenly flush. Cappello, the $30-a-week machinist at General Electric, now claimed to have $6,000 in savings and an equal amount in stocks and bonds. If Mary DeSisto was taken aback by the small fortune Cappello had amassed, Justice Schenk was outwardly impressed.

"Are you willing to take on all three children now?"

"More than willing," replied Cappello.[14]

On September 6, 1935, Justice Schenk ended the custody suit by maintaining the status quo. As the children appeared to be content in their present surroundings, any change, he believed, would do irreparable harm. "The real issue here," he wrote in his four-page decision, "is the welfare of the infants." Financially, the DeSistos, observed Justice Schenk, were of modest means and in all likelihood could care for all three children. The Cappellos appeared to be financially well off and desperate to keep the child who had been in their care since he was ten months old. To tear Frankie away from the only family he had ever known would be cruel. "It is my judgment," wrote Justice Schenk, "that the obvious devotion of Mr. and Mrs. Cappello to this little boy who came to them as a baby will, in the long run, have a more wholesome effect in shaping his character. In closing, he expressed the sincere desire that the obvious bitterness between the two families during this "distressing ordeal" would come to an end for the sake of all the children. Their animosity, he wrote, should not "be allowed to affect the happiness of three innocent victims of an unfortunate tragedy."[15]

In the years that followed, the children rarely saw each other and grew apart. In Schenectady, true to his word, Patsy Cappello changed Frank's last name to his own. As a youngster, Frank grew up unaware of his past. It was a schoolyard taunt—"Your mother is a murderer"—that led him to question his past. Frightened and confused, he hurried home and asked Concetta what this meant. Reluctant at first, Concetta knew that the day would come when either she or Patsy had to tell him the truth. As gently as possible, she told him that she was not his real mother nor Patsy his real father. Without delving into a lot of details, Concetta told him what had happened to his parents. It was his mother's wish that his name would be changed to Cappello to save him from the embarrassment he had just encountered. In an instant, the innocent world of a small boy had been turned upside down. He was stunned to learn that the couple he had grown to love as his mother and father were really his aunt and uncle.

Anna's parting words and wish to her son, "I hope you grow up to be a good man," came true. Frank Cappello grew up and went to Nott Terrace High School and, with his uncle's help, got a job with General Electric. In June 1952, he married Evelyn Altieri and together they raised four children. Occasionally prodded about their family history, Frank said little. "He only told us bits and pieces," said one daughter. After the divorce of the aunt and uncle who raised him, Frank sacrificed everything, according to one daughter, to care for Patsy. Frank Cappello died on December 24, 1981, and is buried in the Cappello family plot at St. Anthony's Cemetery in Glenville, near the grave of the mother he never really knew.

Phyllis and Marie didn't need a playground taunt to remind them of their past. They were reminded of it every day by their aunt, Mary DeSisto. When Aunt Mary removed them from St. Vincent Female Orphan Asylum and brought them to her home in the Bronx, she brought Phyllis to the kitchen sink and handed a dish towel to Marie. "She never touched another dirty dish for the rest of her life, or picked up a rag to clean," said Phyllis.

To Mary DeSisto, the two girls she had gained custody of were literally money in the bank. After the custody suit had been resolved, the court ordered Sam Antonio's insurance money be placed in trust for the three children. Each of them was to receive a little more than $2,100 when they reached the age of eighteen. With no foreseeable end to the economic hard times of the late 1930s, Mary DeSisto looked at this money as hers—payment for services rendered for providing room and board to both the girls living under her roof.

Needless to say, life with Aunt Mary wasn't pleasant. She was a spiteful, vengeful, vindictive person with a temper to match. She made no secret of the fact that she hated Patsy Cappello for interfering in the custody battle. Above all, she hated his sister Anna. Phyllis and Marie never heard Aunt Mary utter a sympathetic or kind word about their late mother. Constantly reminding the girls that their mother was no good, Aunt Mary cursed the memory of Anna Antonio, continually referring to her as a *buttann*—a bitch or whore. Their mother, she said over and over, got exactly what she deserved. There would be no name changing like Patsy had done to protect their little brother. Mary DeSisto insisted that as long as they resided under her roof, their name would be Antonio. It didn't bother her one bit that the girls were teased and taunted in school and called "mother killer" because of the name Antonio.

With verbal abuse at home came physical abuse. Aunt Mary had a fiery temper, and when things didn't quite go her way, the girls felt her wrath. Phyllis was still as stubborn as ever and did her best to stand up to her aunt. As she grew older, she became more defiant and on more than a few occasions took a beating to protect her little sister. "I lost track," Phyllis once said, "on how many times I got beat across my back, I think I still have the scars." Timid, shy, and scared, Marie, recalled Phyllis, "tried to blend into the woodwork, always had a book in her hands." Marie never had it easy. It didn't help that as she grew older, she looked more and more like her late mother. The fifteen-year-old was dust mopping under a bed when Aunt Mary's dog savagely attacked her. Clutching a towel to her bloody face, Marie ran outside the house and took a bus to the nearest hospital. Her nose had been almost severed from her face. For months her face was bandaged. The scars remained and so did the dog. Later on, her appendix ruptured. Hospital bills for this operation and her facial surgery never bothered Aunt Mary. Even though Marie was under the age of eighteen, Aunt Mary took the money from the insurance settlement she felt was due her. Vicki Penta was so upset at what had happened that she put a down payment on an apartment for Phyllis and Marie. Aunt Mary countered by threatening to take Marie to court as she was still a minor. Eventually, Aunt Mary was able to drain every dollar from Marie's account.

Despite a horrific home life, both girls did well in school, graduated early, and got jobs. Phyllis and Marie got jobs as secretaries, but they didn't earn enough money to escape Aunt Mary. Each week, Aunt Mary would demand eight dollars for rent. It was only when Phyllis bought her own groceries, a block of provolone, some salami, bread, and butter did things come to a head. "I told her," said Phyllis, "that if she touched my food, I would break her arm." From that moment on, Aunt Mary kept her distance from Phyllis.

If there was a bright spot in the lives of the two girls, it was Vicki Penta. Both of the girls loved her. "She was more of a mother to us," recalled Phyllis. Vicki did their hair and made sure they were clean and had decent clothing. Vicki had, what Phyllis called, "womanly clothes" and passed them down to both girls. "We wore the same threadbare coats every winter," recalled Phyllis of those days. When their shoes wore thin, the girls resorted to putting cardboard in the soles. Once they had jobs, they were able to buy suitable clothing and strike out on their own. When Mary's husband Peter died on December 30, 1948, they attended the funeral along with Vicki and a few cousins. Several years later when Aunt Mary died, both girls stayed away.

It was a hard life, and both girls deserved better. Products of the economic hardships of the Great Depression and harboring memories of an equally difficult childhood, Phyllis and Marie rose above it all, succeeding in life beyond anyone's expectation. Phyllis got married, held several jobs, and in her nineties remains active in her church and civic organizations. She looked to the future, she once said, because "you know, you can't change the past."

Marie, the little girl who never celebrated her birthday, instead celebrated life. She never stopped learning and at the same time never stopped leading. For twenty-nine years she was the vice president of marketing services for the Southern Life Insurance Company. The Society of Financial Service Professionals honored her by having an award presented in her name for those who exemplified "professionalism within the industry, exceptional individual career achievements and service in a prominent capacity in the support of civic, cultural and humanitarian interest." Marie died at the age of seventy-four in 2003.

28

LEHMAN'S PAINFUL DECISION

The first spadeful of dirt hadn't been sprinkled on any of the three caskets when comments, criticisms, and editorials made their way into the press to address the issues of clemency and capital punishment. Leading the way was a statement from the only man who had the means of halting the execution but chose not to.

After Governor Lehman received a telephone call from Warden Lawes informing him that the executions had taken place, the governor placed a call to his private secretary, Joseph Canavan. That same evening, Canavan made a series of phone calls to news agencies in and around the capital region of Albany and informed them that Governor Lehman was prepared to offer his comments on the executions that had just taken place at Sing Sing prison. If the press was eager for a question-and-answer press conference with the governor, they were sadly mistaken. Lehman was an old politician and a seasoned veteran when dealing with the media. He wasn't about to be drawn into a moral debate surrounding the pros and cons of capital punishment. When journalists arrived at the governor's office, they were greeted by Canavan, not Lehman, who in turn presented each reporter with a typed transcript of Lehman's speech.

Lehman, on several occasions in his statements to the press, expressed his belief that he had acted in accordance with the oath to the office he was sworn to uphold. He offered no apologies for what he did or did not do. Lehman reminded the public that following the ruling of the Court of Appeals, he had granted two reprieves and called the Court of Appeals into session a second time to review the motion presented for a reargument of the case against Anna Antonio based on Saetta's confession. Furthermore, Lehman, at the last minute, waited on the ruling of Justice Brewster on the new evidence of Father Brown. "After the most careful scrutiny of the records," concluded Lehman, "I am convinced that each of the defendants is guilty."[1]

Most important, Lehman wanted to clear up any misconceptions the general public may have harbored concerning his refusal to grant executive clemency to Anna Antonio. He was fully aware of the efforts of the Men's League of Mercy and the Allied Italian Society of New York, together with numerous church groups and individuals who were clamoring for him to grant executive clemency or to at least suspend the death sentence. Requests for mercy poured into his office right up to the time of the execution. Typical of these requests was one of the last ones he received from Rev. R. Maxwell Bradner. The rector of St. Margaret's Protestant Episcopal Church in Strasburg, Pennsylvania, implored Lehman "for the sake of her poor children" to spare her. "I feel," he said, "she may be guilty, but I think she should live for the sake of the children."[2] It was precisely because of the sentiment expressed by Reverend Bradner and others that Lehman felt compelled to address why he refused to grant executive clemency. "The law makes no distinction of sex in the punishment of a crime," he said. "Nor would my own conscience or the duty imposed upon me by my oath of office permit me to do so. Each of the defendants is guilty. The crime and the manner of execution are abhorrent. I have found no just or sound reason for the exercise of executive clemency."[3]

If Lehman feared a backlash from the press following the execution, he needn't have worried. Newspapers across the state that had diligently followed the saga of Anna Antonio agreed wholeheartedly with his decision. The *New York Times* expressed its admiration for the governor for performing his duty, which "must have been excruciating to a man with his tender heart." In a small two-paragraph editorial titled "A Painful Duty," the *Times* said that the governor, given the number of appeals and delays, had no other choice. "His statement shows how long and earnestly he wrestled with the question." The paper lauded his efforts and at the same time expressed no sympathy for the latest victims of the electric chair. "If anyone ought ever to be electrocuted," proclaimed the *Times*, "these three should have been."[4]

Nearby, the *Brooklyn Daily Eagle*, which up to this time had been fairly sympathetic to the plight of Anna Antonio, suddenly did an about-face. The governor, they concluded, had acted wisely. "Regardless of what one may think of capital punishment, the woman had been convicted by due process of law and all efforts to win her a new trial had been lost in the courts. Furthermore, it was a particularly cold blooded affair."[5]

The *Poughkeepsie Eagle News* had followed the trial and execution primarily because one of the city's patrolmen, John Campion, had been instrumental in capturing Saetta and Faraci. "Of the guilt of Mrs. Antonio," expressed the *Eagle News*, "there appears to have been not the slightest shadow of doubt." While the newspaper applauded the efforts of Dan Prior in pursuing every possible legal recourse, they concluded that right from the start, it was a hopeless case. Lehman, they said, did the right thing when not swayed by the fact that she was a woman. "Whether capital punishment is right or wrong," said the *Eagle News*, "sex cannot be made the basis of exemptions."[6]

Closer to home, the *Amsterdam Evening Recorder* straddled the fine line between sympathy and condemnation. "There was no question but that she had been abused by her husband. Her home life was unhappy. She had little to live for except her three children." However, as the editorial was titled "One Law for Both Sexes," the *Evening Recorder* was adamant on the subject of the existing law. "A murder is punishable by death whether the killer is a man or a woman. To extend clemency to a slayer merely because of her sex would be to encourage killings by women . . . we must admit that while the death penalty remains on the statute books it must be enforced without regard to sex."[7]

Perhaps the most unorthodox editorial came from one of the most unlikely newspapers. Lionel S. B. Shapiro, a syndicated columnist for the *Montreal Gazette*, was cynically harsh in his assessment of what had occurred at Sing Sing prison. In his column "Light and Shadows of Manhattan," Shapiro criticized the American judicial system by suggesting that profiteering was involved in executions. "The manner of dealing out Canadian justice is definitely superior. Because it is swift and sure, it is more terrifying. In Canada a condemned person is executed as a criminal; here a condemned person becomes a hero or a heroine, just before execution; in fact execution enhances one's estate considerably. Relatives may command fat salaries for appearing on stage."[8] Shapiro never visited the Death House at Sing Sing to see just how terrifying the electric chair was to Anna Antonio, nor did he get a chance to visit with the families of Saetta and Faraci to see what monetary benefits they reaped from their deaths.

Another who expressed his misgivings about the justice system was Hearst Corporation journalist Arthur Brisbane. Earlier when Anna Antonio languished in her cell awaiting the decisions of the Court of Appeals and the governor, Brisbane noted that while she was alive, she sewed clothes for her children. As a newspaperman he pointed out that this wasn't the "real news" that sold papers. "It will be news," he wrote in his column, "when men enter that death cell, take the woman from her sewing machine, shave her head for application of the wet electrodes and send her away from her children." Agreeing with the editors of the *Albany Times Union,* Brisbane dismissed the eye-for-an-eye doctrine of the death penalty. In his "Today" column, he said that the public seemed to forget that the fate of Anna Antonio was tied to her children. "Why not let the mother stay in prison and work for the children?" posed Brisbane. "Perhaps Governor Lehman of New York will decide to save the little boy and his two sisters from the unpleasant memory that their mother was killed in the electric chair. Was it worse for an ignorant mother to kill her husband, than for an enlightened state to disgrace for life, her innocent children?"[9] When it was all over, Brisbane stepped back and, with a certain degree of cynicism, told his readers that the execution "was an interesting demonstration of civilization's conviction that the way to discourage murder is to *imitate the murderer* and kill with electricity, after he has killed with a bullet, club, knife or poison."[10]

Still, some members of the fourth estate took the opportunity to express a certain disdain for what had happened. The *Albany Times Union* had presented to its readers balanced and unbiased reporting throughout the trial and executions. Now that it was all over, the *Times Union* took umbrage with the latest statement from the Associated Press that "the slate is wiped clean in the Antonio case" and "the books in the Salvatore Antonio case have been balanced."[11] The Albany paper didn't accept this eye-for-an-eye attitude, opting instead for a different view. "Are advocates allowed to speak at the last judgment?" Speaking hypothetically, the *Times Union* said that in heaven, Anna Antonio's "celestial lawyer" would guarantee her admittance to the pearly gates. "I cannot deny this woman's guilt, because here, all is known. But it is also known that the husband whose death she bought with money, was a 'drug peddler,' dealer in narcotics, condemning his customers and victims to a lifetime of agony worse than any death. I formally request that the great book about 'what would have happened if' be opened and that the page be read telling the harm this woman's husband would have done in later life, had not her hired murderers cut that life short."[12]

At the same time Governor Lehman informed the public how duty-bound he was to let the execution proceed, Warden Lawes wasted no time informing the public how horrible it was to perform his duty. "With the death of Mrs. Antonio in the electric chair," wrote Lawes from his desk at Sing Sing, "I am more than ever opposed to these legal killings. While I am convinced that the electric chair is the most humane method of execution, it is, after all, but a legal killing. I can reach but one conclusion every time I carry out a death sentence. From every point of view, the death penalty is futile. Someday, perhaps, civilization will find some other way of compensating society. The death penalty has been tried, judged and found wanting."[13]

Ignoring Governor Lehman's press release, the *New York Daily News* came the closest to expressing what had really happened on Marie's birthday. They were appalled by the roller-coaster ride of emotions Anna Antonio had endured while awaiting appeals and hearings. "We in this country make horror spectacles out of murder cases, especially when the condemned killer is a woman. We drag the thing out. We sob and wring our hands. . . . We play cat and mouse with the victim, until we have reduced her to the last extremity of woe, then we kill her."[14]

All of these editorials, and there were many more, missed a singular point. Not one of them said what really killed Anna Antonio. The electric chair killed her, but it was felony murder that brought her there.

Was she indeed guilty, and should she have been punished? In both cases, the answer is yes. Dan Prior made a point during the trial that Anna Antonio should have been charged with conspiracy, not murder. Strong evidence suggests that she was aware her husband was going to be killed. Having three people on trial simultaneously was the same as a three-ring circus. He knew Anna's chances were far better if she were tried alone. If a jury found her guilty, her sentence should have been prison, not the electric chair. Sam Faraci turned state's evidence when he ratted out his friend Saetta and was rewarded with the electric chair. A coward by nature, Faraci was a willing participant, but not a killer. He, too, should have served time in prison. However, Vincent Saetta was a killer. Whether he felt cheated out of money owed to him by Sam Antonio or the promise of insurance money, he planned the murder. Pumping five slugs into an unarmed man is a clear indication of intent. Saetta should have been punished and was when he sat in the electric chair. What killed each of these individuals—felony murder—should have been etched into the electric chair. Regardless of the circumstance, if one was guilty of murder, all involved paid the same price.

The death of Anna Antonio faded from the headlines but not from memory. Felony murder was still the law, but the man who rocked the cradle of Albany politics was determined that such a spectacle as was witnessed at Sing Sing would never happen again under his watch.

Before he published *Legs*, a novel about the life and times of legendary gangster Jack "Legs" Diamond, author William Kennedy had an opportunity to interview a contemporary legend of sorts, Dan O'Connell. The man behind the scenes of Albany politics since 1919, Dan "Boss" O'Connell was in failing health when Kennedy interviewed him in 1974. With surprising candor and clarity, the eighty-nine-year-old offered his comments on everything from machine politics to scandals and murder. For Kennedy, this was perhaps the last chance he would ever get to talk to anyone who remembered the death of Legs Diamond.

According to Boss O'Connell, the only way to prevent gangsters from gaining a foothold in Albany was to maintain a strong police force. For instance, when Dutch Schultz made inroads to extend his operations into the capital region, he was met at the Albany train station by several grim-faced plainclothes detectives. They gave the Dutchman a stern warning, and Schultz got the message. He never got off the train and instead hurried back to New York. Legs Diamond, however, wasn't as easy to convince.

The reason underworld figures never took credit for the slaying of Legs Diamond was simple—they didn't do it. Lt. William Fitzpatrick, of the Albany Police Department, was the triggerman. "[Dan] Prior, brought him around here," said O'Connell, "but he brought him around here once too often. Fitzpatrick finished Legs."

Kennedy then asked the Boss about another case Dan Prior was involved in after the Diamond affair. It, too, was a murder, only this time, Prior's client went to Sing Sing prison. "I heard years ago," said Kennedy, "from an Albany policeman that because some witnesses from Albany saw a woman electrocuted at Sing Sing, and because she exploded when the current hit her, there had never been any capital punishment in Albany since."

"It was me," said O'Connell, "I wouldn't stand for it. We never had a first degree [murder prosecution] for thirty years. Not since that little woman. Delaney executed her. Lehman would have commuted that. There were probably a dozen who would have gone to the chair, but I wouldn't let them. And they won't try them now."[15]

29

THE TRIAL IN RETROSPECT

On May 22, 1936, candidates slated for graduation at Albany Law School staged a mock trial in which they reenacted the Antonio murder trial. "When the jury came in with the verdict," noted the *Albany Times Union*, the ghost of Anna Antonio "must have felt great regret that the same jury could not have sat on her case in real life." The jury acquitted the defendant. If the same trial were to take place today, would a jury acquit Anna Antonio? Would they do the same for Vincent Saetta and Sam Faraci?

To Delaney's credit, the prosecution throughout the trial avoided ethnic stereotypes, thus sparing the inhabitants of Albany's Little Italy a degrading and disgraceful insult. By the 1930s, the image of the Italian people had already suffered irreparable harm due to the antics of Al Capone, Charles "Lucky" Luciano, and the like. Delaney's plan was to not have Sam Antonio cast as a stereotypical gangster. Dan Prior and, to some extent, Henry Lowenberg thought otherwise. Although they never used the term *Black Hand* or *Mafia*, the subliminal message was present. The Steamburg arson and narcotics peddling were offered up to the jury as proof that Sam Antonio, a second-generation Italian American, and Sicily-born Saetta and Faraci were somehow involved with organized crime. Nativist fears that dated back as far as the Irish diaspora (potato famine) insisted that the influx of immigrants directly corresponded to an increase in crime. It wasn't true in the 1840s and it wasn't true when the next great wave of immigrants came to America from southern and eastern Europe between 1900 and the mid-1920s. Being a poor immigrant didn't necessarily mean you were a potential felon. Like most cities, Albany had their fair share of homegrown law-breakers. As far as Delaney was concerned, the character and past of Sam Antonio were not on trial; Anna Antonio was.

One of the greatest legal travesties that took place before the trial began was the denial of due process rights to Vincent Saetta and Sam Faraci. Lowenberg and Duncan introduced motions during the trial to have the charges dismissed against their clients because they were held for sixteen days without being charged. John T. Delaney maintained that Saetta and Faraci "were being held for questioning" when in fact they were under arrest the moment they were brought to the Third Precinct. Long before the Supreme Court ruled on *Miranda v. Arizona,* the accused had a right to know the charges against him or her and to have an attorney present when being questioned by the police. It was only after sixteen days of questioning that they signed their confessions, were formally charged with murder, and allowed to contact an attorney.

The real tragedy of Anna Antonio was her own naivety. Vincent Saetta and, to a much larger extent, Sam Faraci knew what to expect from the legal system. Anna didn't have a clue. She never in her short life had a brush with the law and in all likelihood never knew of anyone who had. Whereas Saetta and Faraci were locked up in the Third Precinct and denied the right to contact lawyers, Anna wasn't. Brought to the precinct on several occasions, she had plenty of time to obtain legal representation. When Jimmy Hynes brought in Julius Kommit for questioning, the interview was abruptly cut short due to the presence of the pawnshop owner's attorney. Delaney didn't like it, but that's the way the system works. No one—not one policeman, detective, or even the district attorney—told Anna she was entitled to legal representation. When Delaney brought Anna to the Third Precinct to identify Saetta and Faraci, she must have known she was in trouble, yet she did nothing. When the district attorney asked if she knew of her husband's enemies and if she herself used drugs, Anna Antonio should have stood up and screamed at the top of her lungs, "I want to see a lawyer!" She didn't because she didn't know she could. Delaney took advantage of her ignorance of the law. Anna's rights were secondary to his wants. Delaney wanted a confession.

The most critical piece of evidence against all three was their own words. District attorney John T. Delaney had three signed confessions, and in his mind that was enough to prove their guilt. If this trial were to take place today, all three confessions would be inadmissible in court under the Fruit of the Poisonous Tree Doctrine. The first confession was obtained by the police when Gertrude King was able to convince Sam Faraci to come clean and tell the truth. Granted, it was a confession in which Faraci did his best to shift all the blame to Saetta, but it was a confession. When this confession was read to his cohort in crime, Saetta wanted to set the record straight and in turn signed a confession. When Faraci heard Saetta's confession, he recanted and signed yet another. The "poisonous tree" was Faraci's confession, and it yielded "fruit"— that of Saetta's confession. When the police took Saetta's confession and read it within earshot of Anna Antonio, essentially the same thing took place. In this instance, Saetta's confession became the "poisonous tree," and Anna's confession bore the "fruit" of a confession.

Throughout the trial and into the appeal, the attorneys for Saetta and Faraci vigorously opposed the methods used by the police to obtain their clients' confessions. Each claimed that their clients were physically abused by the authorities to obtain these sworn statements. They never mentioned the Fruit of the Poisonous Tree Doctrine because they couldn't—at least not in 1932. Although the Supreme Court ruled on evidence obtained without a warrant in *Silverthorne Lumber Company v. United States* in 1920, it wasn't until *Nardone v. United States* that the high court used the phrase "fruit of the poisonous tree" in describing evidence that had been "tainted" in its 1939 decisions. Had this ruling been in place in 1932, all three confessions would not have been allowed. This would not necessitate Anna Antonio and Sam Faraci taking the stand to testify. Delaney's case against them would have been far more challenging.

When the trial got under way, judge Earl Gallup expressed his confidence that the three defendants would receive a fair trial with a single jury. Gallup was basing this on the precedent that he had established in the 1927 trial of Charles Doran, Floyd Damp, and Theodore "Chickie"

Harrington. Dan Prior was correct in his assertion that this gas station robbery gone wrong wasn't the same as the Antonio case. All three were active participants in the crime whereas Anna Antonio was not. If the trial were to be held today, given the facts and circumstances, there would be three separate juries. When testimony and evidence had been presented for one defendant, the juries for the other defendants would be dismissed. In this way, the jury would consider the evidence against one and not be overwhelmed or confused by the introduction of witnesses and evidence against the other defendants. Having three separate trials or even three juries at the same trial would have taken more time and cost the taxpayers more money.

There were several instances in the trial where the "missing witness" or "uncalled witness" charge could have been used. A defense attorney can ask a judge to give the jury a directive stating that a witness who would be normally called to the witness stand in the case was not called because his or her testimony would support the other side's position. This can only be used if the other side cannot locate the witness. In the Antonio trial, every "missing witness" was available.

A questionable piece of physical evidence lodged against Anna Antonio was the Anna Winters letter. On the surface, this piece of evidence indicated that Anna Antonio wanted a divorce. Lowenberg interpreted this to mean that she wanted a divorce to marry Tony Penta. Prior was admirable in his efforts to impress upon the jury that this was not the case. Tony Penta was not a "missing witness." He was readily available and could have been subpoenaed. The district attorney knew his address (he had visited the Albany jail), and Anna Antonio knew where he was. If his testimony could have helped Anna Antonio, we will never know. However, Dan Prior was probably relieved that Anna Winters was a "missing witness." Her testimony would have been damaging as she harbored a deep resentment toward Anna Antonio. If she liked Anna Antonio, she wouldn't have sent the letter to Delaney.

The "missing witness" status of Gertrude King worked for everyone at the trial, including her. It was doubtful that anything she could have said under oath would have helped Sam Faraci. Delaney knew where she was but wasn't about to put on the witness stand the woman who helped him obtain a confession from Sam Faraci. Charles J. Duncan had no need for her testimony nor did prostitute-hating Henry Lowenberg. After the trial, Gertrude King maintained her "missing status" by legally changing her name. She married and drifted off into obscurity.

Violations of the rights of the accused, illegally obtained confessions, three people on trial with one jury, and missing witnesses would not have been allowed to happen in a court today. The introduction of two new pieces of last minute-evidence in a death penalty case (Saetta's confession and Father William A. Brown's affidavit) would have either been the basis of a new trial or received more scrutiny by the Court of Appeals. If the trial took place today, Anna Antonio may have been punished, but she certainly would not have gone to the electric chair.

A NOTE ON SOURCES

In the mid-1950s, retired city editor of Albany's *Knickerbocker News*, Charles L. Mooney, authored a weekly column titled "The City Editor Reminiscences." Mooney missed the good old days. He liked cops, lawyers, and, above all, a good murder. On more than one occasion, he dusted off the old files to reminisce about the Antonio case. It was easy to retell the story, but Mooney would have preferred to offer his readers fresh insight into a decades-old case. "The late Dan Prior," typed Mooney, "a shrewd criminal lawyer we encountered on a lot of stories, promised one time he'd give us an interesting column, but we never could seem to get together with him long enough to get an interview." Prior's only comment to Mooney was that the Antonio case was by far the most interesting and challenging of his legal career. "We're sorry," Mooney later wrote, "we couldn't have obtained some of his memoirs."[1]

This was indeed unfortunate, but it was equally unfortunate that Henry Lowenberg had his published. Shortly before he died in 1971, Lowenberg, with the assistance of Robin Moore, published *Until Proven Guilty: Forty Years as Criminal Defense Counsel*. Here, Lowenberg took the opportunity to set the record straight on just why he refused to represent prostitutes, procurers (johns), and gamblers, yet eagerly defended racketeers accused of murder and kidnapping. "I have represented notorious underworld figures—among them Frankie Carbo, Billy the Kid Lustig, Louis Lepke and (Legs) Diamond."[2] He was correct in his assertion that these were notorious individuals. In all likelihood, Lowenberg defended Paul John "Frankie" Carbo when he was accused of the murder of gambler Michael J. "Mickey" Duffy in 1931. The same could be said of Louis Lepke Buchalter. As the triggerman for Murder, Inc., Lepke had an arrest record almost three pages long. Lowenberg could have been one of many lawyers to defend him.

The impressive list of societal losers he represented should be treated with caution. With the passage of time and with his body ravaged with cancer from years of smoking, Lowenberg's memory faltered. For instance, William "Billy the Kid" Lustig, an independent gang leader from Manhattan's Lower East Side, was murdered on August 16, 1913. It's difficult to defend someone who was killed in 1913, especially when you haven't passed the bar. Lowenberg graduated from Fordham Law School in 1925. As for his most famous client, Legs Diamond, Lowenberg was correct in his assertion that Legs and his associate Eddie "Fats" McCarthy were transporting and hijacking alcohol in upstate New York. After this, he erred tremendously. "Later," recalled Lowenberg, "both Legs and Fats were shot and killed on a road in the Catskill Mountains." Diamond was in fact murdered in his Dove Street apartment, and Fats McCarthy was killed in a gun battle with police in Colonie in July 1932.

The misrepresentation of facts and details in his memoirs carried over to another client, Vincent Saetta. "I was acquainted with the Saetta family," recalled Lowenberg, "who lived on the lower east side of Manhattan. . . . Vincent had been a client of mine once before, and on that occasion he had been acquitted by a jury."[3] It is doubtful that Saetta's case was "acquitted by a jury" as it was more likely that it was dismissed before it went to trial. If Delaney and Casey could dig up a criminal past on Sam Faraci, they most certainly would have done the same with Saetta, if it were possible.

Lowenberg devoted an entire chapter of his memoirs to the Antonio case. In "Voice of the Accused," he relied on the voice of the trial transcripts to tell the story, not on his defense of Vincent Saetta but on his cross-examination of Anna Antonio. Ignoring Sam Antonio's dope-peddling activities in the Gut, Lowenberg never mentioned the latter's partnership with his client in the Steamburg arson. Instead, he spent a great deal of time on Anna's alleged relationship with Tony Penta. In his final address to the jury, Lowenberg stated that Anna would not hesitate to go to Tony Penta. "Anna jumped to her feet and started toward me, her black eyes snapping in fury, 'You lie,' she screamed," recalled Lowenberg. "Two court attendants grabbed her by the arms and half dragged and half led her back to the table."[4] This dramatic episode was partially correct. Anna did jump to her feet, she did scream, but it was Dan Prior who eased her back to her seat.

"When Anna was seated," continued Lowenberg, "I turned to the jury and I said, 'There's an old maxim you've heard many times. The truth hurts.' You saw the actions on the part of that woman. She wanted to assault me. I must have been telling the truth. Then I went on with my summation, advancing my argument that it was her sweetheart who killed Salvatore Antonio and the only reason that my client, Vincent Saetta, was in this courtroom was because Anna knew him and he was a convenient scapegoat."[5] A careful review of the court transcripts reveal that this never happened. Not only did Lowenberg not make this statement to the jury, he never accused Tony Penta of murdering Anna's husband. It was unfortunate that this and other fabrications appeared in his memoirs and that his efforts to save his own client during his interview with Governor Lehman were omitted.

The most prolific writer associated with the story of Anna Antonio at that time, other than the press, was Lewis Lawes. In almost all of his writings—books, newspaper articles, or interviews—the "firm but fair" warden of Sing Sing never passed up an opportunity to condemn the practice of capital punishment. It was Lawes more than anyone else in the late 1930s who was responsible for preserving the image of Anna Antonio in the mind of the public. In *Meet the Murderer*, Lawes wrote, "No inmate, male or female, ever endured such tortuous suspense as she did. Yet, in spite of her sufferings, she bridged the gap between this world and oblivion with the strength of not one man, but ten."[6]

Lewis Lawes stands in the middle of one of the most oft-quoted questionable statements attributed to Anna Antonio. It was Dale Harrison of the Associated Press who claimed that Anna, as she was about to be led to the electric chair, confided in Lawes, "I did not tell those men to kill my husband for insurance money of $5,000. I could have killed him a dozen times, the house was always full of dope and guns." At the time, no one saw fit to question this statement. Other than the fact that the insurance figure was wrong and that she lived in an apartment and not a house, at no time during the trial did she ever indicate that there were "dope and guns" present. Surely if she had, her attorney would have used this in her defense as it presented a dangerous environment for her children. As to her boast of having the opportunity to kill her husband "a dozen times," this seems out of character. On the witness stand, Anna never spoke about her husband in a threatening manner. Detectives who testified at the trial interviewed her neighbors at 3 Teunis Street and none of them reported any instances of domestic abuse.

In 1935, Dr. Amos O. Squire published his memoirs. In *Sing Sing Doctor,* Squire devoted one chapter to the events leading up to the execution of Anna Antonio and was the first of many to include the "dope and guns" quote. Carefully paraphrasing what Dale Harrison had written earlier, Squire recalled, "there were plenty of guns and dope in the house to do it with." The doctor concluded that this admission on her part was, as he said, "as close as she ever came to confessing to the murder."[7] Lawes read this book and borrowed much of Squire's material for his December 1938 newspaper installment, "The Warden Speaks." In "Bravest of the Brave," Lawes cited entire passages from Squire with one exception. He never used the "dope and guns" quote here, nor did he use it in his own book, *Meet the Murderer.*

Several years later, Robert G. Elliott had his memoirs published. With the assistance of Albert R. Beatty, the book was a compilation of short articles that had previously appeared in *Colliers* magazine in the fall of 1938. Appropriately entitled *Agent of Death,* the book was released in 1940 to mixed reviews. Fletcher Pratt, writing for the *Saturday Review,* called it "a curious book, of more than morbid interest."[8] What struck *Time* magazine was how cold and impersonal Elliott had become in detaching himself from his work with the electric chair. "Elliott wrote as matter-of-factly as though he were describing the operation of an electric toaster. Few readers could wish for a creepier ending."[9] In a plain and somewhat dry fashion, in *Agent of Death,* Elliott devoted three and a half pages to the "frail mother" he executed. Like Dr. Squire, he, too, used the "dope and guns" quote.

With the death of Elliott in 1940 and that of Lewis Lawes seven years later, the general public forgot about the leading critics of the death penalty. They also forgot about Anna Antonio. It wasn't until 1958 that the public became reacquainted with Anna. In that year, Wenzell Brown published *Women Who Died in the Chair.* Brown, who had already established himself as one of the premier pulp-fiction authors of the 1950s in the genre of juvenile delinquency, now expanded his repertoire to include true crime stories. Brown presented the stories of six women who were electrocuted at Sing Sing prison between 1928 and 1951. He copied liberally from the capital region newspapers to tell the story of Anna Antonio. His peers, members of the Mystery Writers of America, awarded him the Edgar Allan Poe Award for Best Fact-Based Crime Book in 1959. Brown followed suit by using the "dope and guns" quote, but this was overshadowed by the sheer number of glaring errors in his work.

> Salvatore (Sam) Antonio was certainly no great loss to the community. He was a short swarthy man, about five foot seven, but heavily built weighing close to 180 pounds. He had a broad coarse face, a dome shaped forehead and jet black thinning hair. Nominally he was a railroad brakeman, but his really significant income came from peddling dope around the railroad station. Allegedly a "kingpin" of the rackets, he had a long criminal record, filled with acts of viciousness.[10]

Brown was correct in his assertion that Sam Antonio was a brakeman for the railroad and that was about all. He was never a "kingpin" of the rackets, nor was he foolish enough to peddle dope in the railroad yard where he was employed. The "long criminal record" Brown attributed to Sam Antonio in fact never existed. Sam Antonio had a clean record and was unknown to the Albany police at the time of his murder. It was federal narcotics agent Richard Kelly who told the police that his agents had been watching Sam Antonio's activities in the Gut area of Albany, not the railroad yards. On the eve of her arrest, Anna Antonio stripped her apartment of all family photographs, locking them away to keep them from the district attorney and the press. No photographs of her husband were introduced at the trial, and only one appeared in the *Albany Times Union*. Sam Antonio was of medium build, had short thick black hair, and for all intents was a handsome man.

The physical description Brown presented of Anna Antonio was equally as bad, reflecting his pulp-fiction style of writing. Anna was "haggard and worn. Her hair was jet black, her deep brown eyes deep set and expressive . . . she looked more Gypsy than Italian. Her excessively wide mouth seemed even wider because of a drooping lower lip." Vincent Saetta had "high cheek bones, heavily lidded eyes, puffy cheeks and a long, thin mouth that gave his mouth a masklike expression." Sam Faraci "was thin, wiry little man with a mop of bushy hair and deep set dog like eyes." The description of all three were merely Brown's interpretations of the pictures that appeared in the press during the trial and sentencing.[11]

For someone who copied so diligently from the newspapers, Brown made critical errors in his retelling of the events leading up to and including the trial. When Saetta, Faraci, and King were being held by the Poughkeepsie police, Brown claimed that both men were drug addicts as they "began complaining about stomach cramps, sweating profusely and drinking great quantities of water—typical withdrawal symptoms of confirmed drug addicts."[12] Brown claimed that the "candy pills" Faraci used were heroin. Patrolman John Campion testified at the trial that Saetta complained of ulcers and did have a glass or two of water. He belched frequently, a clear indication that he was suffering from stomach problems, not from the effects of drugs. As for the "candy pills," it was later learned that they were prescribed by a physician for Faraci.

This was mild when compared to what Brown erroneously said about Anna and Sam's relationship. "His [Sam's] brutality had caused the death of one of her children. He kept her in virtual slavery, forbidding her to leave the house; he beat her and otherwise abused her." None of this was true. Tragically, Anita died of a medical condition. Anna took the Quarter Cab to run errands and go shopping, and there is no record of her being beaten by her husband. At her trial, Anna never said that her husband physically abused her. She was aware of some of her husband's activities, but at no time during the trial had Anna "muttered incoherently about the Black Hand."[13]

Perhaps Brown's greatest error was when he stated that Vincent Saetta testified at the trial. "His testimony," wrote Brown, "was almost identical with his confession. . . . Try as he could, Dan Prior could not shake Saetta's story."[14] In short, Brown's book contained too many errors to be of any use to future historians.

Throughout the 1940s and 1950s and well into the early 1960s, a collection of true crime and true detective magazines became the mainstays of newsstands. It was merely a question of time before one of them latched onto the Antonio murder case. In January 1963, *Detective*

Cases magazine included "How Much to Kill My Husband?" by John R. Billings.

The author began his story with a dramatic rendition of the final moments of Sam Antonio. After approximately four paragraphs, the story went downhill about as fast as Antonio was driven to Memorial Hospital by "two young men." It was state trooper Cassen, said Billings, who intercepted the car carrying Antonio on the outskirts of Albany doing almost ninety miles per hour. Cassen escorted the car to Memorial Hospital and after determining that the two law students hadn't hit the victim with their car, called his superior—Sgt. William Flubacher!

Aside from the fact that Flubacher was a corporal at the time of the murder, Billings mentions him only once, leading everyone to believe that the investigation was led by Chief Smurl and his assistant, John J. Peacock. Griggs, Herzog, and Genova were mentioned, but not Jimmy Hynes. As for Richard Kelly, Billings concluded that Mrs. Antonio was oblivious to the dope racket and expressed serious doubts that her husband was involved with drug trafficking in the Gut. Billings went on to say that the police immediately suspected Saetta and Faraci. They followed them throughout Albany and arrested them in the Gut. The inconsistencies and inaccuracies are simply too numerous to count. William H. Flubacher kept a copy of this article in his personal papers as a souvenir because that was all it was worth.

After that January 1963 issue, the story of Anna Antonio wasn't retold for years. As more states argued the merits of reinstating or abolishing the death penalty, several death row books came into print. While some were social commentaries dealing with a controversial subject, others concentrated on telling the story of those who walked that last mile. In 2002, Marlin Shipman published *The Penalty Is Death: U.S. Newspaper Coverage of Women's Executions.* Although the title of the book leads one to believe Shipman used many newspapers in his research, he used only one, the *New York Times,* in his three-and-a-half-page essay on Anna Antonio. Shipman chose to ignore the "guns and dope" quote but did include small vignettes of the custody quarrel that took place after Anna's execution. Seven years later, L. Kay Gillespie published *Executed Women of the 20th and 21st Centuries.* In a "Who's Who" of executed women, Gillespie offers a tight five- to six-paragraph sketch of Anna Antonio.

For a gut-wrenching rendition of Anna Antonio's last days in Sing Sing, Mark Gado's *Death Row Women: Murder, Justice and the New York Press* is a must-read. Gado, a twenty-nine-year veteran of the New Rochelle police and a frequent contributor to *Crime Library,* relied on the memoirs of Elliot, Squire, and at least a dozen New York newspapers for his research.

With the absence of letters and diaries from the key participants of this case, the best primary source material is the court transcripts. The multiseries set, a copy of which is housed in the New York State Archives, numbers 3,146 pages. In addition to the transcripts, the archives house several hundred more pages of the appeals and rearguments of the case. Therein lie the confessions, background information relating to Anna Antonio, a chronological approach to the investigation that led to the arrest of all three suspects, and the constant bickering that took place among the attorneys. As voluminous as they appear, the transcripts should be viewed with caution when attempting to ascertain who was telling the truth and who was lying to save themselves.

NOTES

INTRODUCTION

1. "Williams, 'Ex-Czar' of Tenderloin, Dies," *New York Times,* Mar. 30, 1917.

2. William Kennedy, *O Albany* (New York: Washington Park Press Ltd., Penguin Books, 1983), 157.

3. "The Gut," *Time,* July 23, 1928. Edwin Corning (1883–1934) was lieutenant governor of New York from 1927 to 1928. His son, Erastus Corning (1907–83), served as mayor of Albany for forty years. During this time Daniel P. O'Connell (1885–1977) was "Boss" of the Democratic Party. For a complete history, see Frank S. Robinson, *Machine Politics: A Study of Albany's O'Connells* (New Brunswick, NJ: Transaction Books, 1977).

4. "Lowell Smith Probes Agent Slaying," *Syracuse Journal,* July 14, 1928.

5. Irving Washburn (1894–1928) resigned from the New York State Police and joined the Department of the Treasury as a Prohibition agent on July 31, 1924. His wife, the former Mary Van Wormer, was with him when he died. See "Irving Washburn, Prohibition Man, Dies from Wounds," *Troy Times,* July 14, 1928. John T. Delaney (1891–1966) was a 1914 graduate of Albany Law School and a veteran of the First World War. At one time he served as Albany city judge, but he resigned when judge Earl Gallup "championed him" in 1928 for the position of district attorney. An integral part of the O'Connell political machine, Delaney served as secretary to the Albany Democratic Party. He resigned as district attorney in 1944 amid allegations that he "neglected and refused to take appropriate action after the theft of $650,000 from the N.Y. central railroad." See "Boyle, 7 Others Indicted in $650,000 Scrap 'Racket,'" *Knickerbocker News,* July 13, 1944, and "John Delaney Dies, Former Albany DA," *Knickerbocker News,* Sept. 9, 1966.

6. "The Gut," *Time,* July 23, 1928.

7. "Smith Arms Dry Sleuths for Battle," *Syracuse Journal,* July 15, 1928.

8. "Hint Additional Arrests Shortly in Albany Murder," *Troy Times,* July 16, 1928.

9. "Hint Additional Arrests Shortly in Albany Murder."

10. "The Gut," *Time,* July 23, 1928.

11. "Diamond Slain; Aids Suspected," *New York Evening Post*, Dec. 18, 1931. John Thomas Diamond (1897–1931) was a high-profile gangster during the Prohibition era. For a complete biography, see Patrick Downey, *Legs Diamond Gangster* (Scotts Valley, CA: Create Space Publishing, 2011).

12. Charles Mooney, "Only Yesterday," *Knickerbocker News*, May 26, 1956.

13. "Prior Is Named City Court Judge," *Albany Evening Journal*, Nov. 24, 1916. A small biography of Daniel H. Prior (1888–1953) appears in *The History of New York State: Biographical*, ed. James Sullivan (New York: Lewis Historical Publishing Company, Inc., 1927), 180–81.

14. Mooney, "Only Yesterday."

15. Mooney, "Only Yesterday."

16. "Diamond Plans Long Rest Trip," *Albany Times Union*, July 15, 1931.

17. "Legs Diamond Slain in Albany," *Amsterdam Evening Recorder*, Dec. 18, 1931.

18. "Diamond Murdered at Albany Rooming House; Wife Was Questioned," *Troy Times*, Dec. 18, 1931. Marion "Kiki Roberts" Strasmick was a former Ziegfeld Follies showgirl and paramour of Legs Diamond. After the death of Diamond, she drifted and disappeared. While researching his novel *Legs*, William Kennedy was unable to discover what had become of her. See "Sad Legacy of 'Legs' Gangster Moll/Dancer 'Kiki Roberts,' Hoofed Way into—and out of—Valley," *Morning Cal4 Allentown Leigh Valley and Pennsylvania News*, Dec. 26, 1996.

19. "Diamond Slain, Aids Suspected," *New York Evening Post*, Dec. 18, 1931.

20. "Diamond Murdered at Albany Rooming House; Wife Was Questioned." Alice Kenny Schiffer Diamond (1902–33) was one of the few mourners at her husband's funeral. On June 30, 1933, she met the same fate as her husband when unknown gunmen shot her in her Brooklyn apartment. She is buried next to her husband in Mount Olivet Cemetery, Queens, New York. See "Diamond's Widow Murdered in Home," *New York Times*, July 1, 1933.

21. "Diamond Murdered at Albany Rooming House; Wife Was Questioned.".

22. "Guard Diamond Home to Foil Baby Killers," *New York Sun*, Sept. 3, 1931. Vincent " Mad Dog" Coll (1908–32) was a ruthless Irish gangster equal to Legs Diamond. Arrested for the death of young Vengelli, Coll went on trial and the charges against him were eventually dismissed. In 1932, Coll died in a hail of bullets inside a phone booth in a New York City drugstore. See "Coll Is Shot Dead by Rival Gunmen," *New York Times*, Feb. 8, 1932.

23. "Diamond Slain, Aids Suspected."

24. "D'Urgolo Freed by Jury Here in 49 Minutes," *Troy Times*, June, 24, 1932.

25. "D'Urgolo Freed by Jury Here in 49 Minutes."

26. Frankie Y. Bailey and Alice P. Green, *Wicked Albany* (Charlestown, SC: History Press, 2009), 45.

27. "Syracuse Nearly Free of the Detestable Drug Dealer," *Syracuse Journal*, June 28, 1927. David L. Smurl (1876–1940) served with the Albany Police De-

partment for twenty-six and a half years, thirteen of which were as chief of police. See "City Funeral Arranged for Chief Smurl," *Knickerbocker News*, Feb. 26, 1940. Richard A. Kelly (1881–1946) had an impressive 90 percent conviction rate on the narcotics raids he orchestrated. See "Kelly, Narcotics Officer Dies in Syracuse," *Knickerbocker News*, Mar. 14, 1946.

28. "Police Catch Man as Albany Drugs Runner," *Albany Evening News*, June 4, 1931.

29. "Six Chinese Arrested in Raid; Opium, Knife and Gun Seized," *Albany Evening News*, June 30, 1930.

30. "237 of 389 Taken for Parking in City Are Free," *Albany Evening News*, June 4, 1931.

31. "Albany Seen Full of Vice by Federal Narcotic Agent," *Albany Evening News*, Feb. 27, 1931.

32. "Chief Denies Story That He Fails to Aid," *Albany Evening News*, Sept. 19, 1930.

1. FROM RAILROADS TO THE RACKETS

1. Census Records, 1890, 1900, 1915.

2. Meaka Penta discovered how family disputes were not necessarily confined to the four walls of one's own home. In an embarrassing exposé, the *Savannah Times* reported a domestic dispute in which Meaka allegedly "refused to share her bed in a wifely manner." In the screaming match that ensued, husband Michael slapped his wife with such force as to knock her to the kitchen floor. Meaka picked herself up and as her husband was about to strike her once more, grasped a nearby flatiron. Michael screamed as Meaka pressed the hot iron against his bare hand. He then grabbed her arm and bit it hard enough to leave teeth marks. Although the *Times* somewhat sympathized with the plight of "henpecked husband" Michael Penta, one who was driven upstairs and "denied even the comfort of suitable bed, clothing and luxury of a wife to nestle close to his manly bosom," the courts thought otherwise and fined him sixteen dollars for the assault. He paid the fine and went home to an empty house. Meaka and her five children temporarily moved into her parents' farmhouse. See *Savannah Times*, Aug. 16, 1907.

3. Census Records, 1915.

4. Marriage Registrations Jan. 1874–Dec. 1932, Antonio-Turano 022232-16, Archives of Ontario, Toronto, Ont.

5. *Savannah Times*, June 5, 1917, Selective Service Records, 31-7-17-A, New York State Archives, Albany, NY.

6. *Savannah Times*, June 17, 1921; *Lake Shore News*, June 17, 1921, death certificate, Town of Wolcott, New York State Department of Health.

7. *Savannah Times*, June 17, 1921.

8. Ellis Island Immigration Records.

9. Marriage license, Antonio-Cappello, no. 2312, New York State Department of Health.

10. Certificate of birth, Phyllis Frances Antonio, Town of Wolcott, New York State Department of Health.

11. *The People of the State of New York against Vincent Saetta, Sam Faraci and Anna Antonio. Case on Appeal 1934*, vols. 113–16, p. 2081–82 (hereafter cited as Trial Transcripts).

12. On May 8, 1912, Meaka Penta was attempting to rekindle a fire with kerosene when her clothing caught fire. A local physician who dressed her wounds estimated that she had suffered burns on "one third of the surface of her body." The overseer of the poor brought her to St. Mary's Hospital in Rochester. "There is plenty of room for the activities of the charitable in this family," reported the *Savannah Times* on May 10, 1912, "as there are four small children who appeal for aid. Better to look after this quartette of helpless and orphaned children than send money to convert the Chinese to Christianity!"

13. Certificate of death, Anita Antonio, 45535, New York State Department of Health.

14. "Wife Declares Husband Forgave after Slaying," *Evening Recorder*, Amsterdam, Apr. 15, 1932.

15. Trial Transcripts, 2092.

16. Trial Transcripts, 2095–96.

17. Trial Transcripts, 2097.

18. "Dairy Farm Plant Destroyed by Fire," *Schenectady Gazette*, Dec. 22, 1931.

19. Trial Transcripts, 2098.

20. Trial Transcripts, 2100.

21. Trial Transcripts, 2103.

2. SAM FARACI

1. Trial Transcripts, 2340.

2. Ellis Island Immigration Records.

3. Trial Transcripts, 2336.

4. "Alderman Michaelson Attacked and Robbed," *Geneva Daily Times*, Dec. 24, 1917; *Auburn Citizen*, Nov. 13, 1918.

5. "Firuggi Is Sent to State Prison," *Geneva Daily Times*, Mar. 5, 1918.

6. "Two Italians Here Get Miller's First Clemency," *Auburn Citizen*, Jan. 13, 1921.

7. *Public Papers of Nathan L. Miller, Forty-Sixth Governor of the State of New York* (Albany, NY: J. B. Lyon Company, Printers, 1924), 280–81.

8. "Two Italians Here Get Miller's First Clemency."

9. "Minister Is Sent to Jail," *Geneva Daily Times*, Feb. 16, 1922.

10. "Jail Delivery at Canandaigua Frustrated," *North Tonawanda Evening News,* Jan. 26, 1922.

11. Trial Transcripts, 2504.

12. Trial Transcripts, 2340, 2594.

13. Trial Transcripts, 2341, 2592.

3. "ARE WE READY FOR A GOOD TIME?"

1. Trial Transcripts, 2109.

2. Trial Transcripts, 2112.

3. Trial Transcripts, 2114.

4. Trial Transcripts, 645.

5. Trial Transcripts, 2083, 2146.

6. Trial Transcripts, 2114–18.

7. Trial Transcripts, 3025–26.

8. Trial Transcripts, 391, 3051.

9. Trial Transcripts, 391, 2346, 3052.

10. Trial Transcripts, 3080–81.

11. Trial Transcripts, 2061.

12. Trial Transcripts, 2064.

13. Trial Transcripts, 2066–68.

14. Trial Transcripts, 2084–85.

15. Trial Transcripts, 3056.

16. Trial Transcripts, 392.

17. Trial Transcripts, 3023.

18. Trial Transcripts, 3029, 3118.

19. Trial Transcripts, 393–94, 3121.

20. Trial Transcripts, 394.

21. Faraci Confession, William H. Flubacher Papers, New York State Police (hereafter cited as Flubacher Papers).

22. Trial Transcripts, 453.

23. Trial Transcripts, 3065.

24. Trial Transcripts, 3067.

25. Trial Transcripts, 3067–68.

26. Trial Transcripts, 2125.

27. Trial Transcripts, 984–85.

4. "MY NAME . . . SAM ANTONIO"

1. Trial Transcripts, 126.

2. Author's interview with John Crary, Feb. 26, 2015.

3. Trial Transcripts, 108.

4. Trial Transcripts, 98, 110.

5. Trial Transcripts, 112.

6. Trial Transcripts, 127.

7. Trial Transcripts, 112.

8. Trial Transcripts, 113.

9. Trial Transcripts, 131.

10. Trial Transcripts, 130.

11. Trial Transcripts, 131.

12. After a brief stint in the army, William H. Flubacher (1900–1978) joined the ranks of the New York State Police on November 1, 1923, was posted to Troop G, and later became one of the first officers in the Bureau of Criminal Investigation (BCI) in the state. After his retirement on February 2, 1952, Flubacher served as justice of the peace for the town of East Greenbush, New York. See "State Police Sgt. Flubacher Retires," *Knickerbocker News,* Nov. 15, 1952.

13. Flubacher Papers.

14. Trial Transcripts, 178.

15. John C. Crary Jr. (1909–85) and William L. McDermott (1910–82) graduated from Albany Law School in June 1932 and were lifelong friends. Immediately following graduation and passing the bar exam, both men accepted positions with the new "racketeering bureau" in the State Attorney General's Office. Crary eventually rose to become an assistant in the Attorney General's Office. He married Cornelia Halpen in 1936. McDermott returned home to Olean, New York, where he practiced law and later served twenty years as a police judge. In 1958 he accepted the position as administrative director of the newly formed New York State Lottery Commission. See "Son of Former *Times* Reporter Gets Assignment," *Troy Times,* Oct. 21, 1933, and "Olean Man Will Run Lottery Commission," *Tonawanda News,* Apr. 24, 1958.

16. Flubacher Papers.

17. Det. George Griggs said this; see Trial Transcripts, 1353.

18. The son of John Crary, in an interview with the author, related how his father and the son of Dan Prior, Dan Prior Jr., were good friends. Crary enjoyed hearing stories from Prior Jr. of the meetings Legs Diamond had with his father. Young Prior recalled how his mother was frightened half to death by the machine gun–toting bodyguards who surrounded their home whenever Legs and his father met.

19. Trial Transcripts, 196.

20. Trial Transcripts, 188.

21. Trial Transcripts, 193.

22. Trial Transcripts, 188.

23. Trial Transcripts, 1051.

24. Trial Transcripts, 1053.

25. Flubacher Papers.

26. Flubacher Papers.

27. "Dope Smugglers Sought in Albanian's Murder," *Albany Times Union*, Mar. 29, 1932.

28. "Albanian, Suspected Member of Dope Ring, Left Fatally Wounded on Castleton Road," *Albany Times Union*, Mar. 29, 1932; *Troy Times*, Mar. 28, 1932.

29. Flubacher Papers.

30. "Dope Smugglers Sought in Albanian's Murder," *Troy Times*, Mar. 30, 1932.

5. "MRS. ANTONIO, YOU ARE NOT HELPING US"

1. George Griggs (1887–1950) was a First World War veteran who had worked as pressman before joining the ranks of the Albany police force in April 1923. Assigned to the Gut as a patrolman, Griggs called it the "tough beat." On one occasion he singlehandedly rounded up a half-dozen hoodlums, earning praise from his superior. His aggressive style earned him the catch phrase "Go get 'em George." See "Up from the Ranks," *Albany Times Union*, Nov. 4, 1931, and "Sgt. Griggs Is a Tough 'Softie,'" *Albany Times Union*, Oct. 7, 1945.

2. Flubacher Papers.

3. Flubacher Papers.

4. Flubacher Papers; Trial Transcripts, 1255.

5. Flubacher Papers.

6. Trial Transcripts, 1255.

7. Flubacher Papers; Trial Transcripts, 1256.

8. Trial Transcripts, 1257.

9. Trial Transcripts, 218.

10. Trial Transcripts, 220.

11. Trial Transcripts, 227.

12. Trial Transcripts, 223.

13. Trial Transcripts, 1268.

14. Trial Transcripts, 1480.

6. LIES, ALIBIS, AND GERTRUDE KING

1. John T. Delaney to Capt. John R. Kelley, Apr. 16, 1932, Flubacher Papers.

2. Flubacher Papers.

3. Trial Transcripts, 1652–53.

4. Trial Transcripts, 1653–54.

5. At the trial, Griggs testified that it was seventy-five dollars and James Hynes recalled the amount as being seventy dollars, while Flubacher neglected to mention the amount. See Trial Transcripts, 1328, 1683, 283.

6. Trial Transcripts, 1329.

7. Trial Transcripts, 1329.

8. Trial Transcripts, 1301.

9. Trial Transcripts, 1489.

10. Trial Transcripts, 265.

11. Trial Transcripts, 1314–16.

12. Trial Transcripts, 2869.

13. Trial Transcripts, 1316.

14. Trial Transcripts, 299.

7. "AT LAST, A BREAK"

1. Flubacher Papers.

2. Trial Transcripts, 1718, 1720, 1722.

3. Trial Transcripts, 1723.

4. Trial Transcripts, 1725.

5. Trial Transcripts, 336.

6. Flubacher Papers.

7. Trial Transcripts, 336.

8. Trial Transcripts, 3130.

9. Trial Transcripts, 1727–28.

10. Trial Transcripts, 3122.

11. Trial Transcripts, 1728.

12. Trial Transcripts, 1541–42.

13. Trial Transcripts, 452.

14. Trial Transcripts, 1571–72.

8. THREE CONFESSIONS

1. Trial Transcripts, 3078.

2. Trial Transcripts, 3081.

3. Trial Transcripts, 3087.

4. Trial Transcripts, 1747–48.

5. Trial Transcripts, 1747–48.

6. Trial Transcripts, 416.

7. Trial Transcripts, 1750.

8. Trial Transcripts, 1752; Flubacher Papers.

9. Trial Transcripts, 3105–6.

10. Trial Transcripts, 443.

11. Trial Transcripts, 3105.

12. Trial Transcripts, 3106.

13. Trial Transcripts, 462; Flubacher Papers.

14. Trial Transcripts, 463; Flubacher Papers.

15. Trial Transcripts, 465.

16. Trial Transcripts, 1775.

17. Trial Transcripts, 1777–78; Flubacher Papers.

18. Trial Transcripts, 1501.

9. THE GATHERING OF LEGALS

1. Henry A. Lowenberg, as told to Robin Moore, *Until Proven Guilty: Forty Years as Criminal Defense Counsel* (Boston: Little, Brown and Co., 1971), 34. Henry A. Lowenberg (1903–71) was a graduate of Columbia University and Fordham Law School. He was the only attorney associated with this trial to publish his memoirs.

2. Lowenberg, *Until Proven Guilty*, 74–75; Trial Transcripts, 2–4.

3. *People of the State of New York Against Vincent Saetta, Court of Appeals* (Walton, NY: Reporter Co., 1934), 78.

4. Lowenberg, *Until Proven Guilty*, 77.

5. Lowenberg, *Until Proven Guilty*, 77.

6. Lowenberg, *Until Proven Guilty*, 78.

7. "Fight to Halt Saetta Case," *Albany Evening News*, June 14, 1932. Judge Earl H. Gallup (1880–1970) graduated from Albany Law School in 1905 and clerked for former governor of New York David B. Hill. After serving in various state offices, he was appointed City of Albany judge in 1922. A product of the O'Connell political machine, Gallup was afterwards elected to this position and retained it until he retired in 1950. See "Lawyers Fete Judge Gallup on Retirement," *Albany Times Union*, Dec. 29, 1950; "Earl Gallup, Ex-judge, Dead at 89," *Albany Times Union*, Feb. 3, 1970.

8. Trial Transcripts (Clerk's Minutes), 61.

9. Trial Transcripts (Clerk's Minutes), 63.

10. Trial Transcripts (Clerk's Minutes), 64, 66.

11. Bailey and Green, *Wicked Albany*, 57–58.

12. Trial Transcripts (Clerk's Minutes), 65.

13. Trial Transcripts (Clerk's Minutes), 69. Charles J. Duncan (1893–1964) was a graduate of Christian Brothers Academy in Albany and received his law degree from Catholic Union Law School in 1916. See "C. J. Duncan, Well-Known, Dies at 70," *Knickerbocker News*, Dec. 8, 1964.

14. Trial Transcripts (Clerk's Minutes), 70.

15. "Fifth Juror Is Named for Antonio Case," *Albany Evening News*, Mar. 23, 1933.

16. Trial Transcripts (Clerk's Minutes), 78.

17. Trial Transcripts (Clerk's Minutes), 79.

18. *People of the State of New York Against Manning Strewl, Return on Appeal* (Albany: The Argus Co., 1936), 96.

19. Trial Transcripts (Clerk's Minutes), 89.

20. Trial Transcripts (Clerk's Minutes), 90–91.

21. Trial Transcripts (Clerk's Minutes), 93.

22. "Mrs. Antonio to Testify in Own Defense," *Albany Evening News*, Mar. 27, 1933.

10. FLUBACHER AND THE ITALIAN DETECTIVE

1. Trial Transcripts, 146.

2. "Corp. Flubacher Trooper Sergeant," *Albany Evening News*, July 18, 1932. It should be noted that almost every newspaper that followed the Antonio trial went back and forth in using the names Sam and Salvatore.

3. Trial Transcripts, 494.

4. Trial Transcripts, 494–95.

5. Trial Transcripts, 497.

6. Trial Transcripts, 500.

7. Trial Transcripts, 597.

8. Trial Transcripts, 527.

9. Trial Transcripts, 533, 547.

10. "Wife Declares Husband Forgave Her After Slaying," *Amsterdam Evening Recorder*, Apr. 15, 1932.

11. Trial Transcripts, 576–77.

12. "At Greggio Trial in County Court," *Utica Dispatch*, Jan. 16, 1914. Joseph Genova (1880–1954) was born in Reggio, Calabria, Italy, and came to America at a young age with his family. In 1910, he became a detective for the New York Central Railroad and served in that capacity, rose to the rank of lieutenant, and retired in 1953. "His ability as an investigator," noted the *Amsterdam Evening Recorder*, "was well known throughout the state and his services were frequently loaned by the New York Central to private detective agencies as well as county and state police who wanted Lt. Genova's help in investigations. He also worked with the F.B.I. at various times." See "Funeral on Tuesday," *Amsterdam Evening Recorder*, Aug. 23, 1954.

13. "Prosecution Rests Case in Trial of Alleged Amsterdam Slayers," *Schenectady Gazette*, July 2, 1930.

14. Boyden Sparkes, "Train Robbers Routed by Science and Brawn," *Popular Science*, July 1931, 135.

15. "Week's End Chit-chat," *Amsterdam Evening Recorder*, June 20, 1931.

16. Trial Transcripts, 434.

17. Trial Transcripts, 434.

18. Trial Transcripts, 436.

19. Trial Transcripts, 428.

20. Trial Transcripts, 436.

21. Trial Transcripts, 428.

22. Trial Transcripts, 428.

23. Trial Transcripts, 1591.

24. Flubacher Papers.

25. Trial Transcripts, 1591–92.

26. Trial Transcripts, 1599.

27. Trial Transcripts, 1608.

28. Trial Transcripts, 1607.

29. Trial Transcripts, 1600.

30. Trial Transcripts, 1610.

31. Trial Transcripts, 1618.

11. JIMMY HYNES, THE ICE CREAM BOY

1. James J. Hynes (1894–1954), reported the *Albany Times Union*, "was assigned to duty in the South End. Through his police work he knew many famous gangsters of the era including Legs Diamond and Dutch Schultz." Hynes spent more time on the witness stand during the Antonio trial than any other member of the Albany Police Department. See "James Hynes, Long Il., Dies," *Albany Times Union*, Jan. 10, 1954.

2. Trial Transcripts, 1799.

3. Trial Transcripts, 804.

4. Trial Transcripts, 813–15.

5. Trial Transcripts, 819.

6. Trial Transcripts, 2844.

7. Trial Transcripts, 1801.

8. Trial Transcripts, 1826.

9. Trial Transcripts, 1772.

10. Trial Transcripts, 1697.

11. Trial Transcripts, 1838.

12. Trial Transcripts, 1770.

13. Trial Transcripts, 1846.

14. Trial Transcripts, 2796.

15. Trial Transcripts, 2739.

16. Trial Transcripts, 2740.

12. THE FIFTY-CENT KNIFE

1. Trial Transcripts, 1694.
2. Trial Transcripts, 1927–28.
3. Trial Transcripts, 1917.
4. Trial Transcripts, 1918.
5. Trial Transcripts, 1924.
6. Sara Mara (1891–1939) served as secretary to John T. Delaney for seventeen years. When she died, Delaney closed the district attorney's office so he and his staff could attend her funeral. Respected and admired, her funeral was "attended by prominent figures in the legal, political and religious life of Albany." See "Death Record in Albany Area," *Knickerbocker News,* Nov. 15, 1939.
7. Trial Transcripts, 1893.
8. Trial Transcripts, 1893.
9. Trial Transcripts, 2787.
10. Trial Transcripts, 2770.
11. Trial Transcripts, 2821.
12. Trial Transcripts, 1994.
13. Trial Transcripts, 2000.
14. Lowenberg, *Until Proven Guilty,* 74–75.
15. *Albany Evening News,* Apr. 10, 1933.
16. Trial Transcripts, 2010.
17. "Defense Opens with Pleas in Antonio Case," *Albany Evening News,* Apr. 10, 1933.
18. Trial Transcripts, 2014.
19. Trial Transcripts, 2015.
20. Trial Transcripts, 2016.

13. ANNA ANTONIO

1. "Changes Urged in County Prison," *Albany Evening News,* Feb. 20, 1931.
2. Trial Transcripts, 2047.
3. Trial Transcripts, 2079–80.
4. Trial Transcripts, 2084.
5. Trial Transcripts, 2125.
6. Trial Transcripts, 2127.
7. Trial Transcripts, 2139.
8. Trial Transcripts, 2133.
9. Trial Transcripts, 2137.
10. Trial Transcripts, 2138.
11. Trial Transcripts, 2142.

12. Trial Transcripts, 1184.
13. Trial Transcripts, 1178.
14. Trial Transcripts, 2145.
15. Trial Transcripts, 2146.

14. HENRY LOWENBERG

1. Lowenberg, *Until Proven Guilty*, 75, 81.
2. Lowenberg, *Until Proven Guilty*, 83–84.
3. Lowenberg, *Until Proven Guilty*, 84.
4. Trial Transcripts, 2155.
5. Trial Transcripts, 2158.
6. Lowenberg, *Until Proven Guilty*, 64.
7. Trial Transcripts, 2159–60.
8. Trial Transcripts, 2164–65.
9. Trial Transcripts, 2161.
10. Trial Transcripts, 2168.
11. Trial Transcripts, 2168–69.
12. Trial Transcripts, 2171.
13. Trial Transcripts, 2208.
14. Trial Transcripts, 2174.
15. Trial Transcripts, 2178–79.
16. Trial Transcripts, 2194.
17. Trial Transcripts, 2207.

15. "WHO IS TONY PINTO?"

1. Trial Transcripts, 2218. Joseph J. Casey (1904–89) graduated in 1922 from Christian Brothers Academy, where he was the valedictorian. Three years later, he was the valedictorian at Albany Law School. From 1932 to 1935, Casey served as an assistant district attorney in Albany County and afterwards went into private practice. In addition to practicing law, Casey was the vice president of the City and County Bank in Albany. A devout Catholic, he was a generous contributor to organizations associated with the church. John Yanas and Kathy Yanas interviewed by author, Mar. 3, 2017.
2. Lowenberg, *Until Proven Guilty*, 89.
3. Trial Transcripts, 2837, 2857.
4. Trial Transcripts, 2218.
5. Trial Transcripts, 2219. Tony Penta (1907–41) remained in Albany and became a driver for the Pearl Taxi Company. When he died, his fellow drivers served as pallbearers at his funeral. See *Knickerbocker News*, May 10, 1941.

6. Trial Transcripts, 2220.

7. Trial Transcripts, 2219.

8. Trial Transcripts, 2225.

9. "Love for Old Suitor Denied by Mrs. Antonio," *Albany Evening News*, Apr. 11, 1933; "Mrs. Antonio Denies Intent to Re[-]wed on Husband's Death," *Albany Times Union*, Apr. 11, 1933.

10. Trial Transcripts, 2228.

11. Trial Transcripts, 2229.

12. Trial Transcripts, 2229–30. For some unexplained reason, Lowenberg included this letter in his memoirs but omits the line "Also I went to New York alone for the funeral." The funeral Anna is referring to was for her father-in-law, Frank Antonio. He died of a heart attack on December 27, 1931, at the home of his daughter, Mary DeSisto, in the Bronx. As for Mrs. Anna Penta Winters, oldest daughter of Meaka Penta, hers was a troubled marriage. During the Antonio trial, her husband, Joseph Winters, was being investigated for welfare fraud in the city of Buffalo, having received $249 when in fact he had $1,884 in a Rochester bank. Ordered to make restitution, he was arrested two years later when he was accused of stealing a ring and a wristwatch from a neighbor who had dozed off while sleeping in her car. See "Fine of $100 Imposed," *Buffalo Evening News*, Jan. 31, 1933; "Pleads Not Guilty in Jewelry Theft," *Rochester Times Union*, Nov. 22, 1935.

13. Trial Transcripts, 2233.

14. Trial Transcripts, 2249.

15. Trial Transcripts, 2313.

16. Trial Transcripts, 2285.

17. Trial Transcripts, 2286.

18. Trial Transcripts, 2283–84.

19. Trial Transcripts, 2284.

20. Trial Transcripts, 2323–24.

16. THE RAT

1. Trial Transcripts, 2439.

2. Trial Transcripts, 2346.

3. Trial Transcripts, 2365.

4. Trial Transcripts, 2366.

5. Trial Transcripts, 2371.

6. Trial Transcripts, 2372–73.

7. Trial Transcripts, 2376.

8. Trial Transcripts, 2392.

9. Trial Transcripts, 2393.

10. Trial Transcripts, 2394.

11. Trial Transcripts, 2397.

12. Trial Transcripts, 2852.

13. Trial Transcripts, 2447.

14. Trial Transcripts, 2440, 2460.

15. Trial Transcripts, 2460.

16. Trial Transcripts, 2445.

17. Trial Transcripts, 2461–62.

18. Trial Transcripts, 2463.

19. Trial Transcripts, 2477.

20. Trial Transcripts, 2478, 2480.

21. Trial Transcripts, 2590–91.

22. Trial Transcripts, 2537.

17. PERJURY AND ATTORNEY CONSPIRACY

1. Trial Transcripts, 2606.

2. Trial Transcripts, 2609.

3. Lowenberg, *Until Proven Guilty*, 77.

4. Trial Transcripts, 2631.

5. Trial Transcripts, 2632.

6. Trial Transcripts, 2633.

7. Trial Transcripts, 2641.

8. Trial Transcripts, 2701.

9. Trial Transcripts, 2707, 2757.

10. Trial Transcripts, 2711.

11. Trial Transcripts, 2712.

12. Trial Transcripts, 2712.

13. Trial Transcripts, 2715.

14. Trial Transcripts, 2717.

15. Trial Transcripts, 2720.

16. Trial Transcripts, 2732.

17. Trial Transcripts, 2744–45.

18. Trial Transcripts, 2745–46.

19. Trial Transcripts, 2752.

20. Trial Transcripts, 2761.

21. Trial Transcripts, 2762.

22. Trial Transcripts, 2763.

23. Trial Transcripts, 2761.

24. Trial Transcripts, 2768.

18. "WHO IS VINCENT SAETTA?"

1. Trial Transcripts, 2770.
2. Trial Transcripts, 2773–74.
3. Trial Transcripts, 2776.
4. Trial Transcripts, 2787.
5. Trial Transcripts, 2791–92.
6. Trial Transcripts, 2792.
7. Trial Transcripts, 2824.
8. Trial Transcripts, 2794.
9. Trial Transcripts, 2794.
10. Trial Transcripts, 2799.
11. Trial Transcripts, 2801; "Mrs. Antonio Weeps during Delaney Talk," *Albany Evening News*, Apr. 15, 1933.
12. Trial Transcripts, 2801.
13. Trial Transcripts, 2802.
14. Trial Transcripts, 2807.
15. Trial Transcripts, 2807–8.
16. Trial Transcripts, 2807.
17. Trial Transcripts, 2811.
18. Trial Transcripts, 2814.
19. Trial Transcripts, 2814–15.
20. Trial Transcripts, 2823.
21. Trial Transcripts, 2834.

19. "DO EQUAL JUSTICE"

1. "Mrs. Antonio Weeps during Delaney Talk," *Albany Evening News*, Apr. 15, 1933.
2. Trial Transcripts, 2835–36.
3. Trial Transcripts, 2857.
4. Trial Transcripts, 2840.
5. "Mrs. Antonio Weeps during Delaney Talk."
6. Trial Transcripts, 2858.
7. Trial Transcripts, 2849.
8. Trial Transcripts, 2854.
9. Trial Transcripts, 2865–66.
10. Trial Transcripts, 2899.
11. Trial Transcripts, 2907.
12. Trial Transcripts, 2917.

13. Trial Transcripts, 2918.

14. Trial Transcripts, 2921.

15. Trial Transcripts, 2916.

16. Trial Transcripts, 2916.

17. Trial Transcripts, 2931.

18. Trial Transcripts, 2958–59.

19. Trial Transcripts, 2983.

20. *Albany Evening News*, Apr. 19, 1933.

21. Trial Transcripts, 2985.

22. Trial Transcripts, 2986.

23. Lowenberg, *Until Proven Guilty*, 97.

20. THE BIG HOUSE

1. Hugh Reilly and Kevin Warnecke, *Father Flanagan of Boys Town: A Man of Vision* (Nebraska: Boys Town Press, 2008), 7.

2. "Brief 'Vacation' Trips to Pleasant Prisons Are Reducing Value of a Human Life to $25, Justice Lewis Tells Municipal Club Diners," *Brooklyn Daily Eagle*, Apr. 29, 1925.

3. Scott Christianson, *Condemned: Inside the Sing Sing Death House* (New York: New York Univ. Press, 2001), 16–17.

4. Ralph Blumenthal, *Miracle at Sing Sing: How One Man Transformed the Lives of America's Most Dangerous Prisoners* (New York: St. Martin's Press, 2004), 137.

5. Lewis Lawes, "The Warden Speaks—Bravest of the Condemned," *Elmira Gazette*, Dec. 14, 1938.

6. Lawes, "The Warden Speaks."

7. Sing Sing Prison Records, New York State Archives.

8. "Indicted in 'Insurance' Murders," *Niagara Falls Gazette*, Sept. 23, 1932.

9. "Claims Murder Deal Made," *Niagara Falls Gazette*, Oct. 14, 1932.

10. "Murder Charge against Staten Island Woman Dismissed; Landers May Be Freed," *New Age*, July 7, 1934; "Doomed Negro Murderer Saved from the Chair," *Amsterdam Record*, July 31, 1934; "Two Women in Death House First in History," *Syracuse Herald American*, Aug. 6, 1934.

11. "Doomed Negro Murderer Saved from the Chair."

12. Lewis Lawes, *20,000 Years at Sing Sing* (New York: Ray Long and Richard Smith, Inc., 1932), 332–34.

13. Sing Sing Prison Records, New York State Archives.

14. Dr. Amos O. Squire, *Sing Sing Doctor* (New York: Doubleday, Doran and Company, 1935), 251. "During the time that Mrs. Antonio was in the death house,

the State spent a total of $4,650 upon her supervision and maintenance—more than was ever spent upon an inmate of the condemned cells at Sing Sing" (Squire, *Sing Sing Doctor*, 250–51).

15. Carrie Stephens (1871–1936), of Ossining, was a matron at Sing Sing for over ten years. Married with no children, she died from injuries sustained from slipping on the ice on the prison grounds after a February 1936 storm. See "1,000 Toil to Free City from Snow," *Yonkers Herald Statesman*, Feb. 15, 1936. Lucy Many (1886–1969), also of Ossining, may have been the longest-serving matron in the history of Sing Sing. She served as a matron to Ruth Snyder in 1927 and ended with Ethel Rosenberg in 1953.

16. "World Famous Warden Never Too Busy to Speak to Inmates," *Daily Argus*, Dec. 26, 1931.

17. Robert K. Elder, *Last Words of the Executed* (Chicago: Chicago Univ. Press, 2010), 141.

18. "Gray and Widow to Hear Doom on Friday the 13th," *Rome Daily Sentinel*, May 12, 1927.

21. THE COURT OF LAST RESORT

1. Steven Chermak and Frank Y. Bailey, eds., *Crimes of the Centuries: Notorious Crimes, Criminals and Criminal Trial in American History* (Santa Barbara, CA: ABC-CLIO, Inc., 2016), 589.

2. Robinson, *Machine Politics*, 66–67.

3. "Strewl Framed Prior Declares Closing Defense," *Amsterdam Evening Recorder*, Mar. 13, 1934. The highlight of the trial was when Dan Prior got in the last word on the family that had been a political thorn in his side. "I know the O'Connell power," he said while addressing the jury. "They own Albany county body and soul. There is not a man in Albany county can be elected to office unless Dan O'Connell puts his OK on it."

4. "Antonio Trio Offers Pleas to High Court," *Albany Evening News*, Apr. 24, 1934.

5. "Antonio Trio Offers Plea to High Court."

6. Trial Transcripts, Court of Appeals, 640.

7. Sing Sing Prison Records, New York State Archives.

8. Trial Transcripts, Court of Appeals, 17–80.

9. "Woman Slayer Still Hopeful of Commutation," *Amsterdam Evening Recorder*, June 26, 1934.

10. "Woman Slayer Still Hopeful of Commutation."

11. "Mrs. Antonio's Fate Now up to Lehman," *Daily Eagle*, June 21, 1934.

12. Austin Sarat, *Mercy on Trial: What It Means to Stop an Execution* (Princeton, NJ: Princeton Univ. Press, 2005), 221.

22. AN UNFORGIVING PRESS

1. "Woman in Death House Stirs Unrest in Sing Sing," *Syracuse American Journal*, May 27, 1934.

2. "Sees Children Last Time Today," *Syracuse American Journal*, June 28, 1934.

3. "Sees Children Last Time Today."

4. Dale Harrison, "Husband Slayer Dies Tomorrow if Plea Fails," *Amsterdam Evening News*, June 27, 1934.

5. Dale Harrison, "Woman Slated to Die Tonight; Mercy Unlikely," *Amsterdam Evening News*, June 28, 1934.

6. "Sees Children Last Time Today."

7. Harrison, "Woman Slated to Die Tonight; Mercy Unlikely."

8. H. Eric Liljeholm, "Mrs. Antonio Awaits Death," *Albany Times Union*, Aug. 9, 1934.

9. Liljeholm, "Mrs. Antonio Awaits Death."

10. "Albany Woman Asks Clemency," *Amsterdam Evening Recorder*, June 20, 1934.

11. "Retrial Plea Denied upon New Evidence," *Albany Times Union*, Aug. 9, 1934.

12. Vicki Moyer Reed interviewed by author, Aug. 16, 2015.

13. Harrison, "Husband Slayer Dies Tomorrow if Plea Fails."

14. "Appeals to Lehman," *New York Sun*, June 28, 1934.

15. "Two Arrested on Statutory Charges, Jailed," *Geneva Daily Times*, June 16, 1934.

16. "Mrs. Ferugia and Child Visited Doomed Father," *Geneva Daily Times*, June 29, 1934.

23. THE STATE ELECTRICIAN

1. Robert G. Elliott as told to Albert B. Beatty, "And May God Have Mercy on Your Soul," *Colliers*, Sept. 24, 1938.

2. Robert G. Elliott as told to Albert B. Beatty, "As Humane as Possible," *Colliers*, Oct. 15, 1938.

3. Elliott, "As Humane as Possible."

4. Elliott, "As Humane as Possible."

5. Elliott, "And May God Have Mercy on Your Soul."

6. Lewis Lawes, *Life and Death in Sing Sing* (New York: Garden City Publishing Company, Inc., 1928), 168.

7. "Woman Gets Stay at Execution," *New York Times*, June 29, 1934.

8. "Antonio Girl Prays for Mother," *Albany Times Union*, June 22, 1934.

9. "Lehman Studies Saetta Confession," *Albany Times Union*, June 29, 1934.

10. "Woman Gets Stay of Execution in the Final Hours," *New York Times*, June 30, 1934.

11. "Mrs. Antonio First to Die; Faraci Follows; Saetta Is Last," *Albany Times Union*, Aug. 10, 1934.

24. SAETTA SPEAKS

1. Lewis Lawes, "The Warden Speaks—Bravest of the Condemned," *Elmira Gazette*, Dec. 14, 1938.

2. "Woman Gets Stay After 2-Hour Wait at Execution Time," *New York Times*, June 30, 1934.

3. Trial Transcripts, Court of Appeals, Re-argument, 37–39.

4. "Woman Gets Stay After 2-Hour Wait at Execution Time."

5. *Beaver (PA) County Times*, Feb. 9, 1981.

6. Robert G. Elliott, *Agent of Death* (New York: E. P. Dutton and Company, 1940), 213.

7. "Woman Gets Stay of Execution in the Final Hour," *New York Times*, June 30, 1934.

8. "Mrs. Antonio and Two Companions Get Short Stay," *Troy Times*, June 29, 1934.

9. Trial Transcripts, Court of Appeals, Re-argument, 46–47.

10. "Text of Saetta's Statement That Halted Execution," *Albany Times Union*, June 29, 1934.

11. "Woman Gets Stay of Execution in the Final Hour."

12. "Mrs. Antonio Seeks Retrial," *Albany Times Union*, July 1, 1934.

13. "Mrs. Antonio Seeks Retrial."

14. "Mrs. Antonio Granted Stay; Attorney to Seek New Trial," *Poughkeepsie Eagle News*, June 30, 1934.

25. "THE PORTALS OF MERCY"

1. Trial Transcripts, Court of Appeals, Re-argument, 16.

2. Trial Transcripts, Court of Appeals, Re-argument, 18.

3. Trial Transcripts, Court of Appeals, Re-argument, 18.

4. "Ruth Will Retain Same Legal Staff," *Philadelphia Inquirer*, Nov. 27, 1927.

5. "Woman Won't See Daughters," *Poughkeepsie Eagle News*, July 9, 1934.

6. "Pleads for Mrs. Antonio," *New York Times*, July 9, 1934.

7. The Cardinal Hayes Papers deposited in the Archdiocese of New York at Yonkers, New York, does not have this report. The Clarence Darrow Papers at the Library of Congress and the Darrow Papers at the University of Chicago Library make no mention of Anna Antonio.

8. "Save Mrs. Antonio from Death Chair," *Brooklyn Daily Eagle*, July 8, 1934.

9. "Last Minute Statement Clears Woman," H. F. Wood, *Albany Times Union*, June 29, 1934; "Mrs. Antonio Reprieved Until Tonight," *Saratogian*, June 29, 1934.

10. Trial Transcripts, Court of Appeals, Re-argument, 56.

11. Trial Transcripts, Court of Appeals, Re-argument, 14.

12. Trial Transcripts, Court of Appeals, Re-argument, 7.

13. Trial Transcripts, Court of Appeals, Re-argument, 86.

14. Trial Transcripts, Court of Appeals, Re-argument, 93.

15. "Mrs. Antonio's Appeal Denied by High Court," *Poughkeepsie Eagle News*, July 17, 1934.

16. "New Antonio Trial Appeal Tomorrow," *Albany Times Union*, Aug. 5, 1934.

17. "Priest Gave Mrs. Antonio First News of Murder Says Prior; Asks Retrial," *Albany Times Union*, Aug. 2, 1934.

18. "Albany Mother Scheduled to Die in Electric Chair Thursday Night," *Albany Times Union*, Aug. 6, 1934.

19. "Retrial Plea Denied Upon New Evidence," *Albany Times Union*, Aug. 9, 1934.

20. "Albany Woman Doomed to Die Denied Retrial," *Amsterdam Evening Recorder*, Aug. 8, 1934.

21. "Only Lehman Can Rescue Trio from Chair," *Albany Times Union*, Aug. 8, 1934.

22. "Lehman Weighs Woman's Fate," *Yonkers Herald Statesman*, Aug. 8, 1934.

23. "Albany Woman Doomed to Die; Denied Retrial," *Albany Times Union*, Aug. 7, 1934.

24. "Only Lehman Can Rescue Trio from Chair."

25. "Albany Woman Doomed to Die Denied Retrial," *Amsterdam Evening Recorder*, Aug. 8, 1934.

26. AUGUST 9, 1934

1. "Mrs. Antonio Goes Calmly to Electric Chair," *Amsterdam Evening Record*, Aug. 9, 1934; *Brooklyn Daily Eagle*, Aug. 10, 1934.

2. "Mrs. Antonio to Die Tonight Unless Governor Intervenes," *Amsterdam Evening Recorder*, Aug. 9, 1934.

3. Mark Gado, *Death Row Women: Murder, Justice and the New York Press* (Westport: Praeger Publisher, 2008), 58–59.

4. "Wife Killer Dies in Ossining," *Gloversville Morning Herald*, July 13, 1934.

5. "Mrs. Antonio to Die Tonight Unless Governor Intervenes," *Amsterdam Evening Recorder*, Aug. 9, 1934.

6. "Mrs. Antonio Awaits Death at Sing Sing," *Albany Times Union*, Aug. 9, 1934.

7. Squire, *Sing Sing Doctor*, 244.

8. Gado, *Death Row Women*, 61.

9. Squire, *Sing Sing Doctor*, 244.

10. *Albany Times Union*, Aug. 10, 1934.

11. "Mrs. Antonio First to Die; Faraci Follows; Saetta Is Last."

12. Squire, *Sing Sing Doctor*, 246. Three years later, Lewis Lawes copied this vignette word for word in his column "The Warden Speaks." See "Bravest of the Condemned," *Elmira Star Gazette*, Dec. 14, 1938.

13. "Mrs. Antonio First to Die; Faraci Follows; Saetta Is Last."

14. Vicki Moyer Reed interviewed by author, Aug. 16, 2015.

15. Gado, *Death Row Women*, 62.

16. "Mrs. Antonio Awaits Death at Sing Sing."

17. "Mrs. Antonio and Husband Killers Die," *Elmira Gazette*, Aug. 10, 1934.

18. *Beaver County (PA) Times*, Feb. 9, 1981.

19. Elliott, *Agent of Death*, 213.

20. "Mrs. Antonio First to Die; Faraci Follows; Saetta Is Last.".

21. Lewis Lawes, *Meet the Murderer* (New York: Harper and Brothers Publisher, 1940), 140.

22. "Mrs. Antonio First to Die; Faraci Follows; Saetta Is Last."

23. "Mrs. Antonio's Accomplices Sent to Death in Electric Chair," *Saratogian*, Aug. 10, 1934.

24. "Mrs. Antonio First to Die; Faraci Follows; Saetta Is Last."

25. "Curious Banned from Antonio Funeral," *Albany Times Union*, Aug. 11, 1934.

26. Kimberly Noyes, DeMarco Funeral Home, letter to the author, Feb. 3, 2016.

27. "Mrs. Antonio's Funeral to Be Here Monday," *Schenectady Gazette*, Aug. 13, 1934.

28. "All Nice Girls to Mrs. Lawes," *New York Post*, July 10, 1935.

29. "Ferugia's Body Is Coming Here for Funeral," *Geneva Daily Times*, Aug. 10, 1934.

30. "Jam at Funeral of Mrs. Antonio," *New York Sun*, Aug 13, 1934.

27. THE CUSTODY WAR

1. "Curious Banned from Mrs. Antonio's Funeral."

2. "Antonio Boy and Uncle Hunted," *Albany Times Union*, Aug. 18, 1934.

3. "Grief Stricken over Losing Boys Custody," *Schenectady Gazette*, Aug. 18, 1934.

4. "Police Believe Uncle, Who Disappeared with Antonio Child, Will Return Tomorrow," *Troy Times*, Aug. 18, 1934.

5. "Police Believe Uncle, Who Disappeared with Antonio Child, Will Return Tomorrow."

6. "3 Would Adopt Two Antonio Children," *Albany Times Union*, Aug. 14, 1934.

7. Walter Winchell, "On Broadway," *Syracuse Journal*, Sept. 4, 1934.

8. "Capello, Home Again, Will Fight to Keep Boy, Has Prior's Aid," *Albany Times Union*, Aug. 20, 1934.

9. "Capello, Home Again, Will Fight to Keep Boy, Has Prior's Aid."

10. "Awaiting Ruling from Court on Reuniting Antonio Children," *Troy Times Record*, July 30, 1935.

11. "Mrs. Antonio's Deed Appoints Cappello Guardian," *Schenectady Gazette*, Aug. 21, 1934.

12. "Court Reserves Decision in Antonio Children Case," *Albany Times Union*, July 10, 1935.

13. "Court Reserves Decision in Antonio Children Case."

14. "Uncle Here Is Given Custody of Antonio Boy," *Schenectady Gazette*, Sept. 7, 1935.

15. *Greensboro News and Record*, Mar. 18, 2003.

28. LEHMAN'S PAINFUL DECISION

1. "Lehman Explains Executive Stand," *Albany Times Union*, Aug. 10, 1934.

2. "Asked for Clemency," *Poughkeepsie Eagle News*, Aug. 10, 1934.

3. "Lehman Explains Executive Stand."

4. "A Painful Duty," *New York Times*, Aug. 11, 1934.

5. "Mrs. Antonio's Execution," *Brooklyn Daily Eagle*, Aug. 10, 1934.

6. "Mrs. Antonio Pays the Penalty," *Poughkeepsie Eagle News*, Aug. 10, 1934.

7. "One Law for Both Sexes," *Amsterdam Evening Recorder*, Aug. 11, 1934.

8. Lionel S. B. Shapiro, "Light and Shadows of Manhattan," *Montreal Gazette*, Aug. 13, 1934.

9. Arthur Brisbane, "Today," *Albany Times Union*, July 6, 1933.

10. Arthur Brisbane, "Today," *Albany Times Union*, Aug. 11, 1934.

11. "Three Lives for One Is State's Toll in Murder of Salvatore Antonio," *Kingston Daily Freeman*, Aug. 10, 1934.

12. Brisbane, "Today," Aug. 11, 1934.

13. "Lawes Deplore Legal Murder," *Albany Times Union*, Aug. 10, 1934.

14. "Executing Anna," *New York Daily News*, Apr. 1, 2012.

15. Kennedy, *O Albany*, 299.

A NOTE ON SOURCES

1. Charles L. Mooney, "The City Editor Reminisces," *Knickerbocker News*, Jan. 2, 1954.

2. Lowenberg, *Until Proven Guilty*, 35.

3. Lowenberg, *Until Proven Guilty*, 75.

4. Lowenberg, *Until Proven Guilty*, 96.

5. Lowenberg, *Until Proven Guilty*, 96.

6. Lawes, *Meet the Murderer*, 142.

7. Squire, *Sing Sing Doctor*, 247.

8. Fletcher Pratt, "Instrument of the State," *Saturday Review*, Jan. 20, 1940.

9. "Executioner," *Time*, Jan. 15, 1940.

10. Wenzell Brown, *Women Who Died in the Chair* (New York: Collier Books, 1958), 50.

11. Brown, *Women*, 51, 53, 57.

12. Brown, *Women*, 51.

13. Brown, *Women*, 58.

14. Brown, *Women*, 60.

BIBLIOGRAPHY

Manuscripts

Archives of Ontario, Toronto, ON
Auburn Prison Records, New York State Archives, Albany, NY
Ellis Island Records, Liberty-Ellis Island Foundation, N Y
William H. Flubacher Papers, New York State Police, Albany, NY
William H. Lehman Papers, Butler Library, Columbia Univ., NY
Sing Sing Prison Records, New York State Archives, Albany, NY
Vital Records, New York State Department of Health, Albany, NY

Newspapers

Albany Evening Journal
Albany Evening News
Albany Journal
Amsterdam Evening Recorder
Auburn Citizen
Beaver County Times (Beaver, PA)
Brooklyn Daily Eagle
Buffalo Courier Express
Daily Argus (Mount Vernon, NY)
Daily Eagle (Poughkeepsie, NY)
Daily News (Tarrytown, NY)
Elmira Star Gazette
Evening News (North Tonawanda, NY)
Evening Star (Peekskill, NY)
Geneva Daily Times
Greensboro News and Record (NC)
Herald Statesman (Yonkers, NY)
Kingston Daily Freeman

Knickerbocker News (Albany, NY)
Lake Shore News (Wolcott, NY)
Montreal Gazette
Morning Herald (Gloversville and Johnston, NY)
New York Age
New York Daily News
New York Evening Post
New York Sun
New York Times
Niagara Falls Gazette
Philadelphia Inquirer
Poughkeepsie Daily News
Rochester Times Union
Rome Daily Sentinel
Saratogian
Savannah Times (Wayne County, NY)
Schenectady Gazette
Syracuse American Journal
Syracuse Herald American
Syracuse Journal
Times Union (Albany, NY)
Tonawanda News
Troy Times Record
Utica Dispatch

Books and Articles

American Agriculturist Farm Directory of Ontario and Wayne Counties: A Rural Directory and Reference Book Including a Road Map of the Two Counties Covered. New York: Orange Judd Company, 1914.

Bailey, Frankie Y., and Alice P. Green. *Wicked Albany: Lawlessness and Liquor in the Prohibition Era.* Charlestown, SC: The History Press, 2009.

Blumenthal, Ralph. *Miracle at Sing Sing: How One Man Transformed the Lives of America's Most Dangerous Prisoners.* New York: St. Martin's Press, 2004.

Brown, Wenzell. *Women Who Died in the Electric Chair.* New York: Collier Books, 1958.

Bureau of the Census, Washington, DC.

Chermak, Steven, and Frankie Y. Bailey, eds. *Crimes of the Centuries: Notorious Crimes, Criminals and Criminal Trials in American History.* Santa Barbara, CA: ABC-CLIO, Inc., 2016.

Christianson, Scott. *Condemned: Inside the Sing Sing Death House.* New York: New York Univ. Press, 2001.

Downey, Patrick. *Legs Diamond: Gangster.* Scotts Valley: Create Space Publishing, 2011.

Elder, Robert K. *Last Words of the Executed.* Chicago: Univ. of Chicago Press, 2010.

Elliott, Robert G., with Albert R. Beatty. *Agent of Death: The Memoirs of an Executioner.* New York: E. P. Dutton and Company, 1940.

———. "As Humane as Possible." *Colliers,* Oct. 15, 1938.

———. "I Am Against Capital Punishment." *Colliers,* Oct. 22, 1938.

———. "A Life for a Life." *Colliers,* Oct. 5, 1938.

———. "And May God Have Mercy on Your Soul." *Colliers,* Sept. 24, 1938.

———. "Their Last Mile." *Colliers,* Oct. 1, 1938.

"Execution." *Time,* Jan. 15, 1940.

Gado, Mark. *Death Row Women: Murder, Justice, and the New York Press.* Westport, CT: Praeger Publishers, 2008.

Gillespie, L. Kay. *Executed Women of the 20th and 21st Centuries.* Latham, MD: Univ. Press of America, 2009.

"The Gut." *Time,* July 23, 1928.

Hall, Bruce. *Diamond Street: The Story of the Little Town with the Big Red Light District.* New York: Black Dome Press, 1994.

Kennedy, William. *O Albany!* New York: Penguin Press, 1983.

Lawes, Lewis E. *Life and Death in Sing Sing.* New York: Garden City Publishing, Inc., 1928.

———. *Meet the Murderer.* New York: Harper and Brothers, 1940.

———. *20,000 Years at Sing Sing.* New York: Ray Long and Richard Smith, Inc., 1932.

Lowenberg, Henry A., as told to Robin Moore. *Until Proven Guilty: Forty Years as Criminal Defense Counsel.* Boston: Little, Brown and Company, 1971.

Miller, Nathan L. *Public Papers of Nathan L. Miller, Forty-Sixth Governor of the State of New York.* Albany: J. B. Lyon, 1924.

People of the State of New York Against Anna Antonio, Vincent Saetta and Sam Faraci, Court of Appeals, Re-argument. New York: The Reporter Company, 1934.

People of the State of New York Against Manning Strewl, Return on Appeal. Albany: The Argus Company, 1936.

People of the State of New York Against Vincent Saetta, Court of Appeals. Walton, NY: The Reporter Co., 1934.

People of the State of New York Against Vincent Saetta, Sam Faraci and Anna Antonio. Vols. 113–16. Albany: The Argus Company, 1934.

Pratt, Fletcher. "Instrument of the State." *Saturday Review,* Jan. 20, 1940.

Public Papers of Nathan L. Miller, Forty-Sixth Governor of the State of New York. Albany: J. B. Lyon, 1924.

Reilly, Hugh, and Kevin Warneke. *Father Flanagan of Boys Town: A Man of Vision.* Boys Town, NE: Boys Town Press, 2008.

Reports of Cases Decided by the Court of Appeals. Vol. 264. Albany: J. B. Lyon, 1934.

Robinson, Frank S. *Machine Politics: A Study of Albany's O'Connells.* New Brunswick, NJ: Transaction Books, 1977.

Sarat, Austin. *Mercy on Trial: What It Means to Stop an Execution.* Princeton: Princeton Univ. Press, 2005.

Shipman, Marlin. *The Penalty Is Death: Newspaper Coverage of Women's Executions.* Columbia: Univ. of Missouri Press, 2002.

Sparkes, Boyden. "Train Robbers Routed by Science and Brawn." *Popular Science,* July 1931.

Squire, Amos O., MD. *Sing Sing Doctor.* New York: Doubleday, Doran and Company, 1935.

Stubig, Carl. *Curses on Albany.* Albany: Privately published, 1912.

Sullivan, James, ed. *The History of New York.* New York: Lewis Historical Publishing Company, Inc., 1927.

INDEX